EDITOR
Paul Golomb

MANAGING EDITOR
Hara E. Person

BOOK REVIEW EDITOR
Evan Moffic

POETRY EDITOR
Adam Fisher

MAAYANOT (PRIMARY SOURCES) EDITOR
Daniel F. Polish

EDITORIAL BOARD
Mona Alfi, Lawrence Bach, Leah Berkowitz, Daniel Fink,
Joshua Garroway, Elaine Rose Glickman, Jason Rosenberg,
Mark Dov Shapiro, Kinneret Shiryon, Donald M. Splansky

PRODUCTION
Publishing Synthesis, Ltd.

COPY EDITOR
Michael Isralewitz

CCAR ELECTED OFFICERS
Richard A. Block, President
Denise L. Eger, President-elect
David E. Stern, VP Organizational Relationships
Elaine Zecher, VP Leadership
Samuel Gordon, VP Financial Affairs
Deborah Bravo, VP Programs
Stephen Einstein, VP Member Services
Jonathan Stein, Past-President

CCAR RABBINIC STAFF
Steven A. Fox, Chief Executive
Alan H. Henkin, Director of Placement
Hara E. Person, Publisher and Director, CCAR Press
and Director of Strategic Communications
Dan Medwin, Publishing Technology Manager

Arnold I. Sher, Director of Placement Emeritus (1989–2008)
and Interim Executive Vice President (2005)
Paul J. Menitoff, Executive Vice President Emeritus (1994–2005)

PAST EDITORS
Abraham J. Klausner * (1953–58), Joseph Klein* (1958–64),
Daniel Jeremy Silver* (1964–72), Joseph R. Narot* (1972–75),
Bernard Martin* (1975–81), Samuel E. Karff (1981–84),
Samuel M. Stahl (1984–90), Lawrence Englander (1990–93),
Henry Bamberger (1993–96), Rifat Sonsino (1996–2000)
Stephen Pearce (2000–2003), Jonathan A. Stein (2003–2009)
Susan E. Laemmle (2009–2013)

*Deceased

CCAR Journal

The Reform Jewish Quarterly

Contents

FROM THE EDITOR
At the Gates — בשערים 1

ARTICLES

FROM THE SOURCES
A Positive Perspective on the Three Embarrassing
   Wife-Sister Stories in Genesis 5
Henry A. Zoob

Three Biblical Bases of Rabbinic Repentance 34
Scott Hoffman

Legal Authority and Verbal Harm in a Talmudic Narrative ... 47
Karl A. Plank

Chesed Shel Emet: Reconsidering the Future
   of Jewish Burial 57
Yoni Regev

A TRIBUTE TO DAVID ELLENSON
Tradition in Transition: The Incredible Journey of
   President David Ellenson 63
Robert Levine

For These I Weep: A Theology of Lament 73
Rachel Adler

At the Turning: Reflections on My Life 94
David Ellenson

CONTENTS

THIS PEOPLE ISRAEL
**The Unholy Scramble for Pulpits: A History
of Reform Rabbinic Placement (Part 1): 1893–1961** 107
Alan Henkin

Kaskel's Chutzpah 133
Gary Stein

The Sigd: From Ethopia to Israel 149
Shai Afsai

POETRY
To a Grandson Yet to Be Born 169
Reeve Robert Brenner

Rising Higher 171
Israel Zoberman

BOOK REVIEWS
***Women's Bible Commentary*, 3rd edition** 172
Edited by Carol A. Newsom, Sharon H. Ringe, and
   Jacqueline E. Lapsley
The New Reform Judaism: Challenges and Reflections 174
Dana Evan Kaplan
Reviewed by David J. Zucker

Join the Conversation!

Subscribe Now.

Engage with ideas about Judaism and Jewish life through essays, poetry and book reviews by leading scholars, rabbis, and thinkers.

A Journal for All Jews
The CCAR Journal: The Reform Jewish Quarterly
$125 for one year subscription
$175 for two year subscription

For more information and to order, go to:
www.ccarpress.org or call 212-972-3636 x243
CCAR | 355 Lexington Avenue | New York, NY 10017

At the Gates — בשערים

In 1873, Isaac Meyer Wise convoked a meeting of the representatives of thirty-four congregations in order to form a confederation of synagogues. "It is the primary object of the Union of American Hebrew Congregations," they wrote into their founding Constitution, "to establish a Hebrew Theological Institute . . . to establish, sustain, and govern a seat of learning for Jewish religion and literature."[1] Two years later, a renamed Hebrew Union College was founded. Wise recognized that a growing American Jewish community could not possibly develop without its own seminary and that no such institute could survive without a firm financial foundation. Once a coalition of synagogues could be formed (effectuated principally by Wise's own congregational president, Moritz Loth) dedicated to the founding—and funding—of an institute, the actual creation of the program would follow close behind.

I am personally intrigued that it took eight years from the opening of the College in order to ordain its first class. What did the students study over that span of time? Historian Michael Meyer asserted that Wise planned for an eight-year curriculum from the start: four years of preparatory education and four years collegiate. All of the classes, however, would be given in conjunction with classes to be taken at a high school and then the University of Cincinnati. The motivation for this course of study, Meyer suggests, was "the type of rabbi called for . . . was not the legal scholar and decisor . . .The rabbi was to preach, to conduct services, to teach children, to be a pastor to his flock. He was also to be a scholar, but his scholarship was expected to extend to secular learning as well as to Jewish studies."[2]

Today, nearly 140 years since Rabbi Wise and an assistant, Solomon Eppinger, presided in the basement of the Mound Street Synagogue over a class of "fourteen noisy boys . . . Four of them wanted to study; ten wanted to make noise,"[3] HUC developed a campus in Cincinnati, merged with New York's Jewish Institute of Religion, and opened centers in Los Angeles and Jerusalem. It is the oldest rabbinic seminary in North America and one of the oldest in the world. Yet, it is remarkably true to the initial vision of

Isaac Meyer Wise. It is founded on the financial support of a union of North American congregations, and it seeks to train rabbis (as well as cantors, educators, and Jewish nonprofit managers) who are not just legal scholars and decisors.

From Wise's death in 1900, HUC (and after 1950, HUC-JIR) has been led by seven presidents. The sixth of those presidents, Dr. David Ellenson, took on leadership at the beginning of the twenty-first century. For the twelve years he led the institution, he had to confront the myriad challenges of preserving and developing an international institution through a period of pronounced changes—economic, intellectual, and spiritual—in the Reform Movement. And through that time, he also managed to teach, study, and publish at the highest level of scholarship. In 2012, Rabbi Ellenson announced his plan to retire by 2014. In anticipation of his retirement, I asked him and a few colleagues to each write a paper for the *Journal* as a tribute to his service to the College-Institute. David has kindly contributed a reflection on the forces and influences that moved a small-city Orthodox Jew to the leadership of the premier scholarly institute of Reform Judaism. Robert Levine has provided a personal reflection on his friend and colleague, a relationship that reaches back to their first days together at the New York school of the College-Institute. Rachel Adler, who acquired her doctorate under Rabbi Ellenson's supervision, adds a scholarly consideration of the Talmudic concept of lament, a reflection of Ellenson's academic influence.

Having established a confederation of synagogues and a rabbinic seminary, Isaac Meyer Wise, in 1889, completed the triad by organizing a rabbinic collegium, the Central Conference of American Rabbis. Only a few years later, the Conference began to entertain the idea of setting up a process that would regulate the search and hiring of rabbis. It took a mere seventy years in order to turn this idea into a functioning placement system. Alan Henkin, current director of Rabbinic Placement, has captured the fits and starts that characterized this long gestation period in "The Unholy Scramble for Pulpits."

This issue includes a number of articles that analyze classic sources. Two—Henry A. Zoob's reading of the three "wife-sister" stories in Genesis, and Karl A. Plank's discussion of the encounter between R. Eliezer and the Sages over the oven of Aknai—mine new insights from familiar texts. Two others—Yoni Regev's raising the permissibility of cremation, and Scott Hoffman's investigation of the shifting understanding of repentance from biblical to Rabbinic thought—bring to bear less familiar texts to well-known tropes of Jewish practice. While these articles investigate the textually or thematically familiar, two more papers—Gary Stein's explication of the surprising impact of General Grant's Civil War directive to expel Jews, and Shai Afsai's description of an Ethiopian Jewish ceremony—bring to light little-known but valuable elements of the Jewish corpus of knowledge.

There is hardly a single unifying theme that binds together the contributions to this issue of the *CCAR Journal*, and yet seeping through many of the articles is the sense of discovery: David Ellenson finding a liberal vision of Judaism even within an Orthodox household; Shai Afsai uncovering an extraordinary ceremony among an ancient but mostly isolated community of Jews; the CCAR finally hitting upon a formula that will allow for the regulation of the placement of its members in Reform congregations; and many more. I hope that this issue will foster a sense of discovery among you.

Paul Golomb, Editor

Notes

1. Michael Meyer and W. Gunther Plaut, eds., *The Reform Judaism Reader* (New York: UAHC Press, 2001), 22.
2. Michael Meyer, "A Centennial History," in *Hebrew Union College–Jewish Institute of Religion at One Hundred Years*, ed. Samuel E. Karff (Cincinnati: HUC Press, 1976), 9.
3. Ibid., 19.

From the Sources

A Positive Perspective on the Three Embarrassing Wife-Sister Stories in Genesis

Henry A. Zoob

Whenever I read Genesis, I am inspired by God's challenge to the Patriarchs to be moral exemplars by whom "all the families of the earth will be blessed."[1] At the same time, I am troubled by the three embarrassing wife-sister stories in Genesis in which Abraham and Isaac lie about their wives' identities in order to save their own lives. Even more embarrassing than the patriarchal lies is the realization that their ploys put their wives in danger of being seized and raped! How do the high moral expectations of patriarchal behavior accord with these acts of deception? My concern with this conundrum is not unique; it has been a *kushyah* for biblical commentators and scholars down through the ages. After many years of keeping my eyes and ears open to possible solutions, with the help of insights from Benno Jacob, a German rabbi and biblical scholar (1862–1945), and Chanan Brichto *z"l*, my revered teacher from HUC-JIR, I believe I have come to a well-founded positive response to the basic questions raised by these stories: Why are there three wife-sister stories in Genesis? What do they teach us? and How does the Torah help us come to terms with the embarrassing aspects of these stories?

HENRY A. ZOOB (C67) is the rabbi emeritus of Temple Beth David, Westwood, Massachusetts. He is the founding chair of the Rashi School, the Boston Area Reform Jewish Day School.

He wants to extend his appreciation to three colleagues and friends, Rabbis Donald Splansky, Samuel Stahl, and Kenneth Weiss *z"l*, as well as longtime friend and retired English instructor, Judith Robbins, and his wife, Barbara, for offering their constructive suggestions for this article.

Before addressing these questions directly, I believe it is important, with the aid of Rabbinic, medieval, and contemporary biblical commentators, to set forth a clear synopsis and explication of each of the three wife-sister stories.

The First Wife-Sister Story: Abraham and Sarah Encounter Pharaoh (Genesis 12:10–20)

The first and most well-known occurrence of the wife-sister ruse appears in Genesis 12:10–20, where we read that soon after Abraham and Sarah[2] arrive in Canaan, a severe famine compels them to flee to Egypt. Just before they enter Egypt, Abraham asks Sarah to say she is his sister, "so that it may go well with me because of you, and I may remain alive thanks to you."[3]

Umberto Cassuto, a twentieth-century Italian rabbi and biblical scholar (1883–1951), writes that some of his contemporary academicians, who are predisposed to think poorly of the Jewish people, have suggested that the phrase "that it may go well with me because of you," indicates that not only is Abraham anxious to save his life, but he also seeks to enrich himself via Sarah. Cassuto counters by asserting that the succeeding phrase of the verse in question, "and I may remain alive thanks to you," does not refer to a separate objective on the part of Abraham; rather, it is in apposition to the first phrase.[4] Everett Fox's translation supports Cassuto's understanding: "Pray, say you are my sister that it may go well with me on your account, that I myself may live thanks to you."[5] Despite Cassuto's concern about the charge of materialistic motives against Abraham, the patriarch's eventual success in accruing wealth in Egypt and later in Gerar, must have been viewed in the days of the *Tanach* as a sign of success and divine favor.

Barry Eichler, a University of Pennsylvania biblical scholar, in an article entitled "On Reading Genesis 12:10–20," seeks to elucidate the wife-sister story of Abraham and Sarah in Egypt by pointing to parallels in ancient Mesopotamian legal sources, classical Greek literature, as well as anthropological material from the Bedouins and other cultures that speak of the unique role of the "guardian brother" in regard to the unprotected sister. Eichler posits that Abraham uses the stratagem of adopting the status of a "guardian brother" to save his life in the following manner: Abraham fears that if the inhabitants of Egypt believe the beautiful Sarah is his wife, and therefore his exclusive property, lacking morality, they will kill him to take possession of her, but as Sarah's guardian brother, Abraham hopes they will choose to negotiate with him to obtain her as a wife.[6] Eichler is not the first to think of this, for medieval commentators Redak[7] and Sforno[8] as well as the nineteenth-century Italian scholar S. D. Luzzatto advance the idea that by pretending that Sarah is his sister, Abraham seeks to be in a position to prolong marriage negotiations with a potential Egyptian suitor until the famine in Canaan is over, when he and Sarah might return to the promised land with his life and Sarah's honor intact. This understanding implies that even though Abraham lies out of his fear that the Egyptians might murder him in order to take possession of his beautiful wife, he believes that if they think she is his sister, they are sufficiently civilized to choose to negotiate with him for Sarah's hand in marriage. Little does Abraham know that there will be no negotiations, because the head of the land, Pharaoh, will seize her for himself!

Nachmanides is rather critical of Abraham's behavior on a number of points. Initially, he faults Abraham for leaving the promised land of Canaan. Abraham should have had faith that God would have saved him and his household from starvation. Nachmanides also comments that "Abraham committed a great sin, albeit unintentionally," in that he placed Sarah in a very dangerous situation. He maintains that Abraham should not have lied, but should have trusted that God would have protected them from danger in Egypt. The punishment for Abraham's lack of faith in God was that like him, his descendants would be exiles in the land of Egypt.

The Rabbis' understanding of Abraham's flight from famine and the events surrounding his wife-sister ruse is the exact opposite of Nachmanides'. In *B'reishit Rabbah*, they laud the first patriarch, because even in the face of a severe famine, he does not protest or abandon his faith in God.[9] Similarly, in *Pirkei D'Rabbi Eliezer*, we read that Abraham's steadfast trust in God during the famine in Canaan and Sarah's abduction in Egypt merits that these two trials are numbered among the ten rabbinic tests by which the Holy One finds Abraham worthy of being God's covenantal partner.[10]

After Pharaoh's courtiers in Genesis 12:15 praise Sarah's beauty to Pharaoh, she is taken into the royal court. The Torah then tells us that *baavurah* (on account of her),[11] things go well with Abraham; he acquires sheep, oxen, asses, slaves, and camels. One could certainly argue that after Sarah enters Pharaoh's court, the animals and slaves that Pharaoh gives to Sarah's "brother" constitute a bride price, or even gifts as an expression of Pharaoh's physical satisfaction with Sarah. Moreover, Pharaoh's statement to Abraham in Genesis 12:19, "Why did you say, 'She is my sister so that I took her as a wife,'" can be construed as his having consummated their marriage.

The Rabbis, however, contend that Sarah's marriage to Pharaoh is not consummated. They propose that in response to Sarah's pleas to save herself from Pharaoh's advances, God sends the "harsh plagues" mentioned in Genesis 12:17 on Pharaoh and his household. As part of the plagues, the Rabbis say that Pharaoh is struck with a severe skin disease.[12] Rashi comments that this punishment is designed to make it next to impossible for Pharaoh to engage in sexual relations. The Rabbis also envision that with every move that Pharaoh makes to molest Sarah, the matriarch gives an order to a protecting angel to strike her attacker. Eventually, Sarah tells Pharaoh she is a married woman, but even then, he is loath to cease his attempts to overcome her resistance.[13]

Another argument against the consummation of Pharaoh's marriage to Sarah can be derived from the second wife-sister story involving Abraham in Genesis 20. There, after King Abimelech abducts Sarah, God stops him from having relations with her by warning Abimelech in a dream that he is subject to a death sentence because of what he has done and that he is not to touch Sarah because she is a married woman. As I intend to demonstrate, I am convinced that the editor of Genesis has crafted the three wife-sister stories as parallel accounts that when taken together impart a single lesson. Hence, what is true for one story in regard to the basic structure of the plot is likely to be the same for the other two stories. If this is correct, I would contend that since God protects Sarah from being raped in the court of Abimelech in Genesis 20, God must also protect her from the same fate in Pharaoh's palace in Genesis 12.

The only explicit information that we have concerning Sarah's role in Abraham's ploy is that he specifically asks her to say that she is his sister. We can only imagine her remarkable courage and perseverance throughout this ordeal. First, she is to be admired for consenting to participate in Abraham's deception, for she must have been aware of the risks involved. Second, once she is taken into Pharaoh's harem, there can be little doubt that she is terrified about the possibility of being violated. Pharaoh may not rush her to bed since he surely has a bevy of available sexual partners, but the threat is there and does not depart until the plagues (an obvious foreshadowing of the Ten Plagues of Egypt in Exodus) compel Pharaoh to reconsider his plan.

Although God afflicts Pharaoh and his household with severe plagues, Pharaoh remains unaware of the existence and power of the God of Abraham and Sarah. It would appear that he intuits from the plagues that Sarah is Abraham's wife (or perhaps, as the Rabbis suggest, she herself informs him), and by taking her into his court, he has provoked an unknown power, which has let loose a terrible scourge upon him and his household. Pharaoh summons Abraham to explain why he said Sarah was his sister[14] and tells the patriarch that had he known she was a married woman, he would not have abducted her. If taken at face value, Pharaoh's words may indicate that he has a basic appreciation about the sanctity of marriage. It is more likely that he may just be trying to offer an excuse for his seizure of Sarah which has backfired. Even so, he does not express any qualms about his kidnapping of Sarah when he thought she was Abraham's sister. Abraham does not offer a word in his own defense. Perhaps, he is embarrassed by the lie he felt he had to tell to save his life, or he may not have the courage to tell Pharaoh that he did not trust that Pharaoh's subjects would let him live as soon as they saw his beautiful wife. Pharaoh, angered by the entire situation, and/or fearful of what else may happen if he does not release Sarah immediately, issues a brusque command to Abraham: "Now, here is your wife; *kach valeich* (take her and be gone)!"[15] He then assigns guards to hastily escort Abraham, Sarah, and all their newfound wealth out of Egypt, another portent of the Exodus: the despoliation of the Egyptians by the Israelite slaves prior to their flight from Egypt.[16]

The Second Wife-Sister Story: Abraham and Sarah Encounter Abimelech (Genesis 20:1–18)

The second wife-sister story, which is recorded in Genesis 20, takes place when the couple arrives in Gerar in the kingdom of Abimelech, following Abraham and Sarah's expulsion from Egypt and a number of significant events in Canaan. After Abraham spreads word that the beautiful Sarah is his sister, Abimelech abducts her, but God appears to the king in a dream to tell him that he is under a death sentence because he has seized a married woman. When the king learns that he was in danger of committing adultery, in words that are reminiscent of Abraham's intercession with God on behalf of the inhabitants of Sodom in Genesis 18, Abimelech pleads "Oh *YHVH*, will You slay people even though they are innocent?"[17] The king goes on to assert his innocence by pointing out that he was unaware that Sarah was Abraham's wife, because both Abraham and Sarah had told him she was his sister! God then says to Abimelech, "I knew that you did this with a blameless heart, and so I kept you from sinning against Me. That was why I did not let you touch her."[18] (Tikva Frymer-Krensky points out that God's prevention of Abimelech's rape of Sarah also serves to assure us that Isaac, who is born in the very next chapter, is unquestionably Abraham's issue.)[19] Nonetheless, *YHVH* still holds Abimelech accountable because he abducted Sarah in the first place, and continues to hold her captive in his court. God goes on to insist that Abimelech must restore Sarah to her husband. If he obeys, Abraham, whom God identifies as a *navi* (prophet), will offer an intercessory prayer to save his life.[20] If he does not obey, the death sentence against him and his household will be carried out. The next morning, after sharing the frightening news with his servants, Abimelech summons Abraham, and with a deep sense of anguish, demands to know why Abraham acted so deceitfully. "What have you done to us? What wrong have I done you that you should bring so great a guilt upon me and my kingdom? You have done to me things that ought not to be done. What, then," Abimelech demands of Abraham, "was your purpose in doing this thing?"[21] Abraham confesses that he did it because he thought "surely there is no fear of God in this place, and they will kill me because of my wife."[22]

The text then includes a verse wherein the patriarch claims that Sarah really is his sister, since he and Sarah share the same father but a different mother: "And besides, she is in truth my sister, my father's daughter though not my mother's; and she became my wife."[23] Abraham goes on to say that ever since "God made me wander from my father's house" there has been an understanding between him and Sarah that she would identify him as her brother whenever they arrive at a foreign land.[24] Because Sarah's parentage is never mentioned in the *Tanach*, there is no way to prove or disprove Abraham's assertion that they are both the children of Terah. Four verses later, Abraham's claim that Sarah is his half-sister is reinforced when Abimelech, in speaking to Sarah, refers to Abraham as "your brother."[25]

Since marriage to one's half-sister is proscribed in Leviticus 18:9, 20:17, and Deuteronomy 27:22, how can Abraham openly assert that Sarah is both his wife and his half-sister? When we observe that Jacob marries sisters Leah and Rachel, which is also prohibited by the Levitical rules of marriage,[26] we can surmise that the authors and editor of the patriarchal narratives in Genesis either were not aware of the Levitical strictures concerning marriage or assumed they were not in effect during the patriarchal period.[27] The Rabbis, however, are not comfortable with the idea of Abraham's marriage to his half-sister. They therefore provide an explanation of the situation that finesses the transgression of the Levitical rules of consanguinity. Their argument begins with Genesis 11:26–28, where we learn that Terah had three sons, Abram, Nahor, and Haran. Haran dies in Ur. Then we read: "Abram and Nahor took to themselves wives, the name of Abram's wife being Sarai and that of Nahor's wife Milcah, the daughter of Haran, the father of Milcah and Iscah."[28] Since the Torah states that Nahor marries his niece Milcah, the daughter of his deceased brother Haran, the Rabbis propose that Abram marries the other niece Iscah, the second daughter of his brother Haran, whose name is paired with Milcah at the conclusion of Genesis 11:29. Earlier in the verse, however, it says that Abram takes Sarai as his wife! The Rabbis solve this apparent contradiction by declaring that Iscah and Sarai are one and the same.[29] This reading allows the Rabbis to infer that when Abraham says to Abimelech in Genesis 20:12 that Sarah is *achoti* (a word that is most commonly understood as "my sister"), he is actually saying she is "my kinswoman."[30] According to the Rabbis, Abraham's assertion אֲחֹתִי בַת־אָבִי הִוא אַךְ לֹא בַת־אִמִּי/*achoti vat avi hi ach lo vat imi* does not mean "she is my sister, the daughter of my father, but not the daughter of my mother" (i.e., she is my half-sister), but rather "she is my kinswoman (my niece) on my father's side, but not on my mother's side."[31] Rashi understands this to mean that Haran, the father of Sarai/Iscah, shares the same father with Abraham but has a different mother. Thus, the Rabbis, in an effort to sustain Abraham's adherence to the Levitical laws of marriage as well as his credibility, resort to the improbable supposition that Sarai and Iscah are the same person. In this vein, we should be aware that for various reasons the Rabbis are not reticent about identifying very disparate characters as the same individual, as is the case with Hagar, who they say is both a daughter of Pharaoh (the Pharaoh who dismisses Abraham and Sarah in Genesis 12),[32] and Keturah, a wife of Abraham.[33] Against this Rabbinic tendency to conflate biblical personalities, I would point out that in regard to biblical characters who have two distinct names, the biblical text usually specifies the individuals who bear two names. For example, Jethro/Reul is explicitly identified as *chotein mosheh* (the father-in-law of Moses) in connection with the separate appearance of each name, Jethro or Reuel.[34]

Leaving the Rabbinical interpretation aside, I would also argue that if the three wife-sister stories are parallel accounts, as I shall try to demonstrate below, it is unlikely that what is operative for Isaac does not apply to Abraham. Hence, since Rebekah is clearly not Isaac's half-sister because Rebekah and Isaac have different mothers and fathers,[35] it follows that Abraham and Sarah are also the children of four different parents. My understanding of Abraham's last minute justification to Abimelech is that a late biblical editor was so uncomfortable with Abraham's lie, he felt compelled to try to mitigate it by interpolating into the text a verse that indicates that Abraham's original claim that Sarah is his sister is not really a falsehood because she is his half-sister.[36] One could argue that the absence of the same justification in the wife-sister story concerning Pharaoh is because it is from a different documentary source.[37] I would suggest, however, that the editor who interpolated Abraham's half-sister rationale in his response to Abimelech but did not chose to include it when Abraham stands before Pharaoh, probably understood that Abraham was so in awe of Pharaoh that he was unable to say anything in his defense. Indeed, unlike the two wife-sister accounts involving both Abimelech and Abraham, and Abimelech and Isaac, Abraham does not utter a single word to Pharaoh throughout the entire episode!

Following Abimelech's agonized complaint to Abraham about Abraham's subterfuge, Abimelech decides to give Abraham many sheep, oxen, and male and female slaves and restores Sarah to her husband. Benno Jacob identifies these gifts as "compensation"[38] for his offense. Abimelech also grants permission to Abraham to settle wherever he chooses in his land.³⁹ In addition, he tells Sarah he is presenting Abraham with a thousand pieces of silver, as a testament to the fact that her honor has not been sullied.⁴⁰ The voluntary gifts that Abimelech bestows upon Abraham as well as the invitation to settle anywhere in his land provide strong indications that Abimelech is remorseful about abducting Sarah and wants to make amends. Abraham responds to Abimelech's deeds of contrition by praying to God on behalf of the king. Abimelech's life is spared and he is healed (perhaps of impotence),⁴¹ as are his wife and slave girls, who had ceased to bear children because God had barred their wombs as part of Abimelech's punishment.⁴²

The Third Wife-Sister Story: Isaac and Rebekah Encounter Abimelech (Genesis 26:1–11)

Like the second wife-sister story concerning Abraham and Sarah, the third story, featuring Isaac and Rebekah, takes place in Abimelech's kingdom of Gerar. In both accounts involving Abimelech, this area is also referred to as the land of the Philistines.⁴³ Nahum Sarna contends that the Abimelech whom Isaac meets "can hardly be the same king whom Abraham dealt with over seventy-five years earlier."⁴⁴ Sarna proposes that Abimelech may be a dynastic name,⁴⁵ which suggests that this Abimelech is the son of the Abimelech of Abraham's day. With the understanding that when Abraham and Sarah meet Abimelech, Isaac is yet to be born,⁴⁶ Sarna probably derives his view of a minimum seventy-five-year gap between the two Abimelechs by comparing Abraham and Isaac's ages at key junctures in their lives as recorded in the Genesis narrative.⁴⁷ Contrary to Sarna's opinion, I concur with W. Gunther Plaut, who proposes that the Abimelech whom Abraham met is the same king whom Isaac encounters.⁴⁸ The most significant clue in this identification is that Phicol, the chief of Abimelech's troops, appears in the narratives in both stories regarding the continuing controversy over wells of water: an initial argument between Abraham and Abimelech's servants⁴⁹ and a later disagreement, between Isaac and Abimelech's herdsmen.⁵⁰ It could be, as Sarna might argue, that Phicol serves as the head of the troops for King Abimelech, and after his death, for a son by the same name, similar to the situation of Abner, the chief of troops for King Saul and his son Ishbaal.⁵¹ If this were true, however, I would think that the author or editor would have identified the second Abimelech as the son of the first king. I believe it is more likely that the Abimelech and Phicol of Abraham's day are the same two leaders whom Isaac encounters. Considering the longevity of the Patriarchs—Abraham lives to the age of 175,[52] Isaac 180,[53] and Jacob 147[54]—it is certainly possible for the editor of Genesis, if he was at all concerned about the time that elapsed between the two Abimelech episodes, to assume that non-Hebrew leaders in the days of the Patriarchs, such as Abimelech and Phicol, enjoyed the same kind of longevity as the Patriarchs.

With the understanding that Abimelech in stories two and three is the same individual, we are now ready to explicate the third wife-sister story concerning Isaac and Rebekah's sojourn in the realm of Abimelech. When the men of Gerar ask Isaac about his wife, he repeats Abraham's ploy by saying she is "my sister." In sharp contrast to the previous two stories, Abimelech never considers kidnapping Rebekah. After an extended period of time, he happens to look out of his window and sees Isaac *m'tzacheik* (laughing-and-loving)[55] Rebekah, which he correctly interprets to mean that they are married. Abimelech has Isaac brought before him and asks him the same question that he put to Abraham: "Why did you then say: She is my sister?"[56] Isaac responds that he feared for his life, but Abimelech points out that because of Isaac's deceit, *achad haam* (one of the people)[57] in his kingdom might have had relations with Rebekah, which would have brought *asham* (guilt)[58] upon the entire community. Abimelech's reference to "one of the people" is significant, because he is expressing the idea that while one of his subjects might have committed the sins of abduction and rape, there was no danger from him, for he has learned from previous experience not to kidnap a foreigner's sister. Abimelech, perhaps out of fear that some of his subjects might be angry that Isaac impugned their standards of morality, goes on to proclaim that anyone in his kingdom who molests Isaac or Rebekah will be put to death.[59] God then blesses Isaac so that he becomes a very successful farmer (Isaac is the only patriarch to take up husbandry) and herdsman.[60]

The Unity of the Wife-Sister Stories

Having set forth my basic understanding of each of the three wife-sister narratives, I now want to demonstrate that these three stories in Genesis are interrelated analogous accounts, the work of a single editor. While each story contains a number of distinguishing elements, the essential structure of each of the three wife-sister stories is comprised of parallel generic events that appear in the same order:

1. Upon arriving in a foreign country, a patriarch, out of fear for his life, decides to disseminate a lie that the beautiful wife accompanying him is his sister. (To mitigate or to attempt to explain away the patriarchal lies, as some scholars and commentators have done in the past, is contrary to the basic structure of the wife-sister motif.)
2. In the first two stories, the wife of the patriarch is kidnapped and brought into the court of the foreign ruler. This element is not present in the third story.
3. The foreign ruler becomes aware of the patriarchal ruse through divine chastisements, a divine dream, or his own observations.
4. The patriarch is summoned and interrogated by the ruler who is distraught because of divine punishments (actual or threatened) and/or because the sin of adultery has been narrowly avoided.
5. In reaction to the situation, the ruler takes decisive action: Pharaoh's abrupt expulsion of the couple; Abimelech's attempt to expiate his offense via gifts as well as his invitation to Abraham and Sarah to settle in the land; and in the third story, Abimelech's directive to his subjects not to molest Isaac and Rebekah.

In addition, although it does not occur in the same sequence in each story, all three accounts include a reference to the material enrichment of the two patriarchs by direct or indirect involvement of the foreign ruler. Thus, Pharaoh gifts Abraham with herds and slaves on account of Sarah,[61] while Abimelech grants Abraham additional animals and slaves as compensation for his seizure of Sarah[62] as well as a thousand pieces of silver as a testament that Sarah's honor has not been compromised.[63] In the third story, Abimelech's directive to his subjects not to molest Isaac and Rebekah affords Isaac the space and security to become a wealthy farmer with the aid of God's blessing.[64]

Another significant factor indicating that these stories reveal the hand of a single editor is the reiteration of nearly the exact same phrase in each account during the questioning of a patriarch by an indignant foreign ruler. Thus, in Genesis 12:18, Pharaoh says to Abraham מה-זאת עשית לי ("What is this that you have done to me!"). In Genesis 20:9, Abimelech cries out against Abraham, מה-עשית לנו ("What have you done to us?"). And in the third story, in Genesis 26:10, Abimelech exclaims, מה-זאת עשית לנו ("What is this that you have done to us!"). The repetition of this phrase, along with the identical sequencing of the analogous events of each story and the parallel references to the material enrichment of the two patriarchs, makes it very likely that the three wife-sister stories have been shaped by a biblical editor to resemble each other. Their similarity draws our attention, but, as we shall see, it is by means of their differences that the biblical editor seeks to convey a lesson.

Explanations of the Wife-Sister Stories That Fall Short of Providing Satisfactory Answers to the Problem

When I was a rabbinical student in the 1960s, the most popular explanation of the wife-sister motif was that of E.A. Speiser of the University of Pennsylvania. Speiser contends that these stories were influenced by an ancient Hurrian marital convention. The city of Haran, which became the homeland of the Patriarchs following their migration from Ur, was a center of Hurrian settlement. Speiser asserts that fifteenth and fourteenth century B.C.E. texts from Nuzi[65] indicate that among the upper-class Hurrians, "the bonds of marriage were strongest and most solemn" when a man would marry a woman and in a separate ceremony adopt her as his sister.[66] He holds that a wife-sister marriage brought increased stature and was legally beneficial to both marriage partners. Speiser proposes that Abraham and Isaac adopted this unique wife-sister bond from their Hurrian neighbors, but the biblical authors of Genesis, who lived centuries later, did not comprehend the original import of the wife-sister marital status, so they recast it in a very different manner.[67] Thus, according to Speiser, Abraham and Isaac did not lie when they declared that their wives were also their sisters.

David E. S. Stein, the editor of W. Gunther Plaut's *The Torah: A Modern Commentary, Revised Edition,* maintains that Speiser's theory "is no longer held by regnant scholarly opinion."[68] Stein cites the article by Samuel Greengus, an Assyriologist at HUC-JIR, entitled "Sisterhood Adoption at Nuzi and the 'Wife-Sister' in Genesis,"[69] as the source of convincing evidence against Speiser's Hurrian thesis. While Speiser contends that the adoptive sister institution is unique to the Hurrians, Greengus demonstrates that it also occurs in Old Babylonian and Ur III societies.[70] Furthermore, Greengus challenges Speiser's analysis of the evidence from Nuzi. He points out that Speiser's argument is based on material from just three documents involving a single married couple. He also questions Speiser's claim that the dual legal bonds of wife-sister were characteristic of the top levels of Hurrian society. Greengus notes that the relevant Nuzi material that he examined, covering at least twenty-six texts, indicates that the "sister" convention was used primarily for women who were socially inferior, such as freed slaves.[71] He asserts that in the vast majority of the adopted sister texts from Nuzi, the man who adopted a woman as his sister did not also make her his wife, but looked to marry her off in order to receive a bride price for her.[72] In sum, Greengus argues that the adopted sister institution at Nuzi was not part of a regular marriage between an upper-class couple that adds special status to their relationship, rather, it "appears to have been a business arrangement . . . typically involving manumitted slaves or lonely, unattached women who needed familial protection. It was a lower class institution and was not practiced by the highest level of Nuzi society."[73] On the basis of material from other Ancient Near East societies, Greengus suggests that even the three texts relating to the single marital relationship used by Speiser to make a case for his wife-sister argument in Genesis were probably superseded by subsequent documents in which the marital provision of the original wife-sister transaction was nullified, leaving the adopting brother free to marry his adopted sister to another man.[74] In light of Greengus's convincing critique, I concur with Stein as well as Frymer-Krensky[75] that Speiser's Hurrian hypothesis is not tenable.

Umberto Cassuto's approach to the problem as to why there are three versions of this troubling story is to suggest that the editor, being respectful of ancient oral and written traditions, decided that if there were three such stories that were popular with different groups of Israelites, it was important to include all of them, even if doing so seemed excessive.[76]

The Torah: A Woman's Commentary, edited by Tamara Cohn Eskenazi and Andrea L. Weiss, states that Abraham and Sarah are depicted as successful "tricksters" who outsmart Pharaoh and at the same time walk off with a handsome amount of the ruler's wealth.[77] Their commentary goes on to propose that Genesis 12 portrays Pharaoh as "a dupe and deals with the 'us-them' theme in a humorous and thoroughly traditional way," and that "this passage is not a tale about unethical behavior, but a story of marginalized persons who succeed in roundabout, unorthodox ways."[78] At best, the "trickster" theory can only be applied to the story involving Pharaoh, for when we look at the second and third stories, having Abraham and Isaac devise a subterfuge that gains an advantage over a non-Hebrew monarch like Abimelech who seeks to behave in an ethical way does not fit the "us vs. them" trickster typology.

In my opinion, none of the above explanations sufficiently answer the question as to why there are three wife-sister stories or what the editor had in mind when these stories were shaped and included in the book of Genesis.

Rashi, Benno Jacob, and Chanan Brichto Help Reveal the Lesson of the Three Wife-Sister Stories

If I am correct in my understanding of the three wife-sister stories as the work of a single editor who sought to impart a unified teaching in three parts, what is the nature of that lesson? In his commentary on Genesis, Rashi points us in the right direction by comparing Pharaoh's response to Abraham's ruse with that of Abimelech. Rashi notes that in the initial wife-sister story, Pharaoh, in an effort to be rid of Abraham and Sarah as quickly as possible, says to Abraham "take her and be gone!"[79] Rashi then cites Ezekiel 23:20, a verse that refers to the Kingdom of Judah's attraction to the gross, whoring, pagan culture of the Egyptians.[80] Behind Rashi's use of the Ezekiel reference is an allusion to a midrashic tradition that Pharaoh wants to expel Sarah from Egypt as soon as possible, because he knows that his Egyptian subjects are lascivious and might be enticed to repeat his mistake by abducting Sarah, and thereby bring additional plagues upon Egypt.[81] By contrast, Rashi points out that Abimelech says to Abraham, "Here, my land is before you, settle wherever you please."[82] By highlighting the difference between Abimelech's generous invitation and Pharaoh's hostile dismissal, Rashi implies that underlying the words of these two monarchs is the reality that Gerar does not harbor the same kind of immoral society as Egypt.

Benno Jacob's commentary on this passage specifically hones in on the distinctions between the two monarchs rather than their subjects when he writes, "The intention of the Bible is to demonstrate the different reactions of Pharaoh and Abimelech in the same situation."[83] With this comment, Jacob, like Rashi, shifts our focus away from Abraham's deception to the contrasting behavior of the two foreign monarchs. Jacob sees "the Pharaoh of Abraham as a forerunner of the Pharaoh of Moses. [This Pharaoh] does not know of God [and] has no fear of God or sin. No deity appears to him because a Pharaoh regards himself as god."[84] Jacob points out that Abimelech's religious and moral superiority to Pharaoh is expressed in several ways in Genesis 20. Abimelech is open to being "warned by the deity . . . He not only corrects his mistake, but beyond this gives Abraham compensation . . . he abhors sin and fears God."[85] Interestingly, Jacob does not extend his comparison of the two monarchs to the third story involving Abimelech, Isaac, and Rebekah.[86]

Chanan Brichto, in his book *The Names of God* (published posthumously in 1998) concludes, as do I, that the "the three stories are one."[87] Brichto, provides us with a twenty-one-page discussion of the subject under the heading "Three Domestic Triangles" in which he makes an argument, similar to Jacob, for understanding the three wife-sister stories as a means of contrasting the moral and religious attitudes of the hostile, guarded, self-centered Pharaoh to the gracious, morally concerned Abimelech.[88] Brichto sees the Abimelech of stories two and three as a monarch whose stellar qualities are accentuated by the editor's use of the arrogant Pharaoh as "a counterfoil."[89] Brichto makes the astute observation that even though Pharaoh's household has suffered from the plagues, Pharaoh sees his predicament only in terms of his own welfare when he says to Abraham, "What is this that have you done to me!"[90] while Abimelech in the second story shows concern for his entire household by demanding of Abraham "What have you done to us?"[91] I would add that the comparison holds true in the third story as well, when once more, Abimelech reveals his concern for his people when he cries out to Isaac "What is this that you have done to us!"[92]

For Brichto, the moral of the stories arises from the deficiencies of the first two patriarchs, Abraham and Isaac: Both prejudge the ethical standards of a foreign nation (the monarchs and citizens of Egypt and Gerar), a prejudice that leads them to make embarrassing and perhaps unnecessary lies. While I am aware that at different times in our history, Jews have had to lie about their identity or the identity of family members in order to survive, the experiences of Abraham and Isaac in Egypt and Gerar do not seem to be such a time. We cannot know for certain that in Egypt the inhabitants might have tried to murder Abraham if he had not initiated his ploy, but surely in Gerar, it was not necessary. If Abraham had introduced Sarah as his wife, Abimelech, as a leader with an awareness of God and a basic sense of ethics, would not have kidnapped her nor would he have allowed any of his subjects to do so. Difficult as it is, Brichto urges us to accept the idea that Abraham and Isaac are portrayed in the three wife-sister stories in a negative light for a reason, namely, to make a statement against prejudicial attitudes towards foreigners.[93]

Brichto is aware of the problem that this negative lesson poses for us, Abraham and Isaac's descendants. His primary response to this difficulty is to ask us to modify our vision of the Patriarchs as perfect exemplars. He points out that human flaws are to be found in our ancestors from "Abram and Sarah through Jacob and Rachel, Moses and Miriam, Gideon and Sampson, David and Solomon, and Jonah and Jeremiah."[94] He also is critical of the tendency to adopt the simplistic perception that non-Hebrews in the Bible are consistently inferior in regard to their religious and ethical practices.[95] In accord with Brichto's thinking on this subject, I would point out that Genesis, in particular, provides notable examples of characters who serve to counter the bias against non-Hebrews, such as Melchizedek, king and high priest of Salem, who blesses Abraham in the name of *El Elyon*;[96] Abraham's servant (assuming he is not a Hebrew), who prays to God to bless his mission to Haran to acquire a wife for Isaac;[97] and Pharaoh, who demonstrates genuine hospitality when he invites Joseph's family to settle "in the best part of the land."[98] Overall, Brichto argues for a more balanced biblical view of both the Hebrew and the foreigner: "Every moral hero, of the Abrahamic line or outside it, is a model for emulation . . . every antihero, of that line or outside it, embodies traits that are to be shunned; and the most meaningful of lessons for us . . . are in the deficiencies in the best of our ancestral heroes of faith."[99] By means of this rather novel approach, Brichto calls on us to understand that our biblical ancestors who appear "so often [as] models for emulation . . . again and again [are] cast in antihero roles for our self-identification and moral correction."[100] In short, Brichto advocates that without losing sight of the virtues and strengths of our ancestors, the Torah is telling us that we also need to pay attention to the instructive value of their weaknesses.

Beyond Benno Jacob and Chanan Brichto's Teachings about the Wife-Sister Stories

Benno Jacob appears to be the first modern scholar who concludes that the intent of the Torah in the wife-sister stories is to contrast the religious attitudes and behavior of Pharaoh and Abimelech. Jacob, however, draws no edifying conclusions from his insight. Chanan Brichto goes beyond the mere comparison of the two foreign monarchs to the thesis that the editor of Genesis has crafted the three wife-sister stories so as to afford the lesson that morality is not the exclusive domain of the early Hebrews; it exists among some foreign leaders and their subjects, and it should be expected of all of them; it is prejudicial to think otherwise.[101]

While I agree with Brichto's basic conclusion, I would suggest a few additions and criticisms. One addition is that the relationship between Abimelech and God in Genesis 20, as well as Abimelech's effort to make amends for his offense, make Abimelech a unique exemplar among non-Hebrews in the Torah. Even though God reprimands and chastises Abimelech for abducting Sarah, there is a sense of familiarity about God's conversation with this foreign king that gives the impression that God and Abimelech are old acquaintances who need no introduction. Thus, when Abimelech argues with God to dismiss his sin because it was done unwittingly, his manner and even his words are similar to those of Abraham in his *chutzpadich* debate with the Eternal before the wicked city of Sodom.[102] Finally, all God asks of Abimelech is to return Sarah to Abraham, but Abimelech, on his own, goes above and beyond God's expectation by showering Abraham with animals and servants, by providing a thousand pieces of silver as testimony to Sarah's unsullied virtue, and by graciously inviting Abraham to settle wherever he chooses in his land. Even though Abimelech continues to suffer from divine chastisements until the end of the episode when Abraham offers a prayer to God on his behalf, his generosity does not seem to stem from an effort to assuage God's wrath; rather, he appears to be sincerely motivated to seek redemption for his sin.

While Brichto points out that in the third story, Abimelech, whose behavior is beyond reproach, represents the climactic counterpoint to the self-centered Pharaoh,[103] Brichto neglects to delve into the specific differences between Abimelech in the second and third stories, a comparison that I believe offers some valuable inferences. When Isaac and his beautiful wife Rebekah enter Gerar and declare that they are brother and sister, Abimelech probably senses that he has seen this behavior before, but graciously accepts Isaac's statement at face value. Having learned from his past experience with Abraham and Sarah that one should not abduct a stranger's sister, let alone a stranger's wife, the older and wiser Abimelech is now prepared to model the proper ethical behavior towards Rebekah. When Abimelech accidentally discovers Isaac's ruse, he becomes angry with Isaac for exposing Rebekah to the possibility of abduction by one of his subjects, an offense that he believes would have brought divine punishment on his entire nation. Moreover, at the conclusion of the episode, Abimelech tries to ensure that his subjects behave properly by issuing a death sentence to anyone who might think of molesting Isaac or Rebekah. In sum, Abimelech in the third story, as compared to the same monarch in the second account, demonstrates moral growth and leadership that would appear to be a result of what he learned when Isaac's father and mother entered Gerar many years previously.

Another interesting lesson that arises from the three stories is that foreigners display a full spectrum of religious awareness and moral behavior, just as one would expect of Hebrews. Some foreigners may be like Pharaoh: They do not recognize God, and even though they may give lip service to a basic code of right and wrong, they are loath to do anything that conflicts with their personal desires. Others may be like Abimelech when Abraham and Sarah enter his realm: They display an ongoing relationship with God and are anxious to adhere to God's expectations of morality, but need divine guidance and discipline to gain insight into their own behavior so that they may ultimately do the right thing. And finally, there are those like Abimelech in the story of Isaac and Rebekah, who when faced with the same moral challenge that he previously failed, knows what is right and does it, and is determined to make sure that others do the same. I also believe that the editor of Genesis intentionally arranged the order of these three stories from the least religious and most deficient ethical sensitivity of Pharaoh in Genesis 12, to the somewhat above average Abimelech in Genesis 20, and ultimately to the best moral exemplar, the judicious Abimelech of Genesis 26. This progression creates a crescendo that helps express the editor's sophisticated perception concerning the varying levels of awareness of God and ethical behavior among foreigners.

My principal departure from Brichto's analysis of the wife-sister motif concerns his suggestion that "the most meaningful lessons for us . . . are in the deficiencies of our ancestral heroes of faith."[104] Such learning is not easy. As biological and spiritual descendants who lovingly mention the Patriarchs and Matriarchs in daily prayer, we are naturally disinclined to scrutinize the failings of our forebears. Discomfort with the flaws of our biblical ancestors is not new; it also appears in the writings of the Rabbis[105] as well as some contemporary scholars, some of whom, as previously mentioned, have tried to rationalize or explain away Abraham and Isaac's embarrassing lies in the wife-sister stories. While I believe that we learn best from our own failings, our deep-seated reverence for our biblical progenitors may render us incapable of gaining personal insights from their shortcomings.

Another reason that it is difficult to identify with the deficiencies of Abraham and Isaac in these stories is the unique context of their prejudice. When one thinks about historical prejudice, there is a decided tendency to focus on disadvantaged individuals or groups who suffer discrimination at the hands of a narrow-minded, powerful ruler or majority group. In the *Tanach* we think of the enslavement of the Hebrews by Pharaoh or the genocidal plot of Haman. In more recent times, the persecution of European Jewry and the eventual murder of six million of our Jewish brothers and sisters by the Nazis as well as the treatment of African American slaves in this country come to mind. The wife-sister accounts, however, feature a very different setting for historical prejudice: Abraham and Isaac display prejudice against foreigners in whose homeland they hope to find a temporary haven! This is the reverse of customary historical prejudice, for here, disadvantaged individuals bear prejudice against those in power. As such, they are not in a position to directly harm the objects of their prejudice. It is purely by chance that the lies that Abraham broadcasts as a result of his prejudice set off a chain of unforeseen detrimental events: the kidnapping of Sarah by Pharaoh and Abimelech, which is countered by the divine punishment of the two rulers. Perhaps, the subliminal lesson of the wife-sister stories is that prejudice, in one way or another, brings harm to its adherents as well as its targets in the world that God created.

In the two issues described above—our ingrained love for the founders of our faith and the peculiar context for patriarchal prejudicial behavior in the wife-sister stories—have probably contributed to the fact that most commentators and scholars over the centuries have failed to recognize the biblical editor's lesson about prejudice that emerges from Abraham and Isaac's deceptions. In this vein, we should also note that since Pharaoh, in the first and most famous wife-sister story, is such an unsympathetic character, Abraham's prejudice against him and his people seems justified. All of these factors contribute to a lack of clarity and efficacy in regard to the editor's lesson about prejudice, and leads me to believe that there must be other elements of the wife-sister story that have engendered an appeal to readers of the *Tanach*. Nahum Sarna points out that the kidnapping of a beautiful wife is a popular theme in ancient folklore. As examples, he cites the Ugaritic legend in which King Keret mounts a military campaign to recover Hurrai, his stolen wife, as well as the mythic story in the Greek tradition of the abduction of the beautiful Helen (of Troy), the wife of King Meneleus of Sparta. Sarna, therefore, proposes that the wife-sister stories, which recount the remarkable beauty of the first two matriarchs, their abduction, and their redemption,[106] must have been popular among the Israelites and thereby found their way into the Torah.[107] I would add that the wife-sister motif has a number of other dramatic elements that create an aura of suspense that holds the reader's interest. Among them are: How should we view the lies of Abraham and Isaac? Will Sarah survive being kidnapped without being raped? What is God going to do about the situation? Will Pharaoh or Abimelech uncover the ruse, and if they do, how will they react? All of these suspenseful elements in the plot dynamics of the three wife-sister stories probably contributed to their appeal in biblical times and continue to do so down to this day.

The overall moral objective of the wife-sister stories of instructing prejudiced Israelites who were inclined to think of themselves as ethically and religiously superior to foreign peoples resembles that of some other passages in the *Tanach*. I would point to aspects of the books of Jonah[108] and Ruth[109] and the passage from the last chapter in Amos, "To Me, O Israelites, you are just like the Ethiopians . . . ,"[110] all of which seek to counteract prejudice against foreigners. I would liken this kind of biblical prejudice against foreigners to the biases of many Americans who tend to stereotype most adherents of Islam, particularly in the Middle East, as zealous fanatics and terrorists.

Finally, when I ask myself, "Do the prejudicial approach of Abraham and Isaac to foreigners and their acts of deception that threaten to compromise the safety and virtue of their wives still disturb me?" I have to say, "Yes!" I want to believe that the Patriarchs are steadfast moral exemplars, so I continue to experience discomfort when they do not live up to my expectations. And even though, with the help of Chanan Brichto, I have come to understand that in the wife-sister stories, Abraham and Isaac are momentarily cast as antiheroes whose trials teach us not to prejudge foreigners, my awareness of this lesson is not sufficient to prevent me from being upset by our founders' embarrassing behavior.

In order to lessen my unease with patriarchal conduct in the wife-sister stories, I need to fully accept the truth that the *Tanach* in its wisdom intentionally portrays the founding fathers and mothers of our people, as well as almost all other illustrious biblical heroes such as Moses and David, as real human beings with flaws and weaknesses, so that we, their descendants, might identify with them.[111] We also need to remember that, to some extent, our biblical ancestors are heroes, because in spite of their human errors, they succeed in advancing their covenant with God. In conclusion, I believe that because we experience our founders in the Torah as true to life human beings, we can challenge ourselves to emulate their most admirable qualities. At the same time, because of our profound veneration for our ancestors, learning from their weaknesses, as Brichto advocates, is a much harder task, which each of us can only try to do according to our individual willingness to confront the flaws in our founders and ourselves.

Notes

1. This Messianic challenge is issued by God to Abraham in Gen. 12:3, to Isaac in Gen. 26:4 (here the word *goyei* [nations] replaces *mishpachot* [families]), and to Jacob in Gen. 28:14.

2. In Gen. 11:31 the first patriarch and matriarch are introduced by the names Abram and Sarai. In Genesis 17, God blesses them and changes their names to Abraham and Sarah. For the sake of consistency, excluding my discussion of the Rabbis' identification of Sarai as Iscah in Gen. 11:29, I will use the names Abraham and Sarah.
3. Gen. 12:13. I follow the translation according to the New Jewish Publication Society (NJPS, 1962) except where indicated.
4. Umberto Cassuto, *A Commentary on the Book of Genesis, Part Two*, trans. Israel Abrahams (Jerusalem: Magnes Press, 1964), 348–50.
5. Everett Fox, *The Five Books of Moses* (New York: Schocken, 1995), 57.
6. Barry Eichler, "On Reading Genesis 12:10–20," *Tehillah le-Moshe: Biblical and Judaic Studies in Honor of Moshe Greenberg* (Winona Lake, IN: Eisenbrauns, 1997), 23–38. In Genesis 24, we encounter a clear example of the role of the guardian brother in regard to marital negotiations, when Laban takes the lead in precedence over his father Bethuel in dealing with the offer of Abraham's servant to have Laban's sister, Rebekah, marry Isaac.
7. Rabbi David Kimchi from Narbonne (1160–1235).
8. Rabbi Ovadiah ben Yaakov from Italy (1475–1550).
9. *B'reishit Rabbah* 40:2.
10. In *Pirkei D'Rabbi Eliezer* 26–31, the ten trials of Abraham include (1) the threat of death to the infant and child Abraham by King Nimrod; (2) imprisonment and trial by fire by Nimrod; (3) leaving his father's house and native land; (4) famine in Canaan; (5) Sarah's being taken into Pharaoh's court; (6) the war vs. the kings; (7) the covenant between the pieces; (8) the covenant of circumcision; (9) banishment of Ishmael; and (10) the binding of Isaac. Slightly differing lists of the ten trials of Abraham appear in Jubilees 17:17 and 19:8; *Avot D'Rabbi Natan*, chap. 33; and *Midrash T'hillim* 18:25. See also Lewis M. Barth, "Lection for the Second Day of Rosh Hashanah: A Homily Containing the Legend of the Ten Trials of Abraham" published in Hebrew in *HUC Annual* 58 (1987): א – מה. *Pirkei Avot* 5:3 refers to the ten trials of Abraham without delineating them.
11. Gen. 12:16.
12. *B'reishit Rabbah* 41:2.
13. Rather than "*on account* of Sarai," the Rabbis understand *al d'var Sarai* in Gen. 12:17 to mean that YHVH afflicted Pharaoh and his household with mighty plagues "*at the word* of Sarai" in the form of prayers to God or appeals for protection to a protecting angel. *Tanchuma, Lech L'cha* 3:8; *B'reishit Rabbah* 41:2.
14. Although the Torah says that Abraham asks Sarah to say that she is his sister (Gen.12:13), apparently Abraham also participates in

the process of disseminating this deceit, for in Gen. 12:19, Pharaoh accuses him of spreading the lie, "Why did you say 'She is my sister'?" (Gen. 12:19).

15. Gen. 12:19.
16. See Exod. 12:35–36.
17. This exclamation in Gen. 20:4 echoes Abraham's words of protest before God at Sodom in Gen. 18:25: "Far be it from You to do such a thing, to bring death upon the innocent as well as the guilty, so that the innocent and guilty fare alike."
18. Gen. 20:6.
19. Tikva Frymer-Krensky, *Reading The Women of the Bible* (New York: Schocken, 2002), 96.
20. Gen. 20:7. A common role of a prophet is to intercede for the people, as in the examples of Moses (Exod. 32:11–14) and Jeremiah (7:6; 14:11; 15:11; 18:20). In this case, Abraham offers a prayer for an individual, Abimelech. Moses also offers an intercessory prayer for an individual, his sister Miriam, who was stricken with leprosy because she spoke out against him (Num. 12:13).
21. Gen. 20:9–10.
22. Gen. 20:11.
23. Gen. 20:12.
24. Gen. 20:13.
25. Gen. 20:16.
26. Lev. 18:18 prohibits a husband from marrying his wife's sister. It is presumed that one may marry the sister of a deceased wife, since there is no explicit prohibition against it.
27. Even though marriage to a half-sister was not considered appropriate, such marriages apparently took place, since after Amnon rapes Tamar, she pleads with him to retain her implying that she wants him to marry her (II Sam. 13:16).
28. Gen. 11:29.
29. BT *Sanhedrin* 69b.
30. Another biblical context in which the word *achot* does not refer to an actual sister is the Song of Songs, where it is used in a poetic sense, e.g., Song of Songs 4:9: "You have ravished my heart *achoti chalah* (my sister, my bride)." See also Song of Songs 4:10, 12; 5:1, 2.
31. My translation of the verse is based on the discussion in BT *Sanhedrin* 58b.
32. *B'reishit Rabbah* 45:1. The midrash says that when Pharaoh saw what God did for Sarah, he gave his daughter as a maid to Sarah, saying "Better let my daughter be a handmaid in this house than a mistress in another house."

33. *B'reishit Rabbah* 61:4. The Rabbis identify Hagar as Keturah because they do not want the reader to think that after the miracle in which Abraham had a child with Sarah at the age of 100 (Gen. 21:5), at a much older age he had six more children with Keturah (Gen. 25:1–2). Rather, if Keturah is Hagar, these children, along with Ishmael, were born to Abraham and Hagar/Keturah, before the miraculous birth of Isaac.

34. Exod. 18:1: "Jethro, priest of Midian, Moses' father-in-law" and Num. 10:29: "Reuel the Midianite, the father-in-law of Moses." Some other explicit examples of individuals with two names are Jacob/Israel, Jerubbaal/Gideon (Judges 7:1) and Solomon/Jedidiah (II Sam. 12:24).

35. Isaac's parents are Abraham and Sarah. Rebekah's father is Bethuel and her mother, although not named in the Torah, participates in Rebekah's marriage negotiations after Sarah's death (Gen. 24:55).

36. He also may be responsible for removing any information about Sarah's parentage in Gen. 11:29, where we might have expected to find it. Indeed, in that same verse we are told that Nahor's wife, Milcah, is the daughter of Haran, but in regard to the wife of Abram, Sarai, no father is mentioned.

37. See E. A. Speiser, *The Anchor Bible: Genesis* (New York: Doubleday, 1964) 89, 147, who identifies the first story as a J document and the second as coming from E.

38. Benno Jacob, *The First Book of the Bible: Genesis,* abr., ed., and trans. Ernest I. Jacob and Walter Jacob (Ktav: New York, 1974), 134.

39. Gen. 20:15.

40. The text is difficult, but NJPS suggests the following translation for Gen. 20:16: "I (Abimelech) herewith give your brother a thousand pieces of silver; this will serve you (Sarah) as vindication before all who are with you, and you are cleared before everyone."

41. See *Pirkei D'Rabbi Eliezer* 26.

42. Herbert Chanan Brichto, in *The Names of God: The Poetic Readings in Biblical Beginnings* (New York: Oxford University Press, 1998), 264, proposes that the sign of their affliction had to be immediately visible if they were to understand it as a divine punishment for the kidnapping of Sarah, which had only recently taken place. He suggests that the women of Abimelech's court developed swollen bellies but did not give birth, a sign of false pregnancy.

43. In the third wife-sister story, the Philistines are referenced four times: Gen. 26:1, 8, 14, 15. In the second story, there are two references to the Philistines: The first occurs after the conclusion of a peace covenant between Abimelech and Abraham, when Abimelech and his chief of troops, Phicol, return to "Philistine

country" (Gen. 21:32); the second appears two verses later: "And Abraham resided in the land of the Philistines a long time" (Gen. 21:34). The references to Philistines in both stories would seem to be anachronistic, because the Philistines, who originated in the Greek islands, did not gain control of the southern coastal area of Canaan until the time of the Judges and Samuel. Nahum M. Sarna, *The JPS Torah Commentary: Genesis* (Philadelphia: The Jewish Publication Society, 1989), 390, claims these Philistine references are not a mistake; rather, he believes there may have been an earlier settlement of Philistines who were part of "a minor wave of Aegean invaders." He also suggests that they differed significantly from the classical Philistines described in Judges and Samuel who were organized in a five-city confederation: Ashkelon, Ashdod, Ekron, Gaza, and Gath. The later Philistines were inveterate enemies of the Israelites and were not inclined to make peace treaties with their Israelite neighbors. The Philistines of Abraham and Isaac's day lived more inland in the area of Gerar. These early Philistines had adopted the Canaanite culture as may be evidenced from their use of Semitic names (Abimelech, Ahuzzath), and unlike the second wave of Philistines, they were open to making peace treaties with their Semitic neighbors, in this case, the Patriarchs. See Gen. 21:22 and Gen. 26:28.
44. Sarna, *JPS Genesis*, 183.
45. Ibid., 183.
46. If Isaac was present during Abraham and Sarah's encounter with Abimelech, Abraham could not have concealed that they were husband and wife. Isaac is born in the next chapter, Genesis 21.
47. I would surmise that Sarna calculates a seventy-five-year gap between the second and third wife-sister stories in the following manner: immediately after we read of Abraham and Sarah's encounter with Abimelech in Genesis 20, we learn of Isaac's birth when Abraham is 100 (Gen. 21:1–5); Abraham's death at 175 is recorded in Genesis 25, the chapter preceding the episode with Isaac and Abimelech (Genesis 26). Assuming the chapters are in chronological order, one could conclude that at least seventy-five years (the time between Isaac's birth and Abraham's death) separates the occasions when first Abraham, and later Isaac, attempt to deceive the King of Gerar about the identity of their wives.
48. W. G. Plaut, *The Torah: A Modern Commentary*, rev. ed., ed. David E. S. Stern, (New York: URJ Press, 1999), 174.
49. Gen. 21:22–34.
50. Gen. 26:12–33. In the account with Abraham and Abimelech, Phicol is mentioned in Gen. 21:22, 32. In the story concerning Isaac and Abimelech, Phicol's name occurs in Gen. 26:26.

51. I Sam. 14:50 states that Abner serves as the head of the troops for Saul, while the reference regarding his position as chief of the troops for Saul's son Ishbaal occurs in II Sam. 3:1–11.
52. Gen. 25:7.
53. Gen. 35:28–29.
54. Gen. 47:28.
55. Gen. 26:8. Fox, *Five Books of Moses*, 119.
56. Gen. 26:9.
57. Gen. 26:10.
58. Gen. 26:10.
59. Gen. 26:11.
60. Gen. 26:12–14.
61. Gen. 12:16.
62. Gen. 20:14.
63. Gen. 20:16.
64. Gen. 26:11–14.
65. Nuzi was a provincial town where over five thousand tablets have been unearthed dating from the fifteenth and fourteenth centuries B.C.E., when Hurrians controlled the area. The tablets deal with administrative and legal issues of the society as a whole, as well as the legal concerns of individuals and families. Today, the site of ancient Nuzi is in Iraq.
66. Speiser, *Genesis*, 92. For a full presentation of Speiser's theory concerning the Hurrian wife-sister marriage convention and its influence on the wife-sister stories in Genesis, see *Anchor Bible, Genesis*, xl–xli, 91–94, and his article "The Wife-Sister Motif in the Patriarchal Narratives" in *Biblical and Other Studies*, ed. A. Altman (Cambridge: Harvard University Press, 1963), 15–28.
67. Ibid., 91, 93.
68. Plaut, *The Torah*, 104.
69. Samuel Greengus, "Sisterhood Adoption at Nuzi and the "Wife-Sister" in Genesis," *HUC Annual* 46 (1975): 5–31.
70. Ibid., 8–9.
71. Ibid.,12.
72. Ibid.,13–14.
73. Ibid.,18.
74. Ibid., 12. Greengus notes that in the case of Speiser's three wife-sister texts, which deal with a single marriage, documentary evidence from Nuzi of later superseding legal procedures is absent. Nevertheless, he claims that other Mesopotamian societies feature a number of texts that nullify the marital clause of a previous wife-sister bond so that the adopted sister may be married off.

He therefore suspects that documents annulling Speiser's single wife-sister case have been lost. Greengus also cites other texts (Ibid.,13–14, 23) in which a wife adopts a lower-class women as her sister with the intent that the adopted sister might become a second wife to her husband and produce children, a situation that is strikingly similar to Sarah's relationship with Hagar, and Rachel and Leah's relationship with Bilhah and Zilpah.

75. Frymer-Krensky, *Reading the Women of the Bible*, 94.
76. Cassuto, *Commentary on Genesis, Part II*, 337–39.
77. Tamara Cohn Eshkenazi and Andrea L. Weiss eds., *The Torah: A Woman's Commentary* (New York: URJ Press and Women of Reform Judaism, 2008), 63.
78. Ibid., 63.
79. Gen. 12:19.
80. See Ezek. 23:19–21: "But she (Israel) whored still more, remembering how in her youth she had played the whore in Egypt; she lusted for concubinage with them, whose members were like those of asses and whose organs were like those of stallions. Thus you reverted to the wantonness of your youth, remembering your youthful breasts, when the men of Egypt handled your nipples." In the *Jewish Study Bible* (New York: Oxford, 1999), 1084, Marvin Sweeney comments that the dalliance with Egypt in this passage from Ezekiel may refer to Solomon's early alliance with Egypt (I Kings 3:1) and/or Jehoiakim's reliance on Pharaoh Necco before he turned to Babylonia (II Kings 23:21–24:7).
81. See *Midrash Aggadah* (twelfth century) on Gen. 12:19: "Because Pharaoh was aware that there were evil people [in his realm], and if Abraham remained in the land [of Egypt], others would fall [by seizing the beautiful Sarah], he therefore said 'Take her and be gone!'" See also *Midrash Tanchuma* 3:8, which cites the same passage from Ezekiel 23 in reference to Abraham's understanding of the lustful nature of the Egyptians so that he sealed Sarah in a box to conceal her beauty from the Egyptians. Eventually, they opened the box, and when they saw how beautiful she was, they reported it to Pharaoh.
82. Gen. 20:15.
83. Jacob, *Genesis*, 133.
84. Ibid., 133–34.
85. Ibid., 134.
86. Even in his original German commentary, *Das Erste Buch der Tora Genesis, Ubersetz und Erklart* (Berlin: Schocken Verlag, 1934), Jacob does not venture to compare Abimelech in wife-sister stories two and three.
87. Brichto, *Names of God*, 274.

88. Ibid., 259–79.
89. Ibid., 274.
90. Gen. 12:18.
91. Gen. 20:9. Brichto, *Names of God,* 265.
92. Gen. 26:10.
93. Brichto, *Names of God,* 276.
94. Ibid., 274.
95. Ibid., 274–76.
96. Gen. 14:19.
97. Gen. 24:12.
98. Gen. 47:6. In Gen. 39:22, however, the same Pharaoh displays his capacity for cruelty when he executes his baker for no apparent reason.
99. Brichto, *The Names of God,* 276.
100. Ibid., 274.
101. My colleague Rabbi Kenneth J. Weiss has suggested that the presence of *three* wife-sister stories follows a proven pedagogical approach on the part of the editor of Genesis. The effectiveness of the three-part lesson is attested in many other traditional contexts such as the first chapter of *Pirkei Avot*, where most of the rabbinic teachings are arranged in sets of three, as in Hillel's famous aphorism "If I am not for myself, who will be for me? If I am for myself alone, what am I? And if not now, when?" This tripartite structure renders the sayings readily understandable and easy to memorize. Also, having been a steadfast practitioner of the three-part sermon for forty-five years, I believe that there is something about a three-part argument that is especially comprehensible to the listener.
102. See note 17 above, where I point out that Abimelech's words in Gen. 20:4 are very close to those of Abraham (Gen. 18:15) in the course of his argument with God.
103. Brichto, *The Names of God,* 274.
104. Ibid., 276.
105. As noted in this article, the Rabbis absolve Abraham from any wrongdoing in the wife-sister stories.
106. While Sarah is abducted twice, we should be mindful that in the third story, involving Isaac and Rebekah, Rebekah's abduction is only a potential threat that never takes place.
107. Sarna, *JPS Genesis,* 94.
108. Jonah's reluctance to deliver a prophetic warning to the Ninevites concerning their impending doom casts him, like Abraham in the wife-sister stories, as an antihero. As we are challenged to refrain from the kind of prejudice Abraham displayed against

the foreigner in the wife-sister stories, so too, from Jonah's failure to care about the lives of citizens of a foreign city, we are challenged to care for the foreigner.
109. Deuteronomy prohibits Moabites from joining the community of Israel (Deut. 23:4–5) because they did not help the Israelites in the wilderness, and their king, Balak, hired a prophet, Balaam, to curse them. The book of Ruth counters that prohibition by means of the character of Ruth, the Moabitess, who shows loyalty to her Israelite mother-in-law, marries two Israelites (first Chilion, and after his death, Boaz) and becomes the great-grandmother of King David.
110. Amos 9:7–8.
111. Ruth is the only important biblical character whom I can think of who displays no failings. It is also important to note that Abraham's flaws are not limited to his dubious behavior in the wife-sister stories. I would also include his callous decision in Gen. 16:6 to allow Sarah to do with Hagar as she thinks best after Hagar has flaunted her pregnancy, a decision that permits Sarah to treat Hagar so harshly that the Egyptian maid flees alone into the desert.

Three Biblical Bases of Rabbinic Repentance

Scott Hoffman

Both biblical and Rabbinic thought are maddeningly lacking a systematic approach to theological concepts. Finding out what "the Bible says" about a topic or "what the Rabbis believe" means culling through texts that are scattered, variable in provenance, and often contradictory as well.

It is nevertheless possible to determine biblical and Rabbinic ideas—broadly speaking—by noting certain overarching trends and locating them in their proper contexts. Three modern attempts have been made toward this end. The first, Solomon Schechter's *Aspects of Rabbinic Theology*, appeared in 1909; the second, G. F. Moore's *Judaism in the First Centuries of the Christian Era*, in 1927; and the last, E. E. Urbach's *The Sages: Their Beliefs and Opinions*, in 1968.[1]

Our Sages did not typically create what we recognize as our own system of beliefs and practices ex nihilo. Rather, it is fair to say that they looked at Scripture as a guide and then adopted or adapted as they saw fit. Cases in which the Sages either ignored Scripture or, conversely, regurgitated it verbatim, are the exception rather than the rule.[2] In other words, we should see the Sages, wherever possible, as legislating in relation to biblical precedent.

Even as we recognize the relationship between the Sages and Scripture, however, it remains to us to demonstrate the specific contours of that relationship with respect to various concepts that pique our interest. In the following pages, we will explore the ways in which the Sages utilized three scriptural ideas in developing their version of *t'shuvah*. These include the verbal confession, the institution of Yom Kippur as day of repentance par excellence,

---

SCOTT HOFFMAN, Ph.D. (JTS91) is the rabbi of Temple Israel of South Merrick (New York). This article is drawn from his doctoral dissertation.

and the power of repentance in averting, rather than mitigating, divine punishment.

The *Asham* Sacrifice and "Feeling Guilty"

Reading through the minutiae of sacrifice, one point becomes clear. Sacrifice is designed to remedy unintentional sin. Depending upon the nature of the transgression, one brings the appropriate sacrifice to the Temple, where, under the auspices of the priest, atonement is gained for that individual. Deliberate sin, on the other hand, is not typically expiable. The book of Numbers contrasts these two types of sin in this way:

> In case it is an individual who has sinned unwittingly, that person shall offer a she-goat in its first years as a sin offering [*chatat*]. The priest shall make expiation before the Eternal on behalf of the person who erred, for having sinned unwittingly, making such expiation that the person may be forgiven. For the citizen among the Israelites and for the stranger who resides among them—you shall have one ritual for anyone who acts in error. For the person, whether citizen or stranger, who acts defiantly [*b'yad ramah*] reviles the Eternal, that person shall be cut off from among the people. Because it was the word of the Eternal that was spurned and [God's] commandment that was violated, that person shall be cut off—and bears his guilt. (Num. 15:27–31)[3]

In other words, there are only two types of sin—accidental and expiable, and deliberate and inexpiable.

Is it not possible that there exists a third, intermediate category of sin, deliberate yet expiable? Thanks in large part to the work of Jacob Milgrom, we know that it does. Milgrom asks that we consider the case of Leviticus 5:20–26, which concerns a person entrusted with a deposit who then lies about having it in his possession.

> The Eternal One spoke to Moses, saying: When a person sins by committing a trespass [*u'maalah maal*] against the Eternal—by dealing deceitfully with another in the matter of a deposit or investment, or through robbery, or by defrauding another, or by finding something lost and lying about it; if one swears falsely regarding any of the various things that someone may do and sin thereby—when one has thus sinned and, realizing guilt [*v'ashem*], would restore either that which was gotten through robbery or fraud, or the entrusted deposit, or the lost thing that was found,

or anything else about which one swore falsely, that person shall repay the principal amount and add a fifth part to it. One shall pay it to its owner upon realizing guilt [*b'yom ashmato*]. Then that person shall bring to the priest, as a penalty to the Eternal, an unblemished ram from the flock, or its equivalent, as a reparation offering [*asham*]. The priest shall make expiation before the Eternal on behalf of that person, who shall be forgiven for whatever was done to draw blame thereby.

Surely, Milgrom argues, a person knows whether or not an object is in his possession—and lies about it anyway.[4] On what basis, precisely, can this paradox be explained?

In another essay entitled "The Cultic Asham: Philological Postulates," Milgrom argues that the term means "to feel guilty."[5] In other words, a person who transgresses in a matter of lost objects and deposits is not apprehended by witnesses or the discovery of incriminating evidence, but decides as an act of conscience to admit his malfeasance.

Milgrom then argues, on the basis of a parallel passage in Leviticus 5:1 about a person who fails to give testimony, that this "feeling guilty" leads to a subsequent confession (Lev. 5:5). Thus Milgrom argues that deliberate sins can be expiated through a feeling of guilt that leads to a subsequent confession. This is what Milgrom means when he refers to the "conscience" that undergirded the sacrificial cult.

There is evidence that a feeling of guilt, followed by a subsequent confession of sin, led to forgiveness in other cultures of the ancient Near East. In a Hittite text, for example, we read:

> Now, I have confessed before the Hattian Storm god, my lord, and before the gods, my lords, "It is true, we have done it . . ." If a servant has incurred guilt, but confesses his guilt to his lord, his lord may do with him whatever he pleases. But because (the servant) has confessed his guilt to his lord, his lord's soul is pacified, and his lord will not punish that servant. I have now confessed."[6]

In other words, deliberate sins may be atoned for through a feeling of guilt that culminates in a verbal confession. The warning in Numbers 15:30 about brazen, defiant sin being excluded from expiation is taken to mean not that it is the deliberate sinner who is excluded from forgiveness but the unrepentant sinner, who is excluded even (in ancient times) from sacrificial atonement. This is very possibly what the Sages meant when they declared that repentance renders deliberate sins into unintentional sins.[7]

Yom Kippur as the "Day of Cleansing"

Having established at least a rudimentary form of repentance within the rubric of the sacrificial system, we now turn our attention to the yearly observance of Yom Kippur. How is it that the tenth of Tishri (the seventh month, according to the Torah) came to have special significance with respect to repentance? Can we identify the biblical roots of this selection?

In the previous section, we saw that the *asham* differed from other sacrifices in that it offered an opportunity for expiation of deliberate sin, with the stipulation that an appropriate, but unspecified, confession took place. Leviticus 16, which describes the Yom Kippur ritual, specifically states that the sin offering (*chatat*) on behalf of the people was also accompanied by a confession:

> Aaron shall lay both his hands upon the head of the live goat [designated for Azazel] and confess over it [*v'hitvadah alav*] all the iniquities and transgressions of the Israelites, whatever their sins, putting them on the head of the goat; and it shall be sent off to the wilderness through a designated agent [*ish iti*]. (Lev. 16:21)

This goat designated for Azazel was intended as a vehicle upon which the people of Israel could "load" their sins. God could not accept this role as He is depicted in the Torah as the source of order, creation, and good. Banishing evil to the wilderness was a way of exiling it to a region where it could do no harm, a phenomenon attested in the literature of the ancient Near East.[8] The Tabernacle, which acted as a sort of magnet for impurity throughout the year, needed to be cleansed completely on an annual basis each Yom Kippur. This would suggest that the sins "loaded" upon the goat, subsequently confessed over by Aaron the High Priest, included deliberate as well as unintentional sins.

Fortunately, we need not rely upon the power of reason alone. In the above passage, Onkelos translates the word "transgressions" (*pish'aihem*), as *meradayhon* (their rebellious) (i.e., deliberate) sins.[9] Similarly, the Talmud in *Yoma* 37b, commenting upon the word "iniquities" (*avonot*) in the above passage, renders the term as *z'donot* (deliberate sins), citing as proof Numbers 15:30–31.

We can thus see that the characteristics of the *asham* are present also in the Yom Kippur *chatat*. It does not require much imagination to see how a sacrificially based cleansing of physical "outer" space might be transformed into a liturgically based cleansing of personal "inner" space.

But there is still one further aspect of repentance which needs to be explored—the power of repentance. A single scriptural book, really an outlier in many respects, became the basis of our reconceiving its power.

The Book of Jonah—"Strange" Book of the Bible

To determine the biblical understanding of repentance further, we can utilize not a conceptual approach, as we have in the previous two sections, but a philological approach. That is, we can look at the key term denoting the concept of repentance, namely *shuv*, and determine from context how it was understood. It can be shown that, while this root has a number of meanings, *shuv* in the sense we are seeking occurs quite frequently, more than 160 times, with 113 of those found in the latter prophets.[10]

While the prophets are divided as to the means through which repentance will restore the equilibrium to the relationship between God and Israel, on one point they are in agreement. All see Israel as undergoing a certain measure of punishment, with repentance serving to mitigate only its severity. One book, and one book alone, conceives of repentance as actually serving to avoid punishment altogether—the book of Jonah.

The book of Jonah is "strange" for any number of reasons. Is the book early or late?[11] How should we characterize its genre? Is Jonah a satire, as several modern scholars have concluded?[12] And what, exactly, is the "message" of Jonah? Is it a tale, for example, that illustrates that divine capriciousness can on occasion work to man's advantage?[13]

All other things being equal, I would suggest that we simply read the narrative as it is presented. Whatever the "facts" of the case, Jonah is first and foremost about how sincere repentance can avert divinely ordained punishment. In chapter three, verses five through ten, we read:

> The people of Nineveh believed God. They proclaimed a fast, and great and small alike put on sackcloth. When the news reached the king of Nineveh, he rose from his throne, took off his robe, put on sackcloth, and sat in ashes. And he had the word cried through Nineveh: "By decree of the king and his nobles: No person or beast of flock or herd shall taste anything. They shall not graze or drink water. They shall be covered with sackcloth—human and beast—and shall cry mightily to God. Let everyone turn back [*vayashuvu*] from their evil ways and from the injustice of which they are guilty. Who knows but that God may turn [*yashuv*] from devine wrath so that we do not perish. God saw what they did, how they were turning back [*shavu*] from their evil ways. And God renounced the punishment planned to be brought upon them and did not carry it out.

In fact, one may say there are no less than three innovations here. The first is that in Jonah God's mercy is extended even to the people of Nineveh—that is, Israel's historic enemies! God's mercy is not the sole province of the Jewish people. Second, we may see that there is an attempt to balance competing values, such as justice and mercy, or God's decrees and man's response.[14] But most important, it shows that punishment is not the only avenue for cleansing iniquity. Repentance can achieve the same atoning function elsewhere ascribed only to punishment and suffering.

The Sages' "Threefold Cord"

We will now see how the Sages combined these three elements into a unified whole that we readily recognize as our Yom Kippur ritual. I will, however, change the order of analysis to begin with Yom Kippur, as both the confessional and the chanting of the book of Jonah are tied to that day in the calendar.

The Sages referred to the concept of *t'shuvah* with only limited definition, despite the fact that we have seen its contours were only partially developed in Scripture. They assigned it various levels, depending upon the context in which it was performed. Consider, for example, the following Rabbinic source:

> For four things did R. Matia ben Heresh go to R. Elezara ha-Kappary to Laodicea. He said to him, "Master! Have you heard the four distinctions in atonement which R. Ishmael used to explain?" He said to him, "Yes."

> One scriptural passage says, "Return, O backsliding children" (Jeremiah 3:14), from which we learn that repentance brings forgiveness.
> And another scriptural passage says, "For one this day shall atonement be made for you" (Leviticus 16:30), from which we learn that the Day of Atonement brings forgiveness.
> Still another scriptural passages read, "This iniquity shall not be expiated until you die" (Isaiah 22:14) from which we learn that death brings forgiveness.
> And still another scriptural passage says, "Then will I visit their transgressions with the rod, and their iniquity with strokes" (Psalms 89:33), from which we learn that chastisements bring forgiveness.
> How are all these four passages to be maintained? If one has transgressed a positive command and repents of it, he is forgiven on the spot. Concerning that it is said, "Return, O backsliding children."
> If one has violated a negative commandment and repents of it, repentance alone has not the power of atonement. It merely leaves the matter pending and Yom Kippur brings forgiveness. Concerning that it is said, "For on this day shall atonement be made for you." (Leviticus 16:30)
> If one willfully commits transgressions punishable by extirpation or death at the hands of the court and repents, repentance cannot leave the matter pending nor can Yom Kippur bring forgiveness. But both repentance and Yom Kippur together bring him half a pardon and suffering completes the atonement. Concerning this it is said, "Then will I visit their transgressions with the rod, and their iniquity with strokes." (Psalms 89:33)
> However, if one has profaned the name of God and repents, his repentance cannot make the case pending, neither can Yom Kippur bring him forgiveness, nor can sufferings cleanse him of his guilt. But repentance and Yom Kippur can make the matter pending. And the day of death with the suffering preceding it completes this atonement. To this applies, "This iniquity shall not be expiated until you die." (Isaiah 22:14)[15]

Without delving into the exact nature of this hierarchy, it nevertheless posits a special role for Yom Kippur. If one views death and suffering as two related phenomena, it would then stand to reason that repentance at the lowest level is done on an ongoing basis, with a higher level being achieved annually each Yom Kippur. Only an individual's day of death, a one-time occurrence, carried greater weight. This annual spiritual "purging" of sin dovetailed neatly with the "purging" of impurity referred to in Leviticus 16.

Of course, the locus classicus in Rabbinic literature is in the final chapter of *Yoma*; in fact, it is the very last *mishnah* in the tractate. There we encounter the well-known Rabbinic maxim that Yom Kippur is efficacious in cleansing us of transgressions against the Almighty. This should not be taken, however, as a license to sin in the future; repentance can only be applied to past transgressions, and only when a sincere promise has been made to avoid their future repetition. Interpersonal transgressions can be forgiven as well, but only on condition of rapprochement with the offended party. It is interesting that the Sages recognized that Scripture itself did not consider the realm of interpersonal sins—and prove their point by referring to Leviticus 16:30:

> He who says, "I will sin and repent, sin and repent: they give him no chance to do repentance.
> If he said, "I will sin and Yom Kippur will atone"—Yom Kippur does not atone.
> For transgressions done between man and God, Yom Kippur atones.
> For transgressions between man and man, Yom Kippur atones only if the man will regain the good will of his fellow.
> Thus did R. Eleazar expound: "From all your sins shall you be clean before the Lord" (Leviticus 16:30)—for transgressions between man and God Yom Kippur atones, for transgression between man and man, Yom Kippur atones only if the man regains the good will of his colleague.[16]

What changed was the vesting of the day itself with sanctity, independent of the sacrifices. Leviticus 16 also seems to ascribe holiness to the day, but this holiness is inextricably bound up with the presentation of the prescribed sacrifices. The impossibility of fulfilling the ritual necessitated a shift to the sanctity of the tenth of Tishri alone.[17]

Moving to the observance of Yom Kippur, for the Sages nothing was more vital than the confessional. We have seen that without a verbal confession, no repentance is possible. Perhaps that is why the Sages required the confessional to be recited throughout the entirety of the day:

> The obligation of reciting the confessional [*vidui*] applies on the eve of Yom Kippur at dusk. But the sages have said, "A man

should say the confession before eating and drinking, lest he be distracted while eating and drinking."

And even though he has recited the confessional before eating and drinking, he must say the confessional after eating and drinking lest some untoward matter may have affected the meal.

And even though he has recited the confessional in the evening prayer, he must recite it in the *Shacharit* prayer.

And even though he has recited the confessional in the *Shacharit* prayer, he must recite it during the *Musaf* prayer.

And even though he has recited the confessional in the *Musaf* prayer, he must recite it in the *Mincha* prayer.

And even though he has recited it in the *Mincha* prayer, he must recite it in the *Neilah* prayer.[18]

Apparently the nature of the confessional was still fluid, as evidenced by the following source:

What is the confession? Rav said, "You know the secrets of eternity."

Samuel said, "From the depths of the heart."

Levi said, "And in You Torah it is written, 'For on this day atonement will be made for you.'" (Leviticus 16:30)

Rav Judah said, "Our iniquities are too numerous to count, and our sins too many to be numbered."

R. Hamnuna said, "My God, before I was formed, I was of no worth, and now that I have been formed, it is as if I had not been formed. I am dust in my life, how much more in my death. Behold I am before You like a vessel full of shame and reproach. May it be Your will that I sin no more, and what I have sinned wipe away in Your mercy, but not through suffering."

That was the confession used by Rav all year round, and by R. Hamnuna the younger, on Yom Kippur.

Mar Zutra said, "All that is necessary is to state, 'Truly, we have sinned,' but if he had said that, no more would be necessary."

For Bar Hamdudi said, Once I stood before Samuel, who was sitting, and the public reader came up and said, "Truly, we have sinned," he rose. Hence he inferred that this was the main confession.[19]

We learn from this source that, on the one hand, many of the confessional passages in our own Yom Kippur liturgy stem directly from this Talmudic source, but that in the final analysis it is the fact of confession, not its length, that is of primary importance.[20]

Finally, we turn our attention to the book of Jonah. The Sages already recognized its powerful message and included its recitation as part of the liturgy prescribed for the fast day. More specifically, it was recited as part of the service observed during a period of drought, which was regarded as God's response to Israel's sin. Hoping to rescue Israel from drought no doubt held echoes of God's rescue of Nineveh from its imminent destruction. Thus we read in *Mishnah Taanit* 2:1:

> What is the order of the fast day?
>
> The ark is carried out into the open place of the town and wood ashes are sprinkled upon it, upon the head of the *nasi*, upon the head of the *av bet din*.
>
> Everyone present takes some and sprinkles it upon his own head.
>
> The elder among them exhorts them, "Brethren, of the people of Nineveh it is not said, 'And God saw their sackcloth and their fasting,' but 'And God saw their works, that they turned from their evil way.'" (Jonah 3:10)
>
> And in the prophets it is said, "And rend your heart, and not your garments, and turn unto the Eternal your God, for God is gracious and compassionate, long-suffering and abundant in mercy, and repents of the evil." (Joel 2:13)

The connections to Yom Kippur now come into sharper focus. Yom Kippur is not only a fast day, but the fast day par excellence; no other fast day is explicitly mentioned in the Torah. Yom Kippur is also now the day of repentance par excellence. It comes as no surprise, then, that already in the Talmud, Jonah is mentioned as the appropriate *maftir* reading:

> On Rosh Hashana we read, "On the seventh month" (Numbers 29:1) and for haftorah, "Is Ephraim a darling son to me?" (Jeremiah 31:20)
>
> According to others, we read, "And the Lord remembered Sarah" (Genesis 21:1) and for the haftorah the story of Hannah.
>
> Nowadays that we keep two days, on the first day we follow the ruling of the other authority, and on the next day we say, "And God remembered Abraham" (Genesis 22:1) with Jeremiah 31:20 as the haftorah.
>
> On Yom Kippur we read "After the death" (Leviticus 16:1) and for the haftorah "For thus says the high and lofty one." (Isaiah 57:15)

At mincha we read the section of forbidden marriages (Leviticus 18) and for the haftorah the book of Jonah. (BT *M'gillah* 31a)

We now have created a Rabbinic version of repentance which is based on three scriptural ideas. The first is that there is no repentance without a verbal confession. In fact, no other aspect of the liturgy is as prominent as the various confessionals recited throughout the day. Second, we see that Yom Kippur has a special atoning power all its own. One repents on a daily basis, but Yom Kippur alone repairs the breach between the worshiper and God with respect to certain sins and transgressions. Finally, the book of Jonah establishes that fate is in our hands, not God's alone. Our behavior can, and does, determine which punishments are visited upon us, and which we manage to avoid.

From Biblical to Rabbinic Repentance

Much more material than what I have included here can be found in the Rabbinic literature. We have not looked, for example, at the contours of repentance with respect to interpersonal sins, such as the nature of such apology. Must it be specific, or can it be general? Need it be public, or is a private conversation sufficient? How many times must one persist if the victim rebuffs an initial attempt at reconciliation?

What I hope does emerge, however, is the balance our Sages struck between fidelity to tradition and the necessity for innovation. Yom Kippur is a ritual whose hold on the popular imagination demonstrates their success in this endeavor.

Notes

1. Solomon Schechter, *Aspects of Rabbinic Theology* (New York: Macmillan Company, 1909); G. F. Moore, *Judaism in the First Centuries of the Christian Era* (Cambridge: Harvard University Press, 1927); E. E. Urbach, *The Sages: Their Beliefs and Opinions* (Jerusalem: Magnes Press, 1968).
2. With respect to our subject at hand, see, for example, the work of Jakob J. Petuchowski, "Concept of *Teshuva* in the Bible and Talmud." *Judaism* 17 (Spring 1968): 175–85. Petuchowski's contention that the Sages innovated very little with respect to the biblical concept of *t'shuvah* seems strange even at first blush, given that the term is essentially absent from Scripture.

3. All translations follow W. Gunther Plaut, ed., *The Torah: A Modern Commentary*, rev. ed. (New York: URJ Press, 2005), unless otherwise noted.
4. See Jacob Milgrom, *Cult and Conscience: The Asham and the Priestly Doctrine of Repentance* (Leiden: Brill, 1976) as well as "The Priestly Doctrine of Repentance," in *Studies in Cultic Theology and Terminology* (Leiden: Brill, 1983), 47–66; and *Anchor Bible: Leviticus 1–16* (New York: Doubleday, 1991), 1062–63. Compounding this problem is the possibility, based on several parallel passages, that such a denial took place under oath. See for example the commentary of the *B'chor Shor* on Leviticus 4:13.
5. Jacob Milgrom, "The Cultic Asham: Philological Postulates" in *Proceedings of the World Congress of Jewish Studies*, August 1973. This reflects a debate between Rashi and Rashbam, the former holding that the term means "to become guilty" (i.e., by new evidence coming to light) and the latter holding that it means "to feel guilty." See the respective commentaries to Leviticus 5:3, 17, and 24 as well as Martin Lockshin's *Rashbam's Commentary on Leviticus* (Providence: Brown University Press, 2001), 30–33.
6. *Plague Prayer of Mursilis*, 9ff., in *Ancient Near Eastern Texts Relating to the Old Testament*, 3rd ed., ed. J. B. Pritchard (Princeton: Princeton University Press, 1969), 395.
7. See, for example, the statement of Rabbi Shimon ben Lakish in BT *Yoma* 86b.
8. See, for example, H. Tawil's "The Prince of the Steep: A Comparative Study" in *ZAW* 92 (1980): 43–59; and D. P. Wright, *The Disposal of Impurity: SBL Dissertation Series* 101 (Atlanta: Scholars Press, 1987), 15–74.
9. See Israel Drazin's *Targum Onkelos to Leviticus* (New York: Ktav, 1994), 150–51. Drazin's text of Onkelos is based on the manuscripts of Sperber and Berliner. It should also be noted that Rashi reads the term *pish'aihem* in the same manner.
10. See William Holladay, *The Root Shuv in the Old Testament* (Leiden: Brill, 1958). See also *Theological Dictionary of the Old Testament (TDOT)*, ed. G. J. Botterwek and H. Ringgren (Grand Rapids, MI: W. B. Eerdmans, 1978).
11. Early date: Y. Kaufmann, *The Religion of Ancient Israel*, trans. Moshe Greenberg (Chicago: University of Chicago Press, 1960), 284ff.; Late date: G. M. Landes, "Linguistic Criteria and the Date of the Book of Jonah," *Eretz Yisrael* 16 (Orlinsky Volume) (Jerusalem: Israel Exploration Society, 1976).
12. See, for example, J. M. Miles, "Laughing at the Bible: Jonah as Pardoy," *JQR* 65 (1975): 168–81; and David Marcus, *From Balaam to Jonah: Anti-prophetic Satire in the Hebrew Bible* (Atlanta: Scholars Press, 1995).

13. Shmuel Achituv and Moshe Greenberg, eds., *Mikra L'yisrael: Perush Mada'i l'Miqra: Ovadiah v'Yonah* (Tel Aviv: Am Oved, 1992).
14. With respect to the former, see Uriel Simon, *Jonah*, JPS Bible Series (Philadelphia: JPS, 1998); with respect to the latter, see Elias Bickerman's *Four Strange Books of the Bible* (New York: Schocken Books, 1967), 3–49.
15. *M'chilta D'Rabbi Yishmael, Bachodesh* 7:17ff.; Lauterbach edition, 249ff.; Horowitz Rabin edition, 228. There exist a number of parallel versions, including *Mishnah Yoma* 8:8, JT *Yoma* 45b–c and *Kippurim* 4:6–8. There is some disagreement about the exact number of "levels" of repentance, the names of the tradents, and the proof texts. For a description of the textual history, see W. S. Towner, *The Rabbinic Enumeration of Scriptural Examples* (Leiden: Brill, 1973), 140–45.
16. M. *Yoma* 8:9
17. It might be possible to divide Leviticus 16 in such a way that certain sources stress the sanctity of the day while others stress the sacrificial offerings, but scholars today prefer to see this chapter as a unitary text. In any case, it would be impossible to envision the Sages viewing this as a composite text from which they might choose a single strand.
18. *Tosefta, Yoma* 4:15, Lieberman 255.
19. BT *Yoma* 87b
20. In fact, there is an expression found in the *Tosefta* "as long as the confessional of Yom Kippur"—even though the evidence suggests it was quite brief. See *Tosefta, B'rachot* 3:6, Lieberman 13.

Legal Authority and Verbal Harm in a Talmudic Narrative

Karl A. Plank

The narratives of Rabbinic legal discourse function in a paradigmatic way. The Sages' impulse to preserve discussions of particular cases is not motivated by a concern to provide an historical record or to be comprehensive in consideration of the law. Rather, such narratives reflect the Rabbis' conviction that the ways in which a given issue is discussed and resolved may furnish an analogy for how to proceed in comparable instances. As such, the narratives furnish templates that enable the Rabbis to negotiate the challenges of new legal questions arising from their own changing, contemporary context. Accordingly, the ostensible topic under discussion may not be the real matter of concern. When the Rabbis discuss, for instance, laws pertaining to the cult of sacrifices in the Temple, the explicit issue is already obsolete: there is no longer a Temple, owing to the Roman destruction of Jerusalem in 70 C.E. Yet such discussions abound because, in debating this issue, the Rabbis develop a method of talking about their own world. Said another way, Rabbinic legal discourse tends to function as a meta-discourse within which the Rabbis, while discussing a concrete situation, are talking at a fundamental level about how they talk, how they conjugate the situations of their existence.

We find a compelling instance in the Talmudic narrative that rehearses the debate over the oven of Aknai (BT *Bava M'tzia* 59a–b). While set within a larger discussion of verbal harm, the story initially seems remote from that theme. The ostensible issue concerns the purity of an earthenware oven, a *tanur shel aknai* (snake oven), which is constructed in serpentine-like clay coils with a sand mortar between the pieces. Rabbi Eliezer ben Hyrcanos, a first-century

---

KARL A. PLANK is the J. W. Cannon Professor of Religion at Davidson College in Davidson, North Carolina.

Tanna, asserts the oven's purity, a judgment that meets with the disagreement of all the other Sages. Unable to convince his peers that his view is correct, Rabbi Eliezer persists in his cause by performing a series of miracles designed to demonstrate his power and, thus, his authority. He calls for a carob tree to uproot itself and travel a significant distance, for a stream of water to reverse its course, and for the walls of the very academy in which they are debating to begin to fall. Each of these happens, but only to meet the consistent response of the other Sages: these acts prove nothing; they are not germane. At this point, Rabbi Eliezer decides to play the ultimate trump card. He declares, "If it is as I say, let it be proved from heaven."[1] And, unsurprisingly, given his earlier shows of power, a voice from heaven (a *bat kol*) sounds forth announcing its dismay that anyone would disagree with Rabbi Eliezer for his views on all matters are halachic (i.e., correct interpretations of the law).

Hearing the backing of heaven, one would expect the debate to be over and done. But again, the act is deemed to lack pertinence. Rabbi Joshua jumps to his feet and puts the point succinctly, by quoting scripture: "'It is not in heaven'" (Deut. 30:12). Rabbi Jeremiah, a fourth-century *Amora,* then explains: "We do not listen to a heavenly voice, since you [God] already gave it to us on Mt. Sinai and it is written there [quoting another scripture], "'Incline after the majority'" (Exod. 23:2).[2] And how does God respond to this dismissal of his voice? According to no less than Elijah, "God laughed and smiled and said, 'My sons have defeated me, my sons have defeated me.'"

Virtually no arguments have directly addressed the issue of the oven's purity, but rather that issue has become a pretext for a conversation about how the community makes legal decisions and understands its authority to do so. The story puts that understanding at stake and does not quickly, if ever, resolve it. Keeping the question alive may have greater value than establishing an answer (which itself may be a way of answering the question). The narrative of the oven of Aknai begins with a controversy or dispute and, even when the ostensible case comes to judgment—against Rabbi Eliezer, the oven is deemed impure— the tension continues. God, admittedly, concedes the point, but does the reader readily join in God's laughter? How does she or he judge Rabbi Eliezer?

As David Luban has argued, the reader might interpret Rabbi Eliezer in two different ways. The first he names the Platonic interpretation, building upon Plato's distinction between truth and mere opinion. Here, one might envision Rabbi Eliezer as the lonely champion of truth, indeed heaven's truth, playing Socrates to Rabbi Joshua and the other Sages' role as authoritarian sophists who simply identify their own opinions as truth.[3] Or similarly, to follow Robert Cover, is Rabbi Eliezer like Frederick Douglass who stubbornly maintained against all professional and judiciary consensus that the Constitution did not allow slavery?[4] This sympathetic view of Rabbi Eliezer draws support from cues in the story: the initial likening of the Sages' words to snakes, fully intending the pun to the Aknai oven; the unequivocal backing of the heavenly voice; and the story of the controversy's aftermath in which Rabbi Eliezer is banned by his peers who, in turn, receive God's own harsh recompense.[5]

Luban's second reading, the humanistic interpretation, sees Rabbi Eliezer as the true authoritarian.[6] Unable to convince the Sages by argument, Rabbi Eliezer resorts to magic and force in an attempt to coerce the Sages' agreement. He acts as a law unto himself, treating himself as an exception who need not assent to the community's authority or rules of play. In his presumption of autonomy, he endangers any prospect of social order. As the story reminds so vividly, even the voice of heaven must yield to the community's judgment, and here it does so willingly, with an approving laughter and smile.[7]

Though these readings oppose each other, both converge on a common understanding of Rabbi Eliezer's view of truth, separating primarily in how one should evaluate that view. Luban speaks of this view as the "right-answer thesis" which assumes, *pace* Ronald Dworkin, that questions of truth (or of legal meaning) have a single, authoritative answer and, as a corollary, that such an answer is grounded in the intention of the originating source or in its original public meaning.[8] Thus, when Rabbi Eliezer calls for the *bat kol* (the heavenly voice), he does so with confidence that its utterance is finally indisputable and changeless. Luban effectively recalls the parallel in Woody Allen's *Annie Hall*. In that film:

> Woody Allen finds himself standing in a theater line behind an obnoxious man pontificating about the theories of Marshall McLuhan. Allen immediately produces Marshall McLuhan, who tells the man, "You know nothing of my work!" To film this scene, Allen recruited the real Marshall McLuhan for a

cameo appearance as a kind of *bat kol*. The scene delights us because it fulfills an infantile fantasy we all have about finally making the idiots see that we're right and they are wrong. The fable of the *bat kol*, like Allen's cinematic fantasy, answers to a thoroughly objectivist image of the truth and a psychological need all of us sometimes feel to force the disbelievers to see what is indisputable.[9]

But, of course, this is precisely the move the Sages oppose. When Rabbi Joshua exclaims, "'It is not in heaven'" it is as if the obnoxious man turned to McLuhan and said, "Well, what do you know?" and then McLuhan replies, "Oh, yes, I see what you mean. Go ahead."—a liberating thought to some and a source of deep anxiety for others.

As Suzanne Stone has shown, the story of the oven of Aknai resonates within current legal theory as it considers the relation between legal interpretation and legitimate authority. Postmodern perspectives in both literary and legal theory have made untenable confidence in the objectivity of meaning, including legal meaning, while at the same time, emphasizing the constructive nature of truth.[10] Such a collapse of the positivist tradition, marked by the absence of foundational, objective values, threatens truth with chaos and relativism and creates the anxiety of interpretation, namely that a legal decision may not represent the divinely revealed tradition, or said more simply, be true.[11] For the Rabbis, this is not so much a deficit, as the working out of a covenantal logic. As Stone notes, following the work of José Faur, "the covenant creates an author-reader relationship between God and his interpretive community, in which God the author surrenders his work to a community who receives it, thus authorizing interpretation without recourse to his intent."[12] The loss of the author's intention as a curb on interpretation, though now familiar in literary studies as the intentional fallacy, generates the deep worry that, in Boyarin's words, "once that control is gone, it seems that any interpretation is the same as any other, that anything at all can be said to the meaning of the text."[13]

When transferred into the legal context, such anxiety may generate reactionary tendencies such as seen in the judicial decisions and opinions of Justice Antonin Scalia. As Robert Burt has shown, Justice Scalia's dominant perspective resembles Rabbi Eliezer's insofar as it seeks to establish a singular truth through appeal to the original meaning of an originating source.[14] Such foundationalism or originalism, in Justice Scalia's case, takes the form of insisting that the original meaning of the constitution is the only legitimate source of constitutional authority.[15] Accordingly, Justice Scalia is disdainful of arguments from precedent that take seriously the accumulative history of the tradition of constitutional interpretation. For him, constitutional interpretation does not or should not change over time. Once the original meaning is known, it yields an indisputable, singular truth.[16]

Seeing the oven of Aknai through the lens of anxiety and in terms of the Scalia parallel leads to other questions: in particular, does the Talmud passage show itself to be aware of its own anxiety and take steps to respond to it that differ from the reactionary tendencies of Justice Scalia? Also, does the passage see the anxiety as worthwhile? What does the resistance to Rabbi Eliezer's "right answer" orientation enable? How is it liberating?

First, the narrative does show sensitivity to the anxiety it might cause. It, too, has concern that interpretation not devolve into excessive relativism. As soon as Rabbi Joshua exclaims, "'It is not in heaven,'" the passage asks, "What does this mean?"—literally, "What is, 'it is not in heaven'"? Rabbi Jeremiah then explains: "We do not listen to a heavenly voice, since you already gave it to us on Mt. Sinai and it is written there, 'incline after the majority.'" If the first part of his explanation justifies the prerogative and responsibility of the community to interpret the Torah, the second part suggests the context and constraint of such interpretation: legal judgments are made in the midst of a community deliberation and are curbed by the rule of the majority. Though interpretation is not vouchsafed in or by heaven, it yet does not follow the path of idiosyncratic whim or individualism and, as such, will never mean simply what one desires or assumes it to be. The community and its rationality constrain the potential abuse of truth feared in the collapse of Rabbi Eliezer's right-answered foundationalism.

Second, the anxiety of moving to a communally based negotiation of the truth is itself a worthwhile cost to pay in order to avoid certain dangers of foundationalism. The foundational perspective, be it Rabbi Eliezer's or Scalia's, has scary implications: if legal truth cannot change then how can it be responsive to the needs of a new context that the original intention may have been unable to foresee or anticipate? If it cannot change, then can it be self-critical, and if not self-critical, what saves it from being simply ideological? If legal meaning is finally indisputable, what prevents it from becoming oppressively authoritarian? The model of the Sages (a model central to the whole dynamic of Oral Torah) counters by locating truth as something determined in dialogue and renewed in ongoing deliberation. Such truth is open-ended and polyvalent, genuinely contemporary, and, in its own way, democratic.

Were the story to end here with the triumph of a postmodern Rabbi Joshua over a foundationalist Rabbi Eliezer, we would be left with an assuring democratic confidence and a narrative ripe for picking by contemporary legal theorists. But the story continues to deal with the aftermath of the debate over the oven of Aknai. If the first part of the story ended with a laughing God as the model of a good loser, the second part finds the Sages to be unusually bad winners. Because Rabbi Eliezer had refused to comply with the majority (and likely persisted in his view after the judgment), the Sages ban him from the community, burning everything that he had declared to be pure.[17] In short, even though Rabbi Akiba approaches Rabbi Eliezer in the gentlest way, the collective action functions to shame Rabbi Eliezer publicly—and this the text sees in the most serious of ways.

As indicated earlier, the story of the oven of Aknai is set within a larger discussion of verbal harm and wrongdoing. Before we get to the narrative, we read that verbal wronging is more serious than monetary wronging because in the former case, restoration is impossible; that God himself exacts punishment for verbal wrongs; and that *halbanot panim* (literally the whitening of the face, i.e., causing shame) is the archetype of verbal wrong. The shame that causes the blood to flow from one's face in great humiliation is itself tantamount to bloodshed (BT *Bava M'tzia* 58b–59a).[18] Though not wrong in their legal judgment or responsibility, the Sages' ban is an act of *halbanot panim* that Rabbi Eliezer receives in mourning, as if he himself has died.[19]

His tearful mourning unleashes natural catastrophe in the world. As the Sages burned his purities, so now everywhere he turns his eyes becomes consumed with fire. Rabban Gamaliel, the *nasi* (head) of the Sanhedrin and, thus, likely the one to have authorized the ban,[20] nearly drowns at sea, surmising rightly, "I bet this has something to do with Rabbi Eliezer." He is saved only by explaining to God that he undertook his actions to insure that disagreements do not multiply in Israel—a compelling point from a legal point of view, perhaps, but not sufficient to justify the shame of another. The narrative follows the story of Rabban Gamaliel who, we are now told, is the brother-in-law of Rabbi Eliezer; Rabbi Eliezer's wife, Ima Shalom (literally, the "mother of peace") is Rabban Gamaliel's sister. Ima Shalom's fear is that should her husband ever fall to his face to vent his anguish in prayer to God that this would result in her brother's death. She succeeds for a period of time until one day a poor man comes to the door seeking food. She goes to the door to see to his need and then Rabbi Eliezer begins his prostration and prayer. Returning, she tells him, "Stand up. You have killed my brother" and we hear the sound of the shofar going out from Rabban Gamaliel's house announcing his death.

The story of the banning of Rabbi Eliezer contrasts sharply with the narrative of the debate. In the story of the oven of Aknai, we find the empowerment of the community to be authoritative interpreters of Torah, to make legal judgments and decisions that are binding. In the story of the banning, the perspective shifts to confront the limits of the community's legal power, its potential to do verbal harm that is deathly. If, throughout the passage, the Rabbis are engaged in a meta-discourse about their own legal process and practice, they have here shown a concern for a self-critical awareness that situates their authority as itself accountable to moral obligation. They are aware that their power may turn oppressive and destructive.

As Rubenstein has shown, the story of the banning exposes a chain of actions and consequences that are catastrophic: the Sages' banning of Rabbi Eliezer leads to his anguish, the venting of which leads to damage of crops; the resulting scarcity of food creates the condition for the poor man to come to Rabbi Eliezer's house to seek food. And, as we have seen, when Ima Shalom tends to this man, leaving her husband alone, he unleashes the prayer which eventuates in Rabban Gamaliel's death.[21] While the death of Rabban Gamaliel might be understood as divine punishment, the story also wants to emphasize through its chain of events that the act of verbal harm creates its own nexus of destruction. It is a serious matter.

Not once does the story challenge the legal authority of the Sages, but it does issue a strong cautionary warning about how that authority is used. It cannot be used for harm with impunity. In social terms, the vesting of the community with authority for its laws is necessary to avoid the dangers of authoritarianism and ideological oppression. In covenantal terms, it is necessary for the community's mature responsibility in relationship to God.[22] Yet, no amount of necessity and recognized good can finally justify the use of legal power to damage the well-being of human relationships that constitute the very community within which legal power is exercised. As Luban reminds, the fundamental rupture of human relations is always wrong.[23]

Our story dramatizes the tension between legal authority and moral obligation. While they need not come into conflict, the fact that one is legally empowered to undertake a program of action does not mean that one is morally justified in doing so. The shaming of Rabbi Eliezer is a paradigmatic case in point. His excommunication may be socially necessary for the reason that Rabban Gamaliel gave when the waves threatened to drown him: social order requires compliance with the law; the disagreements that signify noncompliance cannot be allowed to persist. Yet, the legal justification runs up against the surpassing moral demand to preserve the fabric of human community, to yield to what Luban aptly calls "the primacy of the personal."[24] Those empowered with legal authority must attend to that fundamental obligation to uphold the dignity of those affected by their decisions, to avoid the verbal wrongdoing of shame and humiliation that tears the fabric of community within which their power to do the good and the necessary ultimately rests.

God, the story suggests, will not tolerate such harm. If the laughing God enjoyed the coming of age of his Sages and did not intervene in their legal debate, such can hardly be said of their banning of Rabbi Eliezer. God returns to the story to exert a moral pressure on the very legal authority he has permitted, or even created in his Torah (as Rabbi Jeremiah suggested). The narrative leaves behind the presenting case of the oven's purity to invite one to hear the meta-discourse, how the Rabbis talk about their own process as legal authorities. Unquestionably, we find the empowerment of their responsibility to serve as an authoritative, interpretive community of Torah. They rule through the consensus of the majority. The final word, however, is that all such power is itself under a transcending obligation. Law, at least as understood in our passage, inevitably leads to theology.[25]

Notes

1. The English translation of this Talmudic narrative, here and throughout the article, is that of Jeffrey L. Rubenstein, *Talmudic Stories: Narrative Art, Composition, and Culture* (Baltimore: Johns Hopkins University Press, 1999), 36–38.
2. Note that these quotations are read against their plain meaning in their scriptural contexts, itself a sign of the Rabbis' freedom to innovate within the tradition.
3. David Luban, "The Coiled Serpent of Argument: Reason, Authority, and Law in a Talmudic Tale," *Chicago-Kent Law Review* 79 (2004): 1256–57.
4. Robert M. Cover, "The Supreme Court, 1982 Term—Foreword: Nomos and Narrative," *Harvard Law Review* 97 (1983): 37–40.
5. One might add here the story's mention that the walls of the academy remain at a tilt in honor of Rabbi Eliezer, even if they don't totally fall either, in honor of Rabbi Joshua.
6. Luban, "The Coiled Serpent," 1257.
7. That God's laughter and smile indicate his endorsement, see David Weiss Halivni, *Breaking the Tablets: Jewish Theology after the Shoah* (New York: Rowan and Littlefield, 2007), 112. An interesting parallel that combines elements of both of Luban's views can be seen in the following saying of Rabbi Ishmael: "Don't judge alone, for only the One [God] may do so. Don't say [to your fellow judges], 'Accept my view,' for it is up to them [to make that decision] and not up to you" (*Pirkei Avot* 4:8; trans. L. Kravitz and K. Olitzky [New York: UAHC, 1993]). With Rabbi Joshua and Rabbi Jeremiah, the saying points to the necessity of majority rule; with Rabbi Eliezer, it suggests the continued efficacy of God's judgment in legal affairs. In neither instance, however, could one find permission for Rabbi Eliezer to rule alone.
8. Luban, "The Coiled Serpent," 1255.
9. Ibid.
10. Suzanne Stone, "In Pursuit of the Counter-Text: The Turn to the Jewish Legal Model in Contemporary American Legal Theory," *Harvard Law Review* 106 (1993): 823.
11. Ibid., 833.
12. Ibid., 844.
13. Daniel Boyarin, *Intertextuality and the Reading of Midrash* (Bloomington: Indiana University Press, 1990), 35. The intentional fallacy states that the meaning of a text is not determined by the author's intention, but creates its meaning as an artifact in its own right, independent of authorial purpose and originating context. An axiom of the New Criticism, the concept was first discussed by

W. K. Wimsatt and Monroe Beardsley in their 1946 essay, "The Intentional Fallacy." See their *The Verbal Icon: Studies in the Meaning of Poetry* (Lexington: University of Kentucky Press, 1954; reprint)
14. Robert A. Burt, "Precedent and Authority in Antonin Scalia's Jurisprudence," *Cardozo Law Review* 12 (1991): 1685–97.
15. One might point to the opinions of Justice Clarence Thomas as being equally originalist, though in a slightly different way. Justice Thomas looks to the original intention of the framers of the Constitution as the criterion for its application. Justice Scalia does not look to authorial intention, but to original public meaning (i.e., how the text would have been understood by its original audience).
16. Burt, "Precedent and Authority," 1685–90. On Scalia's originalism, see his own comments to the Woodrow Wilson International Center for Scholars, Washington, D.C, March 14, 2005: "Constitutional Interpretation the Old Fashioned Way," http://www.cfif.org/htdocs/freedomline/current/guest_commentary/scalia-constitutional-speech.htm. Scalia places his originalism over against the orientation of the "Living Constitution." That such originalism is tied to an anxiety over the perceived loss of controlling, interpretive criteria can be inferred from the following statement: "Now, if you're not going to control your judges that way (originalism), what other criterion are you going to place before them? What is the criterion that governs the Living Constitutional judge? What can you possibly use, besides original meaning?"
17. Rabbi Eliezer appears more than once as an outlier: over-against Rabban Gamaliel, Rabbi Akiba, and Rabbi Joshua, each of whom appears in the oven of Aknai, see the dispute over the eighteen benedictions (*Mishnah B'rachot* 4:3–4); and note also the dispute over the literal interpretation of Exodus 21:23 (BT *Bava Kama* 84a). On the latter see Weiss Halivni, *Breaking the Tablets*, 111.
18. See Rubenstein, *Talmudic Stories*, 61–62.
19. In doing so, Rabbi Eliezer follows the cues of Rabbi Akiba, who had come to him dressed in black, shoeless, sitting at a distance, and with eyes full of tears.
20. Thus, Rubenstein, *Talmudic Stories*, 44.
21. Ibid., 46.
22. This point is worked out fully in David Hartman, *A Living Covenant: The Innovative Spirit in Traditional Judaism* (Woodstock, VT: Jewish Lights, 1998).
23. Luban, "The Coiled Serpent," 1284.
24. Ibid.
25. In concluding in this fashion, I support the argument of Suzanne Stone that, though Rabbinic legal discourse shows affinities with post-modern legal theory, it also resists any easy appropriation by a secular culture because of its persistent theological character.

Chesed Shel Emet: Reconsidering the Future of Jewish Burial

Yoni Regev

At the turn of the twentieth century, an immigrant wrote, "I am an Eastern [European] Jew, and we are at home wherever our dead are buried . . . My son will be a complete American, for that is where I will be buried."[1] Death and burial are critical components of the Jewish life cycle. In burying our loved ones we perform a mitzvah and the ultimate act of חסד של אמת, an act of kindness and care that can never be repaid. From Abraham onward, the Bible is replete with stories of burial in a family plot, where the deceased is "gathered to their ancestors." Over two thousand years later, the immigrant writer recognized that the dead remained a vital anchor in his life. But I don't think the same is true for us anymore, or at least, not in the same way.

Most of us have been trained to officiate at Jewish funerals and counsel the bereaved in our community. I would like to suggest to you that there is a burial crisis looming not too far down the road, and the time has come to for us to reevaluate every aspect of our current burial practices. In the next century, the world will have to contend with ten billion natural deaths, a staggering number. To place that number in context, we can project the passing of at least two million Jews in the United States within the span of our careers, and our national and community infrastructures are unprepared for this reality. As Jewish leaders we will be expected to solve this crisis, though few people outside the funeral industry have publicly spoken about it yet.

YONI REGEV (LA14) is Assistant Rabbi at Temple Sinai, Oakland, CA.

This article is based on the senior sermon delivered at HUC-JIR, LA. The author wishes to thank Dr. Rachel Adler to recommending this paper for publication, and to Hillside Memorial Park Cemetery for providing access, information, and support.

As things stand, Jews are among the most likely to live at a great distance from the burial places of their ancestors. Even those who still live close by are unlikely to maintain a regular practice of visiting their relative's graves, even on their *yahrzeit*. We have effectively transplanted this important tradition and mitzvah from the actual gravesite to the realm of the synagogue and the Shabbat service *Kaddish* list. Our current burial practices are a radical change from what we know in antiquity, and they are passing the point of financial and ecological sustainability.

The problem is not just that we are running out of room, but we are fundamentally running on autopilot without considering the cultural paradigm shift that has happened around us. Did our ancestors really envision a time when we would become so numerous that our dead would fill cemeteries many times the size of their ancient cities? Given the alternatives I will describe, I wonder if we can continue to justify the costly practice of treating our burial plots like a residential address for posterity? I don't pretend to have any definitive answers to these problems, but I know that we simply don't have the luxury of ignoring them any longer.

The tradition is clear about our responsibility to provide our deceased with a dignified and speedy burial. Deuteronomy 21:23 commands that even a man executed by hanging must surely be buried that very day: לא-תלין נבלתו על-העץ כי-קבור תקברנו ביום ההוא ..., but we must look further back to the earliest example of Israelite burial to learn how this was done.

Abraham went to great lengths in order to secure a burial place for Sarah, which would subsequently serve as the first אחוזת קבר (family burial estate) in our tradition. Though the Machpelah cave is not explicitly mentioned in the account of Isaac's death and burial, we may safely infer that Jacob and Esau buried their father near his own parents when he was "gathered to his people."

As the first instance of burial mentioned in the bible, Sarah's burial likely influenced the later development of Jewish law. Although the text makes no mention of it, might we then assume that Abraham set forth the example of burying his beloved Sarah wrapped in a linen cloth inside a simple wooden box under a several feet of earth? Most assuredly not.

Ample archeological evidence supports the use of caves for burial as described in BT *Bava Batra* 101a. The Talmud stipulates that a burial place should be in rock-hewn caves, with separate caves for each family and niches dug in the rock for each body. Further, the Talmud (*Sanhedrin* 47b and *K'tubot* 4b) states that the mourning period officially begins when the *golel* (a large stone), is used to close the opening of the niche. Many of us saw a living example of such a structure at בית שערים during our year in Israel.

It is critical to understand that in ancient Israel, and well into the Rabbinic period, the burial process did not end when the *golel* was set in place. If this were the case, even the scores of burial caves and catacombs scattered around Jerusalem and the Galilee would likely not have sufficed for the Jewish population of the land. Rather, on the first anniversary of the deceased's passing, family members would gather in order to perform a secondary burial. After the flesh decomposed, the family would carefully gather the bones of the deceased and reverently place them in a special niche or ossuary where they would literally be gathered together with the bones of their ancestors.

Clear evidence for this common practice can be found in *Mishnah Mo-eid Katan* 1:5, where Rabbi Meir and Rabbi Yossei disagree on whether the practice should be performed during the intermediate days of festivals. Rabbi Meir goes so far as to declare that such gruesome work is the source of great joy: ועוד אמר רבי מאיר: מלקט אדם עצמות אביו ואמו מפני ששמחה היא לו. The *Y'rushalmi* on the same *mishnah* concludes that one derives joy from knowing their relative is finally free from the judgment of Heaven and all of their sins have been absolved.

Dr. Dorit Gad observes that the practice of secondary burial became deeply linked with the messianic aspirations of resurrection around the Second Temple period, and fell out of favor in the third or fourth century c.e.[2] By the time of Maimonides, the practice of burial had changed dramatically. In his *Mishneh Torah* (4:4 שופטים, הלכות אבל), Maimonides makes no mention of secondary burial, but prescribes a quick return of the body to the earth (though he also permits a simple wood coffin to be used). Later commentators argued that it was a mitzvah to bury the dead directly in the earth, so as to fulfill the precept from Genesis 3:19: כי עפר אתה ואל עפר תשוב ("for you are dust, and to dust you shall return"). It is interesting to note that Maimonides prescribed headstones for the tombs of common people, but not for those of the righteous, because their teachings would serve as their lasting memorial.

Today, most non-Orthodox Jews incorporate customs and sensibilities from the broader community in their burial plans. When we bury in the ground, it is often in a sealed casket with a cement vault to prevent the earth from sinking around the grave. Some choose wall burial in a mausoleum, but a growing number are choosing cremation, which has reached unprecedented levels in the past decade, particularly since the economic collapse of 2008. Across North America, cremation accounted for 42 percent of interments last year, up from just 15 percent in 1985. The number is lower in the Jewish population, but has likely reached 20 percent of non-Orthodox Jewish interments.

Cremation is seen by many as a more affordable option compared with traditional burial; however, any cost benefit is easily offset by the destructive environmental impact of the incineration process. Though Reform responsa do not explicitly prohibit cremation, it is widely viewed as undesirable following the traumatic experience and memory of the Holocaust. Conversely, the "traditional" method of ground burial we commonly perform presents us with a different set of challenges, since the Jewish population is primarily centered in dense urban areas where burial infrastructure is already under duress. In New York City, existing cemeteries within the five boroughs have all run out of plots for sale. Jews, and anyone else who would like to be buried in the ground, must travel two hours outside the city for available land.

In Los Angeles, the Jewish cemeteries project their existing supply of land will only suffice for sales in the next thirty years, and that depends on ongoing construction, like that of a massive two-tiered mausoleum called The Valley of the Prophets at Hillside Memorial Park.

For all of that, we are fortunate that land reserves still exist in the United States. Israel, by comparison, faces a far more immediate challenge, and it has incorporated ancient customs alongside halachic innovation to provide a longer-term solution for the lack of burial land. At the newest and largest regional cemetery complex built for the city of Haifa and its environs, the ministry of religious affairs has constructed a three-tiered cemetery that provides "ground burial" on multiple levels above the surface, as well as several levels of wall burial, which they call קברי סנהדרין after Second Temple practices.

More novel alternatives are beginning to attract consumers who are concerned about the environmental impact of death and burial.

The Green Burial Council advocates un-embalmed interment to create miniature natural conservation zones. So-called green burial options are becoming available in cemeteries around the country, such as the Garden of Eden featured in Hillside Memorial's newest project. Environmentally friendly bamboo coffins and linen or raw silk shrouds replace the wood and steel caskets and promote a speedy return of the body to the earth.

Technology also offers future solutions, such as Promessa Organic Burial, a Swedish company that will freeze your body in liquid nitrogen, subject it to a "vibration of a specific amplitude" and reduce it to powder. Another intriguing option is called Resomation, or alkaline hydrolysis, which chemically reduces bodies with pressure and warm alkaline water, leaving only bones and waste water behind in a matter of hours. The industry is calling this process bio-cremation, because it produces a similar result to cremation with a far lesser environmental impact. Since the process uses water instead of fire to consume the body, it may circumvent our existing cultural and religious bias against cremation.

Though this conversation may be distasteful to some of us, we are entrusted with the sacred obligation to guide our communities as they seek to fulfill our traditions in the modern world. We must debate and decide which sacred values deserve the greatest emphasis and promote a burial practice that is sustainable over time. Here are some questions we might ask as we begin this debate:

- What do we mean when we lay someone to eternal rest, and how do we propose to guarantee such long-term care and maintenance of our cemeteries?
- Can we find any modern use for the ancient practice of secondary burial and the direct contact with the deceased, as found in antiquity?
- Do novel technologies pose the risk of בזיון המת (disgracing of the dead) by actively destroying the body?
- How might our rituals, liturgy, and pastoral care change if we no longer perform graveside interments? Could we achieve the same finality and closer that burial provides?
- Can we justify the great economic burden that ground burial now poses for seniors or their families who wish to adhere to tradition?

- Should we develop new Jewish cemeteries where land is available to allow ground burial but the distance from the cities will undermine any hope of maintaining contact between families and their ancestors' graves?
- How might we honor of the tradition to be gathered up with our ancestors when our families are so spread apart?
- Could we follow the example of Temple Akiba in Los Angeles or Beth El in Florida, where the communities maintain a cremation garden or mausoleum on the grounds of the synagogue and see the duty of honoring the dead as central to their congregation's mission?

Whatever paths we follow, we have the opportunity to provide a meaningful and authentic Jewish response to avert this crisis before it gets worse. Just as we transitioned from family plots and cave burials in the time of antiquity, to the *chevrah kadisha* and public cemeteries we know today, Jewish tradition provides the flexibility to change our customs in the face of necessity and progress.

Though dramatic change is needed, there is no doubt that many will protest against any change to the status quo. The future debate must be sensitive and acknowledge that issues of death and burial spark responses from deep inside our soul. There will be pain, distrust, and confusion. But we will have no choice. Our teachings must reflect the authenticity of our heritage and the genuine caring we feel toward the grieving families. Long before the mourning ribbons are cut, before the next burial plots are purchased, we have to be prepared to help guide families towards meaningful rituals through the ever-present Valley of the Shadow of Death.

Let this be a time for bold initiatives and brave conversations, and may we be guided by the spirit of performing חסד של אמת, a selfless act of goodness to ensure the sacred treatment of our dead in the future to come.

Notes

1. Joseph Roth, *Letters 1911–1939*, ed. Herman Kesten, 1970.
2. http://hofesh.org.il/freeclass/history/bones_gathering.html.

A Tribute to David Ellenson

Tradition in Transition: The Incredible Journey of President David Ellenson

Robert Levine

A Man in a Hurry

David Ellenson has always been a man on a mission, even if it wasn't always possible to foresee all the stations on the journey that have contributed so powerfully to the health and vitality of Reform Judaism in the twenty-first century. I personally met David, who would become my best friend, during the first day of classes on the New York campus of HUC-JIR in 1973. Carting a stuffed blue backpack, David rushed into Intro to Bible class, but not exactly to sit and quietly prepare the Rashi for group discussion. With some urgency he wanted to know just what would be covered that day, because he was also registered for a Hebrew literature class which met at the same time.

This guy's in a real hurry, I thought to myself. At that moment, I did not know that a year later David would simultaneously enroll in the Ph.D. program in the Department of Religion at Columbia University. Though this was an unusually ambitious path, David did not want to become a rabbi in order to be a better scholar. He is a brilliant professor who also embodies all the qualities anyone would ever want in a caring, soulful rabbi.

While some first-rate academics find human contact rather inconvenient, David Ellenson thrives on people. They are a great source of oxygen to him. Just as David reads material once and owns it forever, he also meets someone once and has a friend

---

ROBERT LEVINE (NY77) is senior rabbi of Congregation Rodeph Sholom in New York City. His latest book is *What God Can Do for You Now: For Seekers Who Want to Believe* (Sourcebooks, Inc., 2008).

forever. His ability and need to meld his intellectual and personal talents make him among the most impressive and memorable leaders our Movement has ever produced.

So, David was earning two tough degrees simultaneously. As if his plate was not full enough, David also was the primary caregiver to his daughter, Ruthie. When I was invited to the first of many dinners at his apartment, I learned how deeply he also embraced the role of tender father and true *baal habayit*. David's wizardry in the kitchen dazzled this young rabbinic student. In minutes David had changed a diaper, straightened up the living room, and placed on the table sizzling kosher steaks together with a half dozen cans of Tab, his favorite diet cola. There were so many things that drew me to David, then and now, but when he started cooking for me, I knew for sure I was in love.

As a husband and father there was true urgency to Dr. Ellenson's scholarly pursuits. With a family to support he did not have the luxury of being a perpetual student. Yet, I would contend that David was seeking something more important in those early days than a means to make a living. Speaking personally I enrolled at HUC-JIR less to become a rabbi than to find myself as a Jew. In my judgment David Ellenson entered both the College-Institute and a prominent secular academic institution in an effort to reconcile two often contradictory aspects of his persona.

The Reform in the Orthodox

How far David had already traveled when I met him on that day in New York in 1973 became clear to me four years later when I accompanied him back home to officiate at his father's funeral in the Orthodox synagogue of Newport News, Virginia. There I immediately saw how much a product of the South he really was. David's graciousness was home grown. Growing up in a small community of very few Jews, he learned to intermingle easily with people of other faiths and races. Though he went to an Orthodox shul he was totally integrated into the community.

No matter what was going on beneath the surface in that breezy, friendly Southern environment, David never experienced any overt anti-Semitism. Out and about David felt truly at home. Inside his synagogue David was exposed to a decidedly pre-modern Orthodoxy whose rabbis had not embraced the conflict of living as a Jew in modern times. On the contrary, they saw America as a serious threat to the Judaism they had known all their lives and tried valiantly to maintain. David was incredulous when he heard one of his rabbis proclaim in a sermon, "I can understand why Hitler killed so many Western European Jews; they had assimilated and somewhat deserved their fate. What I can't understand is how the pious Eastern European Jews also were killed." Then and there, the outraged David knew that as much as he loved the people and piety of his hometown shul, he would need to find a way to marry his love of tradition with more modern sensibilities. Reflecting on his youth, David would write, "A sense of distance from my surroundings has always marked me. That description of such tension has allowed me to hold up a candle to my own soul."[1]

David Ellenson was ready to embrace the modern world. He graduated from William and Mary and received a master of religion at the University of Virginia. Judaism and the State of Israel continued to exhibit a strong gravitational pull. His experience at a *kibbutz ulpan* during the first-year program in Israel at HUC-JIR reinforced a fierce and undying Zionism that has informed his personal and professional life. What motivated him most, however, was the desire to move beyond his southern small city Orthodox upbringing and find a way to bring traditional Judaism into the modern era.

Through his academic work David would be determined to work out a healthier and more cogent synthesis between these two worlds. In the introduction to his first book, *Tradition and Transition*, Ellenson wrote:

> Simply put, the Orthodox Jew and Orthodox Judaism have not been sufficiently appreciated as being active participants in the dialectical interplay of tradition and modernity universally acknowledged as characteristic of other movements and denominations within modern Judaism. Thus, whether consciously or unconsciously, the responsa—in as much as they are a genre of Jewish legal literature bequeathed to modern Judaism from a medieval corporate past—are deemed particularly unimportant for an investigation of a modern Jewish condition in which Jews reside as individual citizens within a modern nation-state. In recent years there has been movement within the academic community to correct this misperception.[2]

Dr. Ellenson has steadfastly held to the view that true humanism can be found among these modern traditional *poskim* and has devoted his academic career to a thoroughgoing investigation into nineteenth-century European Orthodox sources pursuing, perhaps cherry-picking a bit, among those thinkers who provide some hope for more Jewish unity, further intra-denominational cooperation, or at least some collegiality.

To that end Ellenson turned his attention to a relatively obscure university trained Orthodox Rabbi who would become the head of the Orthodox Rabbinical Seminary of Berlin, Rabbi Esriel Hildesheimer (1820–1899). Far from being a moderate, Hildesheimer felt that there was no other acceptable foundation of Judaism than *Torah min Hashamayim*. In fact, he granted no legitimacy to liberal Judaism whatsoever. Despite this categorical stance, Hildesheimer still recognized the Jewishness of the Reformers and understood that there were many reasons to work together for the Jewish communal good. "I am of the . . . opinion that . . . one is obligated to act in concert with (Liberal Jews) as far as the conscience permits."[3]

Hildesheimer supported antidefamation efforts regarding both Orthodox and Reform Jews, but he went much further, believing that Jews should work together on matters of charitable and communal concern. Thus, while Hildesheimer supported Samson Raphael Hirsch's successful efforts to help overturn a law mandating that Jews must become members of their Jewish community—a measure that prevented Orthodox Jews from seceding from the community dominated by the Reformers—he refused to press for full implementation of that ruling. He conceded that active participation of Reformers in the community could threaten Orthodox absolutism, but he was willing to take that risk for the sake of the well-being of the Jewish community as a whole. Fully aware of the growing distance between the religious movements of Judaism in today's world, Dr. Ellenson nevertheless regards Hildesheimer as an Orthodox leader worthy of emulation, one clearly not willing to compromise on halachic authority and norms, but whose love for the people of Israel allows him to transcend stricture for the higher purpose of Jewish survival and continuity.

Hildesheimer presages the insights of perhaps the most influential of Ellenson's teachers, Professor Jacob Katz (1904–1998), who chronicled the profound changes modernity had thrust upon the traditional Jewish community. Dr. Katz pointed out that communal leaders no longer held authority over its members. Only the secular State had sanctioning power. So, Jewish associations became more and more voluntary, and no one side of the Jewish spectrum could impose its denominational views upon the other. While Jews increasingly have had an unprecedented choice either to embrace the ethics and practices of Judaism, or to walk away by fully assimilating into majority culture, Katz emphasized in his writings that such monumental change did not lead either to the disappearance of Judaism or the Jewish people. Rather it fostered a reinvention of what it means to identify as a Jew in the modern era. Katz's historical and sociological observations form an intellectual foundation for Ellenson's work and provide the academic linchpin for his fundamental optimism of how the Jewish world could undergo profound change, yet still emerge as a divergent yet mutually reinforcing community.

Dr. Ellenson clearly favors religious leaders who embrace the values of *K'lal Yisrael* and *Ahavat Yisrael*. His search for teachers and *poskim* who embrace the reality of modernity is also driven by his sensible view that contact with the entire Jewish community, even those who don't live Orthodox lives, could help the halachist feel greater personal empathy for fellow Jews and lead to an injection of humanism in the halachic process that is too often lacking.

Ellenson's concerns in this regard became crystal clear to me when just a few years after our ordination, he and I collaborated on two articles published in the *CCAR Journal* that focused on two important modern Orthodox responsa. The first article, written in 1981 concerned a responsum by Rabbi Zvi Hirsch Kalischer (1795–1874), one of his era's leading authorities in Eastern and Central Europe. Kalischer was responding to a ruling emanating from the United States that sons born to Jewish fathers and non-Jewish mothers could not be circumcised by a *mohel* lest these children be mistakenly identified as Jews. Kalischer disagreed. In a letter to Dr. Hildesheimer, he argued that it was in fact a mitzvah to circumcise such children. They should not be discarded by the community; moreover they actually possess *zera kodesh* (holy seed). Such a child is more likely to become Jewish and aspire to holiness with such an embrace. I could see how moved David was by Rabbi Kalischer's evident respect for the father's wanting to circumcise the child and to nourish the spiritual potential the child would hence possess.

The second responsum (published in Winter 1983) was by Rabbi David Zvi Hoffman of Berlin (1843–1921), who had studied in Hildesheimer's yeshivah in Hungary and had succeeded him as rector in the Orthodox Seminary of Berlin. Hoffman was asked to rule in the case of a twelve-year-old boy born to a non-Jewish mother and Jewish father who had been circumcised by a *mohel* at eight-days old. Did such a child have to undergo *hatafat dam* (the taking of a drop of blood) before being permitted to convert? In his responsum Hoffman ruled that it was unnecessary to take the drop of blood. It should be assumed, Hoffman wrote, that the circumcision was done for the sake of conversion. Moreover, if there is even a slight chance that drawing the drop of blood will injure the lad, the *hatafat dam* should not take place. Both responsa highlight what Dr. Ellenson has sought: the capacity for compassion within the strictures of the halachic process.

The Road to the Presidency

Shortly after concluding work on his doctorate, David accepted a position at the Los Angeles School of HUC-JIR. He subsequently achieved the title of Professor of Jewish Thought and Director of the Jerome E. Loucheim School for Judaic Studies. For many years Ellenson had been a brilliant and incredibly popular professor, a most sought after speaker and scholar-in-residence throughout the country. While teaching in Los Angeles, David divorced. Over time he fell in love with one of his most impressive former rabbinic students, Jacqueline Koch (who happened to grow up at Congregation Rodeph Sholom in New York where I now serve as rabbi). Jackie was always incredibly smart, mature, and grounded. Aware that falling in love with David meant inheriting his family as well—oldest daughter Ruth is now a writer and Micah was ordained a rabbi on the LA campus of HUC-JIR in May 2014—she was undaunted. When I had the honor of being *m'sader kiddushin* with Jackie and David under the chuppah at HUC-JIR in New York, it was clear to me what a strong bond they had formed.

Jackie's career has similarly contributed so much to the Jewish world. She has been the rabbi chaplain at the Harvard Westlake School in Los Angeles, chair of Hadassah Foundation, facilitator/leader of VeTaher Libeynu, rabbi/director of Women's Rabbinic Network, talented teacher of Jewish Spirituality far and wide, as well as indispensable spouse and advisor of the immediate past president, now chancellor of HUC-JIR. They went on to have three children together: Hannah, Nomi, and Rafi

I will never forget the hours-long cross-country phone call I had with David as he agonized over whether to become a candidate for the presidency of the College-Institute. He loved being an academic and was aware, at least to some degree, how much his life would change serving the Movement as president. Once Jackie and their five children gave him their blessings, David continued to wrestle until he came to an affirmative decision. His personal statement presented to the Search Committee underscores why he was such a perfect candidate:

> The gratitude and devotion I feel for the College-Institute cannot be fully expressed. I had been raised in an Orthodox synagogue. Yet, I never found the atmosphere of Orthodox Judaism—for all that I respected in it—congenial to my own temperament. I have therefore been grateful that for the last twenty-nine years my life has been shaped by this institution and by the sensibilities and beliefs that mark a liberal approach to Jewish religious tradition . . . If possible, the President should be a rabbi-scholar of international reputation whose character and person command universal respect in both the academic and Jewish worlds. The President should embody these qualities because the President serves as a symbol and representative of what the College-Institute is both within the walls of the College-Institute and beyond. The President must be further able to articulate why HUC-JIR is a precious intellectual-religious resource for the ongoing life of the Jewish people and must be someone who can inspire others to aid in the task of building and sustaining this institution. I feel that I possess these characteristics and talents and I believe I can employ them to inspire and guide others to work with me as a partner in the mission that the College-Institute affirms and the vision that HUC-JIR represents.

Then in the next paragraph David reveals the soul within the scholar:

> My scholarship and my teaching have their origins in and are motivated by existential concerns. My entire adult life has been spent attempting to understand and lecture on the diverse ways in which different Jews have attempted to answer the question of

what it means to be part of a Jewish people that strives however haltingly and imperfectly to live in covenantal relationship with God. I love the Jewish people and I am grateful for the liberal approach HUC-JIR has allowed me to internalize concerning how the Jewish tradition can and ought to be approached. I believe in the deepest recesses of my heart as a rabbi that scholarship and knowledge contribute to the enterprise of religious formation.

Dr. Ellenson's significant challenges and important achievements as president will be chronicled by many, but I know how much he has wrestled with questions of what type of rabbi, cantor, educator, communal leader, and scholar we need to produce to meet the ever-growing challenges of Jewish life in the twenty-first century; how to engage faculty who will educate and inspire these students; how to insure the full equality and opportunity for women and for members of the LGBTQ community, whose dignity is core to the covenantal paradigm he cherishes.

As HUC-JIR is one large international family, David has made a point to be physically present to rejoice with our communities on significant anniversaries, mourn for friends who have died, agonize with parents and students alike who bravely carried on their studies in Jerusalem as the Intifada in 2002 threatened them and their brothers and sisters in Israel. Then, there has been the ever-present burden of raising money in order to support the four campuses, the millions of dollars required to maintain the College-Institute in the face of the steady reduction in the contributions member congregations make to the URJ and are then funneled to the College. Somewhat to his own surprise, David has been a brilliant fundraiser. Donors surely are drawn to his easy southern warmth, his insatiable curiosity, and true love of people. What ultimately wins over the generous benefactor, however, is his vision of what HUC-JIR means for the Jewish future in the face of our own sometimes tragic past and ever-present challenges posed by the modern age. His inaugural address at the Plum Street Temple on October 13, 2002, unveiled the core of his approach:

> Today we witness an era where the rate of Jewish exogamy stands at an all-time high, and the limitations and constraints imposed by a previous age upon complete Jewish integration into all sectors of the American nation have given way to an epoch where Jews take part as complete equals in every walk of American

life. At the same time, the twentieth century has borne witness to the previously unimaginable evil of the Shoah, as well as the genocides of other peoples, and we today cannot share the total certainty our ancestors did in the power of reason to achieve the good. Ours is an age of ambiguity and nuance—one in which we stand at the crossroads of global capitalism and global terror.

Yet, we must not allow the uncertainty of our own age to paralyze us. Our contemporary efforts at the College-Institute must be no less than those of our predecessors. We must recognize our own power, and we must employ our passion and our imagination as well as our knowledge to chart the course of Jewish spiritual and communal life for our own time as well as for the future.

In that same address Dr. Ellenson reminded the world of his steadfast devotion to the State of Israel. As President, David has been a champion of the College-Institute's growing program for Israelis, and he has been unshakeable in his resolve that all students experience their initial year of study at the Jerusalem campus.

Writing about one of his beloved teachers, the late Dr. David Hartman, Ellenson contended, "Israel represents a healthy assertion of vitality and moral responsibility on the part of the Jewish people, because it is only by assuming such 'total responsibility for society' that Jews can 'demonstrate the moral and spiritual power of the Torah to respond to the challenges of daily life.' The State of Israel provides the one genuine crucible where the values of Torah can truly be tested and applied, for only in Israel do Jews possess a political sovereignty that entails full accountability."[4]

As a lover of Zion, David is not afraid to challenge the Israeli government that it live up to the words found in its Declaration of Independence, as well as to the ethics found in Torah. Although his body can often be found in New York, Cincinnati, or Los Angeles, a part of his heart always resides in Jerusalem.

Another part of his heart will always be devoted to HUC-JIR and the Reform Movement. Growing up as an Orthodox Jew, David never fully reconciled the emotional comfort he felt when he would daven among the older men of his shul with his ambivalence over the core beliefs and principles of that Orthodoxy. David thus has felt an eternal gratitude to the Reform Movement for allowing him to navigate successfully the journey through both tradition and modernity, the dialectical dilemmas that have formed the essence of his academic and personal quest for personal and communal synthesis.

David is blessed by this Reform community; by his *ezer k'negdo*, Jackie; his fabulous five children; his extended family; and countless numbers of friends who truly love him. I am thrilled to be counted in that privileged circle. David's career certainly will contain new challenges, but he has already left his indelible mark on our Movement as arguably our most beloved and successful president.

Dr. Ellenson penned these words for David Hartman, but, in my view, they apply equally to him:

> Each generation of Jews has the freedom as well as the obligation to appropriate and employ our inherited Jewish tradition in accordance with its own capacities and comprehensions which can only be done when each current generation recognizes that any attempt to evade responsibility and fit history into a fixed pattern constitutes a delusion. People do not receive community as if by fate. Instead, Judaism impresses upon *Am Yisrael* that the notion of covenant provides for an interpretative tradition that asserts that God empowers the Jewish people to employ such community in freedom.[5]

As a younger man David heard his mother tell him that our ancestors tried to understand God's word in such a way that if God were a human being God would be happy to become your friend. David Ellenson, indeed, has walked with God and we are the grateful beneficiaries of that sacred friendship.

Notes

1. David Ellenson, *After Emancipation: Jewish Religious Responses to Modernity* (Cincinnati: Hebrew Union College Press, 2004), 15.
2. David Ellenson, *Tradition and Transition* (Lanham, MD: University Press of America, 1989), 2.
3. Ellenson, *After Emancipation*, 180, from Eliav, Hildesheimer Briefe, letter 12.
4. Ibid., 434.
5. Ibid., 527.

For These I Weep: A Theology of Lament

Rachel Adler

I first met David Ellenson in 1985 when I was investigating graduate programs in theology and ethics. The University of Southern California and Hebrew Union College/Los Angeles had a very underpublicized joint Ph.D. program in which I ultimately received a Ph.D. with David Ellenson as my thesis director. I also had the privilege of taking many courses with him. As a teacher, David works hard and expects his students to do likewise. He assigned mountains of reading. I always theorized that students waded through it all because no one could bear to hurt the feelings of this gentle instructor. When I began teaching Modern Jewish Thought at HUC, I had to revise the Ellenson syllabus radically upon discovering that students were less reluctant to disappoint me.

I recall particularly David's brilliant seminar in Social Reality and Halachah, in which we read nineteenth and twentieth century t'shuvot through the lens of social theory, a kind of interdisciplinary scholarship for which David is famous. It was a small seminar consisting of Rabbi Daniel Gordis, who was also doing his Ph.D. with David in the joint program, an auditing student who had spent a number of years at Yeshivas Torah V'Das, and me. A young woman came to David asking to join the seminar but confessed that her Hebrew skills were not up to decoding t'shuvot. David overflowed with sympathy. "Don't worry," he told her, "Rachel Adler will translate everything for you!"

David has the most organized mind I've ever encountered. He can give a brilliant and perfectly structured lecture without a single lecture note.

RACHEL ADLER, Ph.D. (LA12) is the Rabbi David Ellenson Professor of Jewish Religious Thought, Professor of Modern Jewish Thought and Feminist Studies at HUC-JIR/Los Angeles.

This paper is based on the Dr. Samuel Atlas Memorial Lecture given at HUC-JIR/New York in 2006. I am grateful to Benjamin Fried for his invaluable assistance in editing the revised, expanded version of this piece; an earlier version appeared in the HUC-JIR *Chronicle*, no. 68 (2006): 16–21.

He reads widely in a variety of fields, and his book reviews attest to analytical abilities that quickly pinpoint faulty logic or weak reasoning. Despite these gifts, David Ellenson is the kindest scholar I have ever known and the least arrogant.

When I first encountered David, feminists were popularly considered a menace to Jewish survival. David, however, was already well-read in feminist theory and in Jewish feminist theology. He was unfailingly supportive of my efforts to add to this literature. I suspect that David had something to do with my hiring at HUC, and I wonder if he might not have put in a word for me when I was selected to deliver the Dr. Samuel Atlas Memorial Lecture for 2006, on which this article is based. Ever candid, David did observe, following the lecture, that Dr. Atlas was probably spinning in his grave. May Dr. Atlas rest well. He contributed valuable scholarship that we still use, and I have not yet destroyed either his legacy nor has feminism destroyed the Jewish people. And may my friend and teacher, David Ellenson, Shlit'a, continue to thrive, to learn and to teach, and to impart to many more students the Torah of his scholarship and the Torah of his radiant character.

In the Book of Ruth, when the two widows, Naomi and her daughter-in-law Ruth, return to Bethlehem, the women of the town greet Naomi, and she laments: "Do not call me Naomi, Pleasantness. Call me Mara, Bitterness, for Shadai has made my lot very bitter. I went away full and Adonai has brought me back empty" (Ruth 1:20–21). Her bitterness and rage are understandable. We spend our lives defending ourselves from the sure knowledge that fullness does not last. All that we love we will lose. We are fated to return empty. We are ill-suited to loss and to emptiness. When we cease to feel held in a web of relationships, when the network of meanings that make the world intelligible are destroyed, we are seized with spiritual vertigo. We don't know where we stand or what can be relied upon. 'What are we? *Mah anu?*' we ask. 'What is our life, *Meh chayenu?*'

Pain Unmakes the Universe

This sense of radical unmeaning, of dangling loose from the web that had safely held us, is almost like physical pain. The cultural critic Elaine Scarry writes about physical pain and its effects on the universe of the sufferer.[1] Intolerable pain, says Scarry, unmakes the universe, expunging thought and feeling, self and world, "all that gives rise to and is in turn made possible by language."[2] In severe torment, the sufferer is utterly isolated, unable to experience relatedness, unable to defend her values from a torturer's insistence that she betray them, or to give or withhold consent to a medical procedure, unable to attend to her surroundings, unable to speak—for language is displaced by gasps, moans, and screams. In contrast, Scarry observes, "to be present when the person in pain rediscovers speech is almost to be present at the birth or rebirth of language."[3]

I want to argue that some of these observations are also germane to sufferings from emotional and spiritual pain. "I am a little world made cunningly," the poet John Donne writes about the delicacy and complexity of the human being. There is more than one way to unmake the little world that is a person or even the larger world that is a people. There is more than one kind of pain that can leave us tormented and bereft. And to be present when the sufferer re-achieves relational speech is to be present at the rebirth of redemption.

According to our mystical tradition, language precedes everything, for the world is created with the alphabet. To unmake a world is to undo the alphabet of creation, to plunge the world constituted by language back into disorder, to strike it wordless. But how can the alphabet so violently broken be reconstituted? How can the broken reenter the realm of language and speak the unspeakable? The doorway, I would maintain, is lament. In lament, the boundary between the made and unmade universe is thinnest, for it is the cultural form closest to the preverbal howl of pain. Lament can be incoherent and chaotic, picking its way through a broken rubble of unbearably vivid happenings and intolerable sensations. Its content is dangerously dark and disordered, and its meaning may be nonexistent, rejected, or found wanting. And yet I want to argue that the doorway through which lament enters the world is a *petach tikvah*, a doorway of hope.[4]

What Is Lament?

What, first of all, is lament? Lament is composed of several subgenres. There are laments for the dead, laments by the sick and the disheartened, communal laments over lost battles, destroyed cities and states, and eventually, for other communal catastrophes. We are not the only culture that has lamented. Lament was common to the entire Mediterranean and Middle East as well as to other cultures across the globe. In laments, human beings bewail all that hurts about being human: having bodies that hurt, being mortal, suffering brutality at the hands of others, losing control over our lives, losing kin, losing home, losing freedom, being tormented by memories of happier times or by memories of horrific occurrences, feeling abandoned by an indifferent or actively punitive God.

Listen and you hear a mighty symphony of the broken and bereft. Here is the author of Psalm 77: "Has God forgotten how to pity?/Has He in anger stifled His compassion?" (Ps. 77:10). And here is King David: "My son Absolom O my son, my son Absolom. If only I had died instead of you. O Absolom, my son, my son" (II Sam. 19:1b). And Job: "Why did I not die at birth?/Expire as I came forth from the womb?/Why were there knees to receive me/Or breasts for me to suck?" (Job 3:11–12). And the man of Lamentations 3, complaining about God: "He is a lurking bear to me,/A lion in hiding;/He has forced me off my way and mangled me,/He has left me numb" (Lam. 3:10–11).

I have called this a symphony rather than a cacophony because these explosions of poignant, bitter, even accusatory utterances are contained in literary forms. Some are identified as *kinot* (dirges) and exhibit the characteristic "limping meter."[5] Others exhibit structures particular to lament psalms: a series of complaints, a statement of guilt, a request for God's favor, a petition against enemies, and an abrupt turn to hope and trust in God. Lament psalms, *kinot,* and other biblical genres, which were intended to be sung, share characteristics we would call poetic: patterned stresses, repetition, alliteration, parallelism, and imagery. Imposing form and structure on lament constrains its wildness and socializes it so that the lament can engage a community as witnesses and as participants.

Varieties of Lament: Lament Singers

I want to speak now about three major varieties of laments, all of which offer some resources for us today. The first of these kinds of lament is the lament for the dead. Rather than talking about literary laments for the dead in the Bible, I want to focus on the social phenomenon they reflect. There really were laments for the dead, and although men also lamented, the fashioning of laments was regarded as a women's genre. Wailing women or "professional mourners" as the word *m'konenot* is often translated, did not just wail or howl wordlessly as popularly supposed; they orally composed and sang funeral poetry.[6] Hence, God commands Jeremiah: "Call the lament-singing women [*m'konenot*],/let the wise women come" (Jer. 9:16–17). Jeremiah exhorts the elegy-makers to teach their daughters the craft because the prophesied devastation will require so many lamenters (9:19). Lament-singing women are referenced in several of the prophetic books but the only full-scale biblical depiction of a female lamenter is of Zion in the Book of Lamentations.

The formal structures of lament and their performance by female artists are familiar to the Rabbis of the Talmud. "What is meant by 'chanting' [*innui*]?" asks *Mishnah Mo-eid Katan*. "When all the women sing in unison. And lament [*kinah*]? When one speaks and all respond after her."[7] For the mishnah what distinguishes *kinah* is not a distinctive meter but a call and response type of structure.

The female lamenter was ubiquitous in both Israelite and Talmudic societies. In *Mishnah K'tubot* (4:4), Rabbi Yehudah rules that even the poorest husband must provide at the very minimum two flute players and one lament-singing woman for his wife's funeral. A funeral may be delayed in order to summon the lament singers (*Sanhedrin* 47a). The position of the lament singers in the funeral procession was pivotal. A *baraita* teaches that they either immediately preceded or immediately followed the corpse, depending on local custom (*Sanhedrin* 20a).

Compare what we have learned so far about Rabbinic lament with the vivid account of travel writer Patrick Leigh Fermor who in the 1950s witnessed a performance of oral lament poetry in Mani, the mountainous, isolated Southern Peloponnese region of Greece.[8] This lament poetry is believed to be descended from the laments of classical antiquity.[9]

> The chief woman mourner . . . begins the *klama*, or weeping . . . [T]he [lament] unfolds in spite of the semi-ecstatic mode of delivery in a logical sequence of proem, exegesis, and epilogue. As the dirge continues, the knees stiffen, the hair falls in disorder, the headkerchief is stretched across the shoulders, an end held in each hand, which work up and down with a sawing motion in

time to the slow beat of the metre. The breast is struck, the cheeks clawed, and very often the [lament] accelerates into a gabble and finally into wails and shrieks without meaning. If the dead man has been killed in a feud, the dirge may finish with terrible curses and oaths of vengeance . . . When she fades out, another woman "takes" the [lament].

Lament and the Preverbal

What do we learn from this? As in the Talmud, Greek lament is a performance by individual women and groups of women, and it has structure and meter. Between this modern Greek lament and the literary lament poetry of *Tanach*, there are a number of analogies. In both traditions, lament is contradictory rather than emotionally consistent. The lamenter is, by turns, accusatory, guilt-wracked, reminiscent, despairing, imploring, vindictive, bitter, hopeful. In both, lament is tumultuous and disordered language interspersed with returns to the preverbal: gasps, sobs, tears, keening, cries of ah, alas, woe, while at the same time, strict literary conventions are maintained. Gail Holst-Warhaft, a classics scholar, writes: "Like the cries that puncture the text, so sobs, sighs and sudden intakes of breath are integral to the performance of lament. Singers of dramatic or plaintive songs from opera to blues will use their breath for heightened emotional effect . . . [B]reathing and singing, like weeping and singing have always been so intimately associated that it may be difficult to determine where a sigh ends and a song begins."[10]

Breathing. Weeping. Music. Throughout the ancient Mediterranean, flutes are used at funerals. They represent the breath, the body's mysterious, God-given internal wind instrument, now stilled.[11] Percussion instruments, like drums, may be used to represent the thumping heart. The third-century Palestinian *Amora* Ulla offers the following details about how Jews grieved at funerals: "*Hesped* means beating on one's heart . . . *Tipuach* means clapping one's hands together.[12] And *Kilus* means [lamenting] with the foot"—either stamping one's foot or, as *Tosafot* suggests, slapping one's thigh (*Mo-eid Katan* 27b). What these actions tell us is threefold. They tell us that grief is expressed with the whole body. They tell us that grief is expressed rhythmically, probably as a percussive accompaniment to the lament music. And they tell us that lament exists at some intersection between art and violence.

I have said that lament is language traumatized, but there is also an impulse to traumatize the body. Many commentators talk about mourners enacting a mimesis of death.[13] Like the dead, the mourner does not bathe, anoint, or have sex. The mourner rips his clothes, a custom that safely channels the mourner's wish to imitate the disintegrating body of the corpse, to be united with her once more. And from Ulla we have heard about striking the body. The little black ribbon the funeral director snips for us today does not even begin to address this desire for violent grief. We must ask ourselves how we are going to make a place for it today.

The Content of Funeral Laments

What did lament-making women say? That is the jackpot question. Dirges for funerals were preserved in the memories of those who performed them and those who participated in refrains or call-and-response. But they were not committed to writing. In *Mo-eid Katan* 28b, however, the fourth-century *Amora* Rava quotes seven snippets of lament sung by the women of a Babylonian town named Shokhenziv. Talmudic scholars lived in this town, and it was a major center of scholarship.[14] The snippets of lament are out of context and very obscure. In fact, they are enigmatic enough to make one wonder if the women of Shokhenziv were having a little fun at Rava's expense. There are many textual variants of these fragments and many commentaries on the enigmatic words of the lamenters of Shokhenziv. The Aramaic is very colloquial and therefore difficult, and there are multiple and conflicting translations. An additional problem is whether translations that theologize are attributable to the female lament singers or to the more theologically invested classical translators and commentators. I will now reproduce the Talmudic text, numbering the quoted laments:

1. מאי אמרן? מרא רב: ויי לאזלא, ויי לחבילא.
1a. אמר רבא: נשי דשכנציב אמרן הכי: ויי לאזלא, ויי לחבילא.
2. ואמר רבא: נשי דשכנציב אמרן: גור גרמא מככא, ונמטי מיא לאנטיכי.
3. ואמר רבא: נשי דשכנציב אמרן: עטוף וכסו טורי, דבר רמי ובר רברבי הוא.
4. ואמר רבא: נשי דשכנציב אמרן: שייול אצטלא דמלתא לבר חורין דשלימו זודיה.
5. ואמר רבא: נשי דשכנציב אמרן: רהית ונפיל אמעברא ויזופתא יזיף.
6. ואמר רבא: נשי דשכנציב אמרן: אחנא תגרי אזוגי מיבדקו.
7. ואמר רבד: נשי דשכנציב אמרן: מותא כי מותא, ומרעין חיבוליא.

The first fragment is contributed by Rav, and then echoed by Rava quoting the women of Shokhenziv, and it is a case in point. Rashi translates it: "Alas for the departed./Alas for his wounds." There is the exclamation of woe, which we know to be common in lament. However, some commentators translate it, "Alas for the departed. Alas for his pledge."[15] The pledge, or item held in safekeeping for someone, is here understood to be the soul, the return of which its owner, God, will demand of the deceased.

The second fragment is more complicated. I will follow Soncino and translate, "Take the soup bone out of the pot/and fill the vessel with water."[16] The irony is that the same pot that made the sick man's broth will now heat the water to wash his corpse. Patrick Leigh Fermor in his account of Greek women's laments notes their custom of making homely objects such as the dead man's tools testify to his death.[17] Here the evidence of the transition from sickness to death is the pot and its two uses. Moreover, in Rabbinic times, before the rise of burial societies, the dead man may have been washed by the same woman who made the soup.[18]

A third quotation is the only one in the grand style, invoking nature to mourn for the deceased: "Cloak yourselves, high mountains, a great man and a noble was he."[19] The fourth snippet is both frank and acidly funny about the dead man's fecklessness: "He rushes and tumbles aboard the ferry/and has to borrow his fare." An interesting detail here is the ferry, a feature of the Hellenistic underworld. As has been noted in the case of Greek lamenters, this lamenter is not particularly orthodox in her theology.[20] There may be an element of satire here that brings to mind that mocking songs were also a women's genre.[21] Or perhaps, as Rabbenu Hananel argues, it is meant to be pathetic and ironic. This man has labored all his life and yet at last has to borrow the money for his final ride.[22]

The fifth lament can be translated, "The grave is a fine robe for a free man, whose traveling outfit is now complete." Rashi explains, "That is to say, death is as beautiful or befitting as an outfit of [finest] Milesian wool. All he has is his shroud, for he is poor."[23] Soncino translates, "borrow [and buy] a Milesian robe/To dress a free-born son: [Give it free of charge] for provision left he none."[24] Soncino has translated *shayul* as "lend" rather than as *Sheol*, "the grave." But this makes less sense than Rashi's translation, for lamenters at a burial would not be taking up a collection to pay for the shroud, although Rabbenu Hananel too translates, "Let us prepare fine garments to lay out this good person who has died." The term *zavdah* can refer to a shroud, a traveling outfit or, metaphorically, a shroud as an outfit for one's final journey.[25] Rabbenu Hananel's translation also removes the irony implicit in Rashi's gloss: for the poor free man, the grave itself is as good as a garment of fine Milesian wool as a traveling outfit for this last journey.

The sixth cryptic lament attributed to the women of Shokhenziv can be translated: "Our brothers are like merchants who are searched at the boundary." In other words, just like traveling merchants who are searched and made to declare their goods at the boundary, our brothers are tested by their characterological "goods" when passing the boundary from life into death.[26] Rabbenu Hananel says the meaning is that our brothers the merchants will be examined or tested by their possessions and their business practices.[27] Rashi translates, "Our brother the merchant will be judged by the brood he left behind," which is puzzling.[28] Soncino translates, "Our brothers are merchants who/at the customs houses are searched."[29] This seems to presume that "merchant" is a metaphor but Soncino does not elaborate further on its meaning.

The final lament of the women of Shokhenziv I will translate following Rabbenu Hananel as "This death is like any other death [i.e., all must die]. Death is the principal and the length of sickness is the interest."[30] Soncino translates: "This death or that death [is the end of the quest]: Our bruises are the rate of interest."[31] In this translation, death is the principal and pain is the interest. In any case, the tone is ironic, and as in the previous lament a financial metaphor is used. Note that all the fragments from the female lament singers are prefaced "And Rava said, the women of Shokhenziv say," as if these quotations from females had to be individually chaperoned into the Talmudic text.[32]

Most of these lament fragments are quite different from the example I shall discuss next. We have seen instances of irony and grim humor colloquially expressed, with domestic or financial metaphors. Both areas were ones in which women participated, although they were disadvantaged in the economic domain.[33] We have seen regret, but a minimum of ornate rhetoric and sentiment and no startlingly beautiful poetry.

The next example is the only one I have found that refers to a biblical lament. This text is from BT *N'darim* 66a–b, and it picks up a quotation from David's lament for Saul and Jonathan,

"Daughters of Israel, Weep for Saul/Who clothed you in crimson and finery/Who decked your robes with jewels of gold" בנות ישראל אל-שאול בכינה/המלבישכם שני עם-עדנים/המעלה עדי זהב על לבושכן (II Sam. 1:24). The text relates that these lines were used to mourn Rabbi Ishmael. The story is told both in the Mishnah and in the Gemara that follows. Rabbi Ishmael was said to have taken an indigent girl into his home and cared for her. He even had a gold tooth made for her to substitute for a missing one. When her uncle saw her made beautiful, he regretted his previous vow to have no benefit from her. Rabbi Ishmael absolved him of the vow on the grounds that he had not vowed concerning the transformed girl he now saw. His vow was therefore an error and thus the man was permitted to marry her. At Rabbi Ishmael's death, it is related, a lament singer sang, "Daughters of Israel, weep over Rabbi Ishmael, who clothed you in crimson and finery." This story suggests that if it were particularly appropriate, a biblical lament might be quoted. Perhaps it is an indication that Rabbinic-period lamenters had biblical laments in their repertoire, since in the story it is the lament singer and not the Rabbis who makes the quotation.

Lament as a Social Practice and Its Demise

In lament for the dead, then, we have a type of social performance led by experts, the lament-making women, but with open participation for everyone, female and male. In this performance, language, weeping, breast-beating, clapping, stamping, and ripped clothing, all express and respond to a world disordered. Death has irrupted into the domain of the living and uprooted a member of a family and a community. All must lament before comforters can begin to console.

Lament of this sort may have continued for many centuries in some communities. A researcher heard lament songs from Iraqi Jewish women as late as 1950.[34] Funeral songs have also been attested among Jews in Southern Iran and among Moroccan Jews. In Ashkenaz, women's lamenting may have succumbed to a one-two combination punch from the newly influential *Zohar* and from the growth of burial societies organized like medieval guilds. The *Zohar* warned that because through Eve's sin, death was introduced into the world, the Angel of Death is present among the women during funerals, and he has permission to kill during the funeral ceremony.[35] Hence separating the women from the men is a matter of life or death. At the same time, *chevrei kadisha* (burial societies), introduced their own customs and theology of reception into the afterlife. The women's "weeping and lamenting" were accused of weakening the song of the seraphim, "who rejoice at the arrival of the deceased."[36]

These developments may explain why several Ashkenazic communities' records from the sixteenth century on confirm that women were placed at the back at funerals. Harsh punishments were prescribed for those who ventured forward among the men: having their cloaks taken away, being sprayed with water, or, in one community, stone throwing.[37] The implication is that the law was difficult to enforce because the women were recalcitrant. Possibly they were lamenters protesting the disvaluing of their expertise.

Lament Psalms: The Hopeful Lament

I want to present rather briefly the second of the lament subgenres I have chosen to address. Here is an individual lament, Psalm 13. The Bible scholar Tod Linafelt makes a distinction between the lament for the dead and the lament psalm.[38] The lament for the dead is focused on death, while the lament psalm is directed toward life and seeks more life. It is, ultimately, hopeful rather than hopeless. The dirge can afford to be hopeless, because the community contains and preserves hope for the mourner. In the individual lament, the lamenter must himself turn toward hope and life.

Hope is intrinsic to the theological work of lament. The Bible scholar Walter Brueggemann contends that lament is a form of protest that "shifts the calculus and redresses the distribution of power between the two parties, so that the petitionary party is taken seriously and the God who is addressed is newly engaged in the crisis in a way that puts God at risk."[39] Because God is a God of justice and not a cosmic bully, God can be confronted by God's covenant partner. According to Brueggemann, rather than presenting a compliant false self and rendering the relationship manipulative and insincere, the lamenter confronts God with the immediacy of suffering in a way that renders retribution unjustifiable. You will notice this motif in Psalm 13:

For the Leader: A Psalm of David
How long, Adonai, will You forget me forever?

How long will You hide Your face from me?
How long will I have cares on my mind
grief in my heart all day?
How long will my enemy have the upper hand?
Look and answer me Adonai my God!
Restore the luster to my eyes,
Lest I sleep the sleep of death;
Lest my enemy say, "I have overcome him!" [or "I have put an end to him!"]
My foes exult when I totter.
But I trust in your kindness [*chasdechah*].
My heart will exult in your deliverance.
I will sing to Adonai
for He has been good to me.

The psalm starts off with a derangement of language, the accusatory and paradoxical question: *"How long, Adonai, will you forget me forever?"* The JPS translation "tames" this question into an exclamation: "How long O Lord; will you ignore me forever!" But this particular expression, *ad ana* (how long), occurs only four times in the Book of Psalms, all in Psalm 13. A similar expression, *ad matai*, occurs in six psalms (6:4, 74:10, 80:5, 82:2, 90:13, 94:3), and it is an interjection of exasperation. *Ad ana*, on the other hand, seems to seek both information and a response. The question "How long will you forget me forever?" has to be located in deep memories of infancy, when mommy's leaving was experienced as if she had dropped into a black hole. But the despair in this personal experience of abandonment "forever" is lightened by the hopeful "how long," which implies an eventual ending. So the lamenter, presenting his most vulnerable self, senses a glimmer of hope even at the opening of the lament. How long will You hide Your face from me? This evokes another deep memory. An infant's first reactions are to faces. Faces reassure the infant in his helplessness. They offer love and attention. The hiding of the face, its going away, is a primal occasion of anxiety. The game of peekaboo is a version of the "gone and reappeared" game that Freud observes a toddler playing.[40] The feared abandonment by the face is overcome again and again by the repeated reappearance. "In the access to the face," the philosopher Emanuel Levinas says, "there is . . . also an access to the idea of God."[41] Human faces bear a hint or recollection of God that can spur the desire for God. For Levinas, relation to the

Infinite is not a contemplation of an abstract idea, but a desire. For our speaker in Psalm 13, the turning away of God's face represents his desire for God thwarted and blocked. He suffers.

"*How long will I have cares on my mind grief in my heart all day?*" The speaker is preoccupied with plans or schemes (*eitzot*). But his is the anxious scheming of one whose insecurity will not let him rest. Instead, persistent grief clings to him, as if his plans had already failed. "*How long will my enemy have the upper hand?*" (*yarum*—be high above me, tower over me). These four repetitions of "how long" present to us a speaker increasingly frantic with anxiety. God's abandonment in his vulnerable situation is intolerable. For there is an enemy, as there often is in Psalms, a person, a conspiracy, or a metaphorical enemy, a sickness, or an obsessive idea that is a mortal threat to the speaker.

"*Look at me, answer me Adonai my God.*" The speaker pleads for recognition and response from the withdrawn Deity. "*Restore the luster to my eyes/Lest I sleep the sleep of death.*" The speaker's eyes are dulled like a fainting or dying person. "*Lest my enemy say, 'I have overcome him!*' [or *'I have put an end to him!*']" "*My foes exult when I totter*" (*emot*, or you might translate it "stumble"). Repetition again expresses anxiety. The repeated word lest (*pen*) introduces what the speaker dreads: defeat and death. In keeping with the disarrangement of lament, the images are out of logical order. First he imagines his death, then, his defeat, and at the last veers back to the nightmare moment when a running man stumbles, begins to fall, and his adversaries close in to drag him down. But at this horrid moment, the speaker pulls his mind away from these despairing images of collapse and ruin. "*But I trust in your kindness* [*chasdechah*]." Instead he calms himself by remembering his trust in God. A similar conjunction of images occurs in Psalm 94: "*When I think my foot has given way, your faithfulness, Adonai, supports me.*" (*Im amarti mata ragli/ chasdechah, Adonai, yisadeni.*) Now the speaker can envision his own joy at the deliverance he trusts to occur: "*My heart will exult in your deliverance/I will sing to Adonai/for He has been good to me.*"

Communal Lament: Making and Unmaking

I want to turn now to the last of the three types of lament: the communal lament for the fallen city in the paradigmatic lament text of the Hebrew Bible, the Book of Lamentations. This will not be a full-scale analysis. I have only a few points. The book's Hebrew name is *Eichah*, and three of its five chapters begin with that word. *Eichah* (How!) is used in the Book of Lamentations, not as a call for reasoned explanations of cause and effect, not as the rational inquiry, *eich*? but as an exclamation of incredulous horror. "How dreadfully everything has changed!" "How awful this is!" The open vowel of the emphatic *ah*, mimics a scream: *Eichaaah*. For when people are truly horror stricken, what astonishes them is how an ordinary day turned into a catastrophe after which nothing will ever be the same.[42]

The liturgical performance of Lamentations is the centerpiece of a mimesis of unmaking and remaking. Hauntingly chanted on the Ninth of Av, it commemorates the destructions of the Temple and other catastrophes of Jewish history. Ashkenazic tradition surrounds its recitation with graphic representations of a dead covenant and a bereaved community. The synagogue, locus of the ordered nomos, is deliberately disordered. The Holy Ark is shrouded like a corpse. Chairs on the altar are overturned and fasting worshipers sit on the ground. The following Sabbath the community rises to re-contract the covenant as the Ten Commandments are read. The liturgical performances that frame Lamentations both present and overcome the terrifying possibilities of cosmic disorder and covenantal rupture.

The Book of Lamentations both bewails and remakes this shattered world quite explicitly by reconstituting the broken alphabet of creation. Four of its five chapters are acrostics. Chapter 3 is a triple alphabetical acrostic. Chapter 5 is not an acrostic but has the same number of verses as there are alphabet letters. The alphabet represents the totality of language, and the acrostic thus represents the gamut of catastrophic experiences and the gamut of human reactions that can be represented in language.

The structure of the book, its strict, alphabetical sequence of verses, barely serves to contain the wildly disordered content. The poet and the two speakers, the woman Zion and the man who has known affliction, pour out a torrent of personal and collective woe: physical torment, humiliation, pity, self blame, accusations hurled at a violent and predatory God, dreadful tableaus of jeering enemies, starving children, cannibal mothers, slave laborers, slaughtered bodies, pleas for mercy, pleas for bloody revenge. Because lament is without rational sequence, this torrent of complaint strikes us as confused and overwhelming. One can see this sequenceless, anarratival quality in Holocaust memories. The postmodern ethnographer Ruth Linden observes that the accounts of the women survivors she records contain fragments of "sheer happenings" whose senselessness and arbitrariness would be falsified by ordering them in narrative.[43] Lament is a repository for "sheer happenings." It curbs narrative's tendency to assign causes and meanings, to use storytelling to mend the unmendable. Lament's capacity to represent non-narratives allows it to preserve what is irreducible and inexplicable about evil.

The first two chapters of Lamentations are a mixture of genres. They are at first death dirges but, as the woman Zion becomes increasingly active and alive, they become laments beseeching life. In Lamentations 1 we see both the isolation of pain and the lack of logical sequence I have been talking about. The first fact we learn about the female figure Zion is her loneliness. The poet's portrait contrasts her present with her former state as a death dirge would do. She was populous and is now lonely, was great and is now a widow, was a princess and is now a forced laborer. Zion is pictured weeping in the night, an image that will recur. We get the first instance of what will become a refrain, *"Ain menachem lah"* ("there is no one to comfort her"). Then suddenly Judah's exile is introduced and Zion is in exile. Verse 4 swerves back to the deserted city. Verse 5 introduces three themes that will persist throughout the book: (1) the triumph of Zion's foes; (2) Zion's punishment for sins; (3) Zion's children going into exile. From these first five verses we can see how the demands of alphabetical acrostic, which constrain the choice of the verse's subject matter, actually enhance the disjointedness that characterizes lamentation.

Linafelt calls the Book of Lamentations "survivor literature," because it is literature written by survivors in the wake of a catastrophe, but also because the literary figure Zion is centrally concerned with the survival of her children.[44] "It is survival," says Linafelt, "rather than the theological categories of guilt or hope that I take to be the hermeneutical key to the poetry of chapters 1 and 2."[45] The outrageousness of pain forms the core of Zion's complaint. She keeps presenting to God the palpable, soul-shattering reality of suffering and death as simply unjustifiable as punishment. She accuses God not of injustice but of compassionlessness. *"Re'eh v'habita"* ("See and look hard") are words that recur along with words for pain, suffering, torment, and agony. Zion interrupts the poet-narrator in verse 9 to say, "See Adonai, my misery; How the enemy triumphs." And in verse 11: "See Adonai, look hard at how abject I have become." She calls on witnesses to her ordeal:

> May it never befall you—
> All who pass along the road
> Look about and see:
> Is there any agony like mine
> which is meted out to me
> when Adonai made me suffer
> on the day of His wrath. (Lam. 1:12)

The poet calls on Zion to mobilize herself in defense of her little ones. Act like a lamenting-woman, he tells her:

> Arise, cry out in the night
> At the beginning of the watches
> Pour out your heart like water
> In the presence of Adonai!
> Lift up your hands to him
> For the life of your infants
> Who faint for hunger
> At every street corner. (Lam. 2:19)

She responds less with pleading than with indignation:

> See O God, look well (*habita*) at whom you have treated so badly
>   (*l'mi 'ollalta ko*)
> Alas women eat their own fruit,
> Their new-born babes
> Alas priest and prophet are slain
> In the Holy Place of Adonai. (Lam. 2:20)

This monstrous inversion—that women are eating their infants rather than infants nursing from their mothers—she construes as God's fault, like the slaying of priest and prophet in the sanctuary. They are evidence of how God has turned the world upside down.

Zion does not let God off the hook. In the concluding chapter, where gendered personifications merge into a communal "we," the lamenting community is poised between hopeful reconciliation and the reiterated testimony of violation and abandonment. It is the liturgical tradition that tips the balance in favor of restoration, by insisting that the penultimate verse, "Take us back O God, and we will turn back./Renew our days as of old" must be repeated *after* the final verse, "for truly you have rejected us, bitterly raged against us." If I orchestrated a performance of Lamentations, I might draft a powerful soprano to sing that last verse over the congregation's repetition of "take us back/renew our days" in order to restore the textual tension that forbids easy recuperation.

The Covenant-Marriage Metaphor and the Possibility of Reconciliation

"Take us back." The covenant is compared to a marriage. What I always find most moving about this metaphor of God and Israel as partners in a marriage is precisely its insistence that the one we hurt is the one with whom reconciliation is nevertheless possible. The covenant-marriage metaphor is troubled and sometimes violent, as many feminist theologians have pointed out.[46] Yet it is the one covenant metaphor that offers God and Israel an opportunity to grow into partnership, to begin to recognize the Other as separate from self and yet intimately bound to self. The metaphor of the sacred marriage whose participants persist, despite violence and betrayal, is applicable to human, political dilemmas as well. In South Africa, Rwanda, Cambodia, and in *Eretz Yisrael*, where civil covenants were intolerably violated, human, political beings struggle with conflicting impulses. Like the violent God of Lamentations, they are caught between the unslakable passion for just retribution and the bitter compassion that counsels us all to pardon the unpardonable, to mediate and mend broken covenants. This is one reason why I believe we need lament.

Lament can help us to bear witness to violence and injustice in the life of the community, to respond with indignation and outrage and then with constructive action. We do not know and will not know why God does not protect us from atrocities or genocide or why God created a world that can be devastated by tsunamis or hurricanes, but we can express our anger, our grief, our sense of abandonment. We can bring to God not only our best behaved happy selves but also selves seized by despair, brokenness, a thirst for revenge, and other so-called unacceptable feelings. This is lament, the first step in reconstituting the broken world.

Reform Judaism and the Reluctance to Lament

We Reform Jews have not made much room for lament in our communal life. Early Reform worshipers, who wanted their services to be "edifying and uplifting," were dismayed by the negativity of lament and by the disorderly universe it depicted. Reform congregations valued decorum and restraint. The anger at God in lament texts and the penitential themes, which were thought to demean human dignity, were removed from Reform liturgy early on. The national events to which lament was tied, the destruction of the Temple and exile, were not seen by Reform theology as tragic, but rather as necessary steps to evolve an international Jewish diaspora that could fulfill its mission to be a light unto the nations. Not until a few years ago did Reform Jews begin to celebrate Tishah B'Av, the holiday that has come to commemorate all acts of destruction against the Jewish people.

Currently, because our psychologically sophisticated community has become more tolerant of public expressions of pain, and because of the healing movement's revelation that many congregants are ill or suffering, Reform is accustoming itself to public acknowledgments of brokenness. There is still work to do. Healing services are often segregated from the rest of the congregation, as if congregants in need of them were undergoing some exceptional misfortune that will not befall the rest of us. And some healing services are relentlessly upbeat and make no room for lament. Lament with its tears, illogic, poignancy, and shadow of death is still an explosive topic. It is an irony. We want to repair the world and yet we are reluctant to acknowledge that everything is broken, including ourselves.

We need laments to vocalize the pain before we can be comforted. We need laments at funerals so mourners can grieve their loss. We need laments for people in persistent vegetative states and those who have become profoundly demented, to give their loved ones words to bewail the loss of those relationships. We need laments for divorces, miscarriages, abortions, diseases, and mutilations. We need laments for communal catastrophes. The history of lament can help us by reminding us how poetry and music open the heart to its pain and give sorrow a voice. Maybe we will once again have music at funerals, and weeping will follow.

When a Torah scroll has an effaced or mutilated letter, a reader may not read from it until it is repaired and made whole. Every human loss is a silencing, a letter of the alphabet of creation effaced, erased, a whole world destroyed. We cannot go on until we can break that silence, until we can speak authentically to God out of our wounds. The language of lament allows us to rearticulate the alphabet of creation and restores for us the hope of redemption. As it says in Isaiah (25:8), "He will destroy death forever. Adonai Elohim will wipe the tears from every face."

Notes

1. Elaine Scarry, *The Body in Pain: The Making and Unmaking of the World* (New York: Oxford University Press, 1985).
2. Ibid., 30.
3. Ibid., 172.
4. Hosea 2:17.
5. Limping meter, first identified by Karl Budde, consists of lines with three stresses followed by lines with two stresses. Karl Budde, "Das hebräische Klagelied" *ZAW* 2 (1882): 1–52.
6. See also Amos 5:16. On women as communal elegists see S. D. Goitein, "Women as Creators of Biblical Genres," *Prooftexts* 8, no. 1 (1988): 1–33.
7. *Mishnah Mo-eid Katan* 3:9. In BT *Mo-eid Katan* 28b some verses of women's lament songs are cited. I am grateful for the help of Professor Gail Labovitz who consulted with me about this difficult material. Professor Labovitz is the editor, translator, and commentator for the yet to be published volume *Massekhet Mo'ed Qatan: Text, Translation, and Commentary (Feminist Commentary on the Babylonian Talmud)*, under contract, Mohr Siebeck.
8. Patrick Leigh Fermor, *Mani: Travels in the Southern Peloponnese* (London: Penguin Books, 1988), 53–62.
9. Gail Holst-Warhaft, *Dangerous Voices: Women's Laments and Greek Literature* (London: Routledge, 1992).
10. Ibid., 70.
11. bid., 71.
12. The wording is obscure. This is the gloss of Rashi, *Mo-eid Katan* 27b.
13. Saul M. Olyan, *Biblical Mourning* (Oxford: Oxford University Press, 2004), 39–46.
14. Adin Steinsaltz, *Masekhet Moed Qatan* (Jerusalem: HaMakhon HaYerushalmi L'Firsumim Talmudim, 1984), *Mo-eid Katan* 27b.
15. Steinsaltz, *Mo-eid Katan* 28b. See *HeChayyim* and *Iyunim S'machot* 2:10.
16. Two sources for a translation are Marcus Jastrow, *Dictionary of the Targumim, Talmud Bavli, Yerushalmi, and Midrashic Literature* (New

York: Judaica Press, 1921) and *Moed Katan*, trans. Rabbi Dayan H. M. Lazarus, *Seder Moed* IV (London: The Soncino Press, 1938). Jastrow's translation is strained. See *antikhi*, p. 83. "Take the bone pin out of the jaw (the base in which the vessel is suspended) and let water be put into the *antichi*" (sic). Soncino emends *mekhaca* to *khacava*, Latin *cacabus*, cooking pot, parallel to *antikhi*. *Moed Katan*,186–87.

17. Fermor, *Mani*, 60.
18. *S'machot* 2:10. It is permissible for a woman to wash either a man's or a woman's body, and before the ubiquity of *chevrei kadisha* and the rising prestige of the mitzvah, it is likely that women often performed that task. Dov Zlotnick, *The Tractate Mourning* [Semachot] (New Haven: Yale University Press, 1966), 1, 10.
19. Following the gloss of Rabbi Chananel *Mo-eid Katan* 28b.
20. Holst-Warhaft, *Dangerous Voices*, 10.
21. Athalya Brenner and Fokkelien van Dijk-Hemmes, *On Gendering Texts: Male and Female Voices in the Hebrew Bible* (Leiden: E. J. Brill, 1993), 43–48.
22. Rabbenu Hananel, *Moed Qatan* Vilna edition 6 (Jerusalem: Pe'er HaTorah, 1929), 28b.
23. Rashi, *Moed Qatan* Vilna 28b.
24. Soncino *Moed Katan*, 186.
25. Jastrow, see *Zavda*, 384.
26. Jastrow, see *Zavzaga*, 378. See also *Ein Yaaqov* (New York: Avraham Yitzchak Friedman, n.d.), Perek Shlishi, *Mo-eid Katan* 28.
27. Rabbenu Hananel, *Moed Qatan* Vilna 28b.
28. Rashi, *Moed Qatan* Vilna 28b.
29. Soncino *Moed Katan*, 187.
30. Rabbenu Hananel, *Moed Qatan* Vilna 28b.
31. Soncino *Moed Katan*, 187.
32. There are too many of them to constitute a scribal error. It is more like a refrain.
33. Judith Romney Wegner, *Chattel of Person: The Status of Women in the Mishnah* (New York: Oxford University Press, 1988), 1–19, 126–127, 172–173.
34. *Zohar, Parashat Vayak'heil* 196a–b. See also Zev Farber, "Women, Funerals and Cemeteries," *JOFA Journal* (Summer 2008): 1–3, 36.
35. *Gesher HaChaim*, 14:15 citing *Zohar, Parashat Vayak'heil*.
36. Ibid. On this issue see Miriam Sarah Feigelson "The Disappearance of Jewish Women from Burial Rites" (unpublished paper presented at WJSA Conference—Loyola Marymount University, Los Angeles, California, April 6–8, 2013), and Miriam Sarah Feigelson, הדרתן של נשים מטקסי קבורה (The Disappearance of Jewish

Women from Burial Rites) (unpublished paper presented at the Sixteenth World Congress of Jewish Studies—Jerusalem, Israel, July 28–August 1, 2013).

37. Sylvie Anne Goldberg, *Crossing the Jabbok* (Berkeley: University of California Press, 1996), 115.
38. Tod Linafelt, *Surviving Lamentations: Catastrophe, Lament, and Protest in the Afterlife of a Biblical Book* (Chicago: University of Chicago Press, 2000), 35–43.
39. Walter Brueggemann, "The Costly Loss of Lament," *Journal for the Study of the Old Testament* 36 (1986): 59.
40. Sigmund Freud, "Beyond The Pleasure Principle," *Standard Edition of the Complete Psychological Works of Sigmund Freud* 18, trans. James Strachey in collaboration with Anna Freud, assisted by Alix Strachey and Alan Tyson (New York: Vintage, 1999), 14–17.
41. Emmanuel Levinas, *Ethics and Infinity* (Pittsburgh: Duquesne University Press, 1985), 92.
42. Joan Didion *The Year of Magical Thinking* (New York: Alfred A. Knopf, 2005), 4.
43. R. Ruth Linden, *Making Stories, Making Selves: Feminist Reflections on the Holocaust* (Columbus: Ohio State Press, 1993), 9, 17–18.
44. Linafelt, *Surviving Lamentations*, 18.
45. Ibid.
46. For an extended discussion of this topic see Rachel Adler, "The Battered Wife of God: Violence, Law, and the Feminist Critique of the Prophets," *Review of Law and Women's Studies* 7, no. 2 (Spring, 1998): 171–201. Some major examples of the literature of feminist critique are: Gracia Fay Ellwood, *Batter My Heart* (Wallingford, PA: Pendle Hill Pamphlets, 1988); T. Drorah Setel, "Prophets and Pornography: Female Sexual Imagery in Hosea," in *Feminist Interpretation of the Bible*, ed. Letty Russell (Philadelphia: Westminster Press, 1985), 86–95; Renita J. Weems, "Gomer: Victim of Violence or Victim of Metaphor?"*Semeia* 47 (1989): 87–104, and *Battered Love: Marriage, Sex, and Violence in the Hebrew Prophets* (Minneapolis: Fortress, 1995); Naomi Graetz, "The Haftarah Tradition and the Metaphoric Battering of Hosea's Wife," *Conservative Judaism* 45, no. 1 (Fall 1992): 29–42; Fokkelien Van Dijk-Hemmes, "The Metaphorization of Woman in Prophetic Speech: An Analysis of Ezekiel xxiii," *Vetus Testtesmentum* 43 (1993): 162–70. See also Susan Brooks Thistlethwaite, "Every Two Minutes: Battered Women and Feminist Interpretation," in *Weaving the Visions*, ed. Judith Plaskow and Carol Christ (San Francisco: Harper and Row, 1989), esp. 312. In response to Naomi Graetz, see Benjamin Edidin Scolnic, "Bible-Battering," *Conservative Judaism* 45, no. 1 (Fall 1992): 43–52.

At the Turning: Reflections on My Life

David Ellenson

When I was appointed as president of HUC-JIR in 2001, I hoped that I would be able to give a decade of service in what I knew would be a challenging and rewarding position. My life had been shaped by the College-Institute. I enrolled as a student on our Jerusalem campus in 1972 and was ordained in New York in 1977. Two years later, I was selected to serve as a professor of Jewish Religious Thought at our Los Angeles school. There I had the privilege of teaching courses in Medieval and Modern Jewish Thought, Modern Jewish History, Modern Liturgy, Modern Religious Movements, and Modern Rabbinic Literature. Much of my work focused across denominations on the efforts and accomplishments of persons such as Esriel Hildesheimer, Zacharias Frankel, and Abraham Geiger—all prodigious scholars who also headed modern rabbinical schools in nineteenth-century Germany.

When the opportunity presented itself almost thirteen years ago to offer myself as a candidate for the position of president of HUC-JIR, I was unsure as to whether I even wanted to consider applying for this post. However, during a dinner discussing the prospects of my candidacy with friends who were intimately familiar with my fields of study, I was struck when one said to me, "You have spent a career as an historian researching and analyzing the careers of men who created the modern rabbinical seminary and who established modern Jewish religious movements. Perhaps it is time for you not only to study history, but attempt to contribute to it as a

---

RABBI DAVID ELLENSON, Ph.D. (NY77) was President, 2001-2013, and is the Chancellor and I.H. and Anna Grancell Professor of Jewish Religious Thought at HUC-JIR.

This article is an adapted version of the introduction to David Ellenson's *Jewish Meaning in a World of Choice*, which is scheduled to be published in 2014 by the Jewish Publication Society/University of Nebraska Press.

seminary president yourself." That conversation, along with many others, persuaded me to apply for the presidency, and on June 6, 2001, I was selected as president of Hebrew Union College–Jewish Institute of Religion.

Now, more than twelve years later, as I turn away from my position as president of the College-Institute and embark on a new chapter in my life, I realize that my soul is bound to this institution and to the holy mission that animates it—the education of religious, communal, educational, and intellectual leadership for the Reform Movement and the Jewish people—in the most intimate ways. It has been the greatest privilege of my life to devote my entire life to this school, and I am grateful for the opportunity and honor I have had to work with so many as president for this sacred cause.

It is surely appropriate that my friend and New York classmate Paul Golomb has now asked me—as I step down—to write an essay for the *CCAR Journal* describing my own assessment of and reflection upon these years in office. Tales of trials and triumphs have surely been intertwined during these years, and my colleague Steven Windmueller has already written a preliminary overview of my years in office.[1] I suspect others will follow, and the day may well soon come that I will feel ready to add my own voice to those of others in assessing these years. However, I must confess that I feel it too early and my years in office too fresh for me to be able to describe as I would like the achievements and challenges, the joys and disappointments of my term in office. Instead, I am going to take this opportunity that Paul has provided me and alter his request. Rather than speaking directly about my presidency, I would like to provide an autobiographical reminiscence—selective to be sure—that will describe the persons and contexts that forged me as a person and that led me to become a rabbi-professor and ultimately president of HUC-JIR.

*****

The forces that have animated my life and work cannot be understood without recourse to my family and my past as a Jewish boy growing up in the South during the 1950s and 1960s and the multilayered world I experienced. Everything in my world talked about difference and exclusion. My grandparents had all emigrated from Eastern Europe to the United States in the early 1900s. My maternal grandparents had settled in Cambridge, Massachusetts, while my paternal grandparents improbably came to Newport News, Virginia. My parents, Rosalind Stern and Samuel Ellenson, met at Harvard Hillel in 1945, immediately after World War II, and they married in 1946. A year later, I was born, and six months after my birth, my father, a degree from Harvard Law School in hand, returned with my mother and me to Newport News, where he began the practice of law.

Newport News and its sister city of Hampton were then small southern towns that were overwhelmingly Protestant. The politics of race was a central issue in the Virginia of my boyhood, and there was strict segregation in the schools and in all public facilities along with ubiquitous signs separating "white" from "colored" people in all these venues. While the landmark 1954 *Brown v. Topeka* decision in which the U.S. Supreme Court reversed *Plessey v. Ferguson* (1896) and held that the doctrine of "separate, but equal" was unconstitutional, Virginia Senator Harry Flood Byrd of Winchester—the dominant political voice in Virginia during those years—nevertheless formulated a policy of "massive resistance" to integration that guided the political direction of the Commonwealth during those years.

Of course, there was resistance to Byrd as well. I still have strong remembrances of students from Hampton Institute (now Hampton University) engaging in nonviolent protests and marches to desegregate public restaurants even as a former governor of Virginia, in a particularly obscene comment, stated that "integration was akin to mixing vanilla ice cream with coal dust. It ruined the ice cream and rendered the coal dust useless," he claimed. I still cringe as I recall his words, and I remember shamefully that Prince Edward County in Virginia at one point during this period closed all its public schools rather than allow integration. It may have been the one place in the English-speaking world that had—for a short time—the disgraceful distinction of having no public school system.

At the same time, I have a vivid memory of how my parents felt about all this and the attitudes they conveyed to me as a young boy over supper at the dining room table, where events of the day were discussed. They were enthusiastic supporters of Governor Lindsay Almond of Roanoke, who, after his election in 1958, abandoned the policy of "massive resistance" that his political mentor

Senator Byrd had promulgated. Instead, Governor Almond stated that Virginia would obey the law of the land as dictated by the Supreme Court. Regarded as a "traitor" by his own class, Governor Almond was a hero in my home and he remains for me a shining model of political and moral courage. When I wrote about this in an earlier writing, my friend Professor Stephen Whitfield of Brandeis sent me an enlarged copy of a *Time Magazine* cover graced by a picture of Governor Almond. It remains at the center of my office today.

During this period of my boyhood, my father took me to a segregationist rally being held in the southern countryside of Virginia. He was uncharacteristically silent as we drove to the rally. He said only that he wanted me to see firsthand and up close how "evil" appeared. My father made no other comment, either at the rally or as we drove home. However, he surely succeeded in his aim. More than half a century later the impression of this ugly event remains at the very core of my being.

As I relate this story and describe this period, I would not want to convey the impression that my parents were outspoken political activists nor that our existence as Jews was anything but comfortable on every visible level. To this day, I cannot fully capture how very much I love the South and the Peninsula. The approximately 2,000 Jews located on the Peninsula lived peacefully and prosperously among more than 150,000 gentiles. My father and one uncle enjoyed successful law practices. Another uncle had a roofing business while yet another was director of public works for the city. My entire extended family lived in the same pleasant neighborhood, and my childhood and adolescence were filled with family gatherings and events at which aunts, uncles, and cousins were present. Every Saturday night I would spend the night with my grandmother.

In 1962, I served as a page in the Virginia State Senate and two years later in 1964 I was a page to the Virginia delegation at the Democratic National Convention in Atlantic City. At Newport News High School I was elected president of the student body—I believe I was the first Jew to ever attain that position. I enrolled the next year at the College of William and Mary. In so doing, I followed my father, my uncle, several cousins, and preceded my younger brother. I assumed during that period that I would become an attorney, practice law with my father and uncle, and hopefully enter Virginia politics. I was and remain at some very deep level of my being a Virginian.

However, I was also a Jew and that was "the rub." I never felt I fully belonged. My being a Jew in a Christian world made me an outsider and different from the time I was a small boy, an observer even as I was an eager participant in the larger world. It left me feeling alienated even as I was overwhelmingly social and active.

Interestingly, there was an extremely strong Jewish religious and communal life there and this ingrained a strong feeling of Jewish identity—Yiddishkeit—in me. There were four synagogues on the Peninsula—two Orthodox (one had mixed seating, though its rabbi was a graduate of Yeshiva University), one Conservative, and one Reform. My family belonged to the Orthodox shul that had a *m'chitzah*, and I loved learning Hebrew and the skills to lead every variety of Orthodox services. My father served as president of our synagogue and my mother was extremely active in our Jewish Federation and Hadassah as well as the National Council of Jewish Women. The celebration and observance of the Sabbath and Jewish holidays were at the very center of our family life, and nothing was impressed upon me more by both my parents than the miracle and importance of the State of Israel and a love for and responsibility to the entire Jewish people.

The influence of my mother was more pronounced than that of anyone. She was a wonderful Hebraist, and I still have a siddur she was awarded as a child, with the inscription in *maskilic* Hebrew, "*Nitnah l'tovah stern, peras rishon l'hitstayenutah bi-sefat 'ever*— Given to Tovah Stern, first prize for her distinction in Hebrew." My mother had attended Hebrew College in Boston, read Hebrew texts with me in an Ashkenazic accent, and regaled me with story after story of her cousin who had fought with the Haganah to secure the independence of the Jewish State. She would remind me that eight days after I was born (November 21, 1947), the United Nations voted to partition Palestine and she would describe how the streets in her neighborhood in Cambridge erupted with joy when Israeli independence was declared in May 1948. When I was a teenager, she was appointed as director of Social Services for the city of Hampton, Virginia. At her interview, she was asked how, as the wife of "a prominent attorney," she possibly could head an agency when a majority of its clients were of a different race and a different socioeconomic class. She replied by saying to the interview committee, "You must not be aware. I am a Jew, and we are told everyday to remember that we were slaves to Pharaoh in Egypt. We are commanded to remember the heart of the stranger, because we were strangers in the land of Egypt." My mother inculcated a love for Israel, a commitment to Jewish values, and a concern for the welfare of the less fortunate in the deepest recesses of my heart. She was completely committed to K'lal Yisrael, and when one of my rabbis wanted me to be active only in the Orthodox National Conference of Synagogue Youth (NCSY), she protested strongly and insisted that I also be engaged in AZA (B'nai B'rith Youth), which brought together teenagers from across the denominational spectrum in our small Jewish community. I was also keenly aware that while my younger brother and I were assigned central roles in the liturgical rites of our synagogue, such roles were completely denied my mother (who was not bothered by this) and my sister (who was hurt profoundly by this exclusion).

In sum, the fabric of my identity was fraught with tensions. The inequities and evils I witnessed as a child and as a teenager in matters of race and gender and the sense of being an outsider as a Jew to the gentile culture in which I was raised all left a permanent mark on me.

*****

It was at William and Mary that I began to acquire the tools I would need to direct my life and answer the questions that lay in my heart. I was fortunate in my junior year to enroll in a course that Professor Ed Crapol taught on the History of American Foreign Policy. At that point, I was an indifferent student. However, Professor Crapol, newly arrived from his graduate work at the University of Wisconsin under the direction of William Appleman Williams, changed all that. His lectures were filled with content and he delivered them with excitement and passion. I still recall with the joy that is always associated with great learning and discovery how he applied the "Frontier Thesis" of Frederick Jackson Turner as a framework for understanding the course of American Foreign Policy from its origins during the early Federalist Period up to the modern day. Ed Crapol modeled the relevance and excitement, the moral dimensions, of what an academic life could and ought to be, and I would not have entered the Academy if it were not for him.

The other teacher I would recall is Professor James Livingston. Dr. Livingston came to William and Mary my senior year to inaugurate the Department of Religious Studies. It was he who taught me for the first time the works of Soren Kierkegaard, Martin Buber, Paul Tillich, and others. It was he who pointed out to me how many of the persons who were the great moral voices of that day—Abraham Joshua Heschel, Reinhold Niebuhr, Martin Luther King—possessed religious educations and commitments. Like Dr. Crapol, Professor Livingston displayed a complete mastery over the materials he presented in a soft yet comparably passionate way. He convinced me that there was no field in the world I would rather pursue than that of religious studies. In his class, while reading *The Shaking of the Foundations* by Paul Tillich, I came across the following paragraph:

> The name of this infinite and inexhaustible depth and ground of all being is *God*. That depth is what the word *God* means. And if that word has not much meaning for you, translate it, and speak of the depths of your life, of the source of your being, of your ultimate concern, of what you take seriously without any reservation.[2]

These words addressed my soul. Beset by conflicts over my identity as an Orthodox Jewish boy raised in Tidewater, Virginia, Tillich prodded me to recognize who I was in the depths of my being. He awakened a nascent recognition in me that I was above all a Jew. While I was surely uncertain about the nature of my faith in God, I had no doubt that it was Judaism—its texts and traditions—and the Jewish people that constituted the core of who I was as a person, my "ultimate concerns" that I took "seriously without any reservation." A lifetime quest to articulate why that was so and the pursuit of explaining why my religious and cultural traditions as a Jew were so significant to me in a world where Jewish meaning could not be taken for granted and where myriad choices and options challenged my commitments and identity as a Jew began in earnest.

I enrolled soon thereafter in the Religious Studies Department of the University of Virginia, where I received an M.A. degree under the tutelage of Alan Lettofsky. A rabbinical graduate of the Jewish Theological Seminary, who went on to work for his doctorate at

Yale University, Alan was the consummate pedagogue and mentor. He guided my nascent interests in Jewish Studies with rigor and compassion. He was both demanding and understanding. It remains one of the signal blessings of my life that I had such a teacher at this point in my career, and I will always be grateful for the nurture and direction he provided. He advised me to enroll in a seminar on the Sociology of Religion taught by David Little. There, for the first time, I read the works of Durkheim and Weber, where I was provided the beginnings of a vocabulary that would allow me to frame and illuminate my concerns. It was also equally clear to me that I had so much more to learn if I was to ever explore seriously the nature of what it was to be a Jew in the modern world.

This led me to move to Israel for two years. The first year I lived on Kibbutz Mishmar Haemek in the Jezreel Valley—where I worked in the fields and advanced my spoken Hebrew—while, in the second year, I enrolled in the rabbinical program at Hebrew Union College in Jerusalem. Although I seriously considered remaining in Israel and making *aliyah* at the end of that year, I decided to return to the United States, where for the next four years I would pursue rabbinical ordination at HUC-JIR in New York and doctoral studies in Religion at Columbia University. I loved the College-Institute and was particularly influenced by Lawrence Hoffman. I immediately recognized him as a kindred spirit, and I marveled at his ability to use sociological and philosophical paradigms to illuminate Jewish texts and derive Jewish meanings and understandings. He genuinely inspired me. At the same time, I had the pleasure of studying Jewish Intellectual History with Arthur Hertzberg and Sociology with Gillian Lindt, Robert Nisbet, and Joseph Blau at Columbia.

The influence of Eugene Borowitz was also profound and enduring. As a second-year rabbinical student, I sat in his Introduction to Modern Jewish Thought class and heard him say that the central problem of modern Jewish thought was that of articulating how to be simultaneously Jewish and modern in a Western world of seemingly endless possibilities. His unadorned and direct statement of the problem resonated in the very depths of my being. His words struck me as clear and profound—true. He gave me an intellectual-theological framework for analyzing the "intellectual arrangements" different Jewish thinkers and movements have advanced over the past two hundred years in their diverse attempts to affirm Jewish meaning in a world where being Jewish is no longer required. My entire scholarly and intellectual project has been informed by my attempts to understand how different Jewish individuals and groups have responded to this challenge and attempted to renew the Covenant between God and Israel in modern times. His teaching touched the recesses of my heart.

*****

The precise character of my work was shaped by two men. Towards the end of my formal graduate education in 1976 and 1977, I came under the tutelage of Fritz Bamberger of HUC-JIR and Jacob Katz of Hebrew University, who was then at Columbia as a visiting professor. Dr. Bamberger was a German refugee scholar who was the embodiment of *Bildung*. Cultured and erudite, he possessed an unsurpassed knowledge of modern Jewish intellectual history. I flourished in my relationship with him as I wrote my rabbinical thesis on Esriel Hildesheimer under his guidance. He commented to me that my treatment of Hildesheimer derived from an overarching intellectual perspective of tension. He identified this perspective as quintessentially "American." I had described Hildesheimer as possessing a "hyphenated identity" in which the German and Jewish elements of his identity did not fit together perfectly. Dr. Bamberger maintained that I was not necessarily incorrect in my portrait of Rabbi Hildesheimer. However, he also assured me that Hildesheimer would not have viewed himself as I viewed him. That is, Dr. Bamberger—despite the dislocation he himself experienced as a German Jew during the 1930s—was convinced that a nineteenth-century acculturated Jew like Hildesheimer was the product of a German-Jewish symbiosis that would have caused him to experience his life as a seamless whole. He told me that it took an American Jew like me who had read Mordecai Kaplan to understand Hildesheimer's life as I had. To this day, I still have my doubts about what Dr. Bamberger said. Nevertheless, his comments did make me aware that the hermeneutic of tension I have employed in all my work is embedded in a narrative that emerged from my own childhood experiences as a Jewish boy in Virginia.

My decision to employ this hermeneutic as the most appropriate one to illuminate the course of the modern Jewish experience in the West was reinforced by my study at the same time with Jacob Katz, who was surely the preeminent historian-sociologist of modern

Judaism. Professor Katz provided me with the content and even more importantly the methodology that would guide and inform my work for decades to come. In his seminar on Judaism in the Nineteenth Century, Professor Katz pointed out that Germany was the crucible in which modern Judaism was born. It was here that the conflict between an inherited Jewish tradition and a highly acculturated Jewish community first played itself out. Katz himself explored the diverse ways Jews emerged from the ghetto from the 1770s on. He contended that what was noteworthy was not that countless Jews ultimately assimilated in light of an open society in which Jews were culturally, politically, and ultimately socially and economically integrated. Rather, what he viewed as remarkable was that Judaism did not atrophy and die in the wake of these changes. Instead, Jews reconfigured their identity and observance in different ways and the study of how they did this—the intellectual arrangements and observance patterns they created—was to become the subject of my own work. Indeed, it is a primary reason that I wrote my dissertation on Rabbi Hildesheimer, an Orthodox Jew completely committed to Jewish tradition, who received a doctorate from a German university and who was completely comfortable in Western culture. A study of his life would indicate precisely how Jewish religious tradition could be and was adapted to the demands of the time and place in which he lived. In so doing, I could hold up a mirror to my own being and provide a case study of how Judaism could be adapted to the modern world.

Professor Katz also provided me with the insight that German Judaism was of special significance for an understanding of modern Judaism. Jews in Germany did not simply acculturate into the mores of the larger society as Jews in France or England had. By an appeal to a history of prior evolution and change, these German Jews provided an ideological platform that could be exported to other Jewish communities. They provided a rationale for religious reform and the emergence of Jewish religious movements that could challenge the hegemony of Rabbinic Judaism with its notion of an unchanging and eternal Jewish law. Professor Katz hammered this point home in his seminar and provided countless examples drawn from his vast knowledge of Talmud and Jewish law, Western languages, Jewish and European history, as well as sociology to demonstrate his position. The transition of German Judaism from the medieval to the modern world grips my attention to this day.

However, it was his seminar on the Uses of Halachah in the Writing of Jewish History that had the greatest impact on the direction of my work. Professor Katz would dissect the halachic writings of great eighteenth- and nineteenth-century Rabbinic decisors and have us see how this approach could be employed in the writing of history. It was an aesthetic delight to see this man—educated as a youth in Hungarian yeshivot and later trained as a sociologist at the University of Frankfurt—at work in this way, a genius at work in his laboratory. Dr. Katz said over and over again that we could assume that all the men whose work we investigated knew the Talmudic and Rabbinic sources we read as well as we did! Thus, if we found a "mistake" or "misreading" in one of these rabbis, Professor Katz said we should pay a great deal of attention to it because something of significance was undoubtedly happening. In order to uncover the reason for the "misreading," it was crucial to have a knowledge of history and sociology—the personal biography as well as the context in which the decisor lived—to successfully dig out nuggets of meaning from the texts we were mining. In addition, Professor Katz stated that what was important about a Talmudic precedent for a ruling was not that something was cited, but rather why the writer chose a particular precedent and not another to justify his ruling. After all, he observed, there was almost always a precedent that would be cited. The historical significance of this choice could only be determined in light of economic, social, biographical, or political factors. Finally, Professor Katz pointed out to us that in looking at this legal material and attempting to define its historical import and meaning, the "ideal type" methodology of Max Weber could be invaluable. In this methodology, an analytical construct not found "empirically anywhere in reality" was employed to isolate elements of social reality to explain their significance and importance. Professor Katz himself employed this method in his famed *Exclusiveness and Tolerance* as well as *Tradition and Crisis*. In both works, he was able to illuminate the transition of European Judaism and its culture and institutions from the relatively closed world of the Middle Ages to the much more expansive horizons of the modern period. He urged us to employ this model in our own work.

I am proud to say that in all these ways my own work follows in the path of Professor Katz. My life, my interests, my education prior to my coming to Columbia prepared me for the lessons he taught. In the years subsequent to Columbia, my decision to center so many of my investigations on responsa literature and modern Jewish prayer books—with their diachronic elements that draw on the past and their synchronic elements that testify to contemporaneous influences—reflects the impress of his influence and method. My decision to employ his model to study Rabbinic responsa and prayer book compositions in Western Europe, North America, and my beloved Israel reflect my deepest personal commitments to Judaism and the State of Israel. It also led me to believe that academic scholarship was a vital means to illuminate an understanding of life for myself, my Jewish community, and others in the larger world. In this sense, I hope that my scholarly work and practical efforts are reflections of the immense shadow and influence of Professor Katz as well as my other teachers.

*****

Elizabeth Costello, the fictional protagonist of South African author J. M. Coetzee's novel, *Elizabeth Costello*, states, after receiving an award for her literary work:

> We all know, if we are being realistic, that it is only a matter of time before the books which you honour, and with whose genesis I have had something to do, will cease to be read and eventually cease to be remembered. And properly so. There must be some limit to the burden of remembering that we impose on our children and grandchildren. They have a world of their own, of which we should be less and less part.[3]

As a Jew who is commanded everyday to remember my bondage and my exodus from Egypt, I cannot agree with the fictional Costello. I cannot forget the books of my Jewish past, nor do I want to. Instead, I hope that my children and my students and their descendants, as our daily liturgy phrases it, will be *"yodei sh'mecha v'lomdei toratecha"* (knowers of God and students of Torah). My years as president of the College-Institute have been an extension of my entire life and all my values. I have aspired as a Jew born in America and connected deeply both to Israel and the larger world to place myself and my students in a chain of Jewish tradition that is humane and inclusive.

Rabbi Leo Baeck provides me with a language for that aspiration. The last duly elected leader of the Jewish community in Germany during the dark years of the Holocaust, Rabbi Baeck saved the life of my teacher Fritz Bamberger by securing a teaching position for him in Chicago. I feel connected to him in the deepest recesses of my soul. In his *This People Israel*, first published in 1948, three years after his release from Terezin, where three of his own sisters perished, Rabbi Baeck wrote:

> Every generation by choosing its way, its present way, at the same time chooses an essential part of the future, the way of its children. Perhaps the children will turn from the eternal way, but in this, too, they will be determined by the direction of their parents. The responsibility to those who follow after us is included in the responsibility to ourselves. The way of the children, whether accepting or rejecting the direction, emanates from our way. Ways bind, wind, and wander. When a man forms his life, he begins to create community. He is not only born into community as if by fate, but he has now been called to the task of molding it.[4]

My own Jewish way has wandered. Surely, the ways of my own children and grandchildren as well as my students will wander as well. Nevertheless, I and they are also bound, and my way, just as theirs, emanates from those who lived before us. I have tried—through my researches and through my work as a teacher and as president of the College-Institute—to honor the way I have inherited even as I have struggled to mold a direction for a way that reflects who I am. I look forward with confidence to how the students and graduates of HUC-JIR, under the leadership of Aaron Panken, will mold their own directions for the Jewish people and humanity in the days ahead.

Notes

1. See Steven Windmueller, "Unpacking a Presidency: Rabbi David Ellenson," *ejewishphilanthropy.com*, August 15, 2013, http://ejewishphilanthropy.com/unpacking-a-presidency-rabbi-david-ellenson/.
2. Paul Tillich, *The Shaking of the Foundations* (New York: Charles Scribner's Sons, 1948), 57.
3. J. M. Coetzee, *Elizabeth Costello* (New York: Penguin Books, 2003), 20.
4. Leo Baeck, *This People Israel* (New York: Holt, Rinehart and Winston, 1965), 393–94.

This People Israel

The Unholy Scramble for Pulpits: A History of Reform Rabbinic Placement (Part 1): 1893–1961

Alan Henkin

Wednesday, June 20, 1951, was a gorgeous day in New London, Connecticut, with temperatures in the mid-seventies and not a drop of rain in the sky. At the Griswold Hotel ("The Finest Summer Resort Hotel in America") a dejected Roland Gittelsohn (1910–1995) stood before his colleagues at the annual convention of the Central Conference of American Rabbis to report on the status of the Conference's placement plan for rabbis. The November 1950 General Assembly of the Union of American Hebrew Congregations had killed the placement plan that he had so painstakingly crafted and shepherded through so many committees and conferences.[1]

Just two years earlier, in 1949, the CCAR convened in Bretton Woods, New Hampshire, at the historic Mount Washington Hotel, which in 1944 had hosted the Bretton Woods International Monetary Conference. In 1949 Gittelsohn had only returned a few years earlier from the Pacific Theater of World War II with three combat ribbons for his service with the Fifth Marine Division on Iwo Jima. An optimistic Gittelsohn and his Committee had presented a detailed plan for rabbinic placement that was well received and provoked such a lively conversation that it had to be continued

---

RABBI ALAN HENKIN, Ph.D. (C80) is director of Rabbinic Placement for the CCAR.

The author wishes to thank Rabbi Gary Zola and Kevin Profitt of the American Jewish Archives, as well as Kathleen Shoemaker of the Manuscript, Archives, and Rare Book Library of Emory University, for their invaluable research assistance.

later that afternoon. The plan attempted to remedy "the chaos and anarchy of the past with a procedure that would be orderly." Since its founding the CCAR had tried many times to institute such a plan but all of its efforts had come to naught. The time was right for the CCAR to join with the congregational arm of the Reform Movement, the Union of American Hebrew Congregations, to correct "a situation which threatens to become intolerable."

The plan called for the establishment of a Placement Bureau composed of representatives of the CCAR, the UAHC, and the Hebrew Union College–Jewish Institute of Religion. The Bureau would hire a full-time director, and it would all be paid for proportionately by the three arms of the Movement. Congregations and rabbis would have to use the Placement Bureau exclusively. "Unless every rabbi and every congregation agree to abide by the same orderly and fair course of procedure, the rule will become nugatory, and the scrupulous penalized." Congregations had the right to describe to the Bureau the kind of rabbi that they were searching for, and the Bureau would have the authority to recommend candidates to congregations in search. The Bureau also would have the power to invoke sanctions on rabbis or congregations who violated its rules.

In the discussion afterwards Gittelsohn told the members that so far, the representatives of the UAHC "approved the report substantially," which Maurice Eisendrath (1902–1973), the president of the UAHC, confirmed. Solomon B. Freehof (1892–1990) expressed concern that the director "will have your career and your fate in his hands." Others voiced worries about the costs of the Bureau and about the necessity of sanctions. Overall, however, a consensus emerged that placement had become "a very sad situation and we have to take some very drastic steps," as Jacob J. Weinstein (1902–1974) put it. In the end the Conference approved the substance of the plan with some relatively minor changes, asking the Committee to send the amended plan to the members for the next Convention.

At the CCAR Convention held at the Gibson Hotel in Cincinnati in 1950 Gittelsohn brought forward the amended plan on Thursday morning, June 8. This too touched off a spirited conversation. Gittelsohn reported that the Executive Board of the UAHC tentatively approved the plan, but James G. Heller (1892–1971) warned the Conference that although the UAHC leaders seemed to favor the plan, "some members of the New York Congregations took a violent attitude against the plan." In other cities the plan received widespread support of synagogue leaders. No wonder Gittelsohn and his Committee felt hopeful about his plan. So confident did the CCAR leaders feel that they included in the plan the establishment of a "temporary placement committee that will go out of existence immediately upon the establishment of the general placement bureau," said CCAR President Jacob Marcus (1896–1995). The vote on the provisional body was overwhelming, 78 to 11.

One year later, however, Gittelsohn's placement plan was dead. Oddly enough, the UAHC had approved a motion to create a placement system. But the plenum had attached several amendments that it knew would make it unacceptable to the CCAR. Among the "poison pills" were: the placement system would be optional for rabbis and congregations; and congregations could go into placement before they had resolved the status of their current rabbis. Years later James G. Heller would describe this UAHC meeting as "one of the most frustrating, and to a certain extent most depressing, meetings that we have ever had in Reform Judaism." Gittelsohn's Placement Committee voted 7 to 2 against accepting the UAHC amended motion, and it urged the CCAR Convention to reject it as well. The Convention turned down the UAHC-amended plan but it also voted to keep in place the provisional placement system set up just a year earlier. With that, admitting that he was "weary after three years of onerous and at times disheartening attempts" to construct a placement system for the Movement, Gittelsohn resigned as chairman.

The Early Years

By 1889, when Isaac Mayer Wise (1819–1900) turned seventy, the Hebrew Union College had ordained twenty rabbis, and Wise turned to organizing the American rabbinate. In July of that year he and his disciple David Philipson (1862–1945) gathered the rabbis attending the council of the UAHC to ascertain their interest in a rabbinic conference. A motion to create a Central Conference of American Rabbis passed unanimously, and the CCAR came into existence.

Although the CCAR's first two conventions were held at Young Men's Hebrew Associations in Cleveland and Baltimore, the third convention in 1892 met at Temple Beth-El in New York City. Beth-El's new synagogue had just been built at the cost of $350,000 (about $9 million in 2014 dollars), and the building was dedicated only the year before. In 1879 Kauffman Kohler (1843–1926) succeeded his father-in-law David Einhorn (1809–1879) as rabbi of Beth-El. Eventually Beth-El would merge with Temple Emanu-El, but when in 1891 Beth-El was dedicated, the *New York Times* called it "magnificently decorated."[2]

At this third CCAR Convention the members took up for the first time the issue of rabbinic placement. On Sunday morning, July 10, 1892, Maurice Harris (1859–1930) and Joseph Silverman (1860–1930) introduced a resolution on rabbinic ethics, though three of its six operative clauses dealt with placement. The first clause asked that no CCAR rabbi accept a position in a congregation "that sends adrift a colleague who has grown old in its service" unless that rabbi has been offered a decent pension. The second called on rabbis not to accept an invitation to serve a congregation "while the incumbent is still in office" and wait until "after the pulpit is declared vacant." Third, when two rabbis are both candidates for the same congregation, "they should extend to each other all the courtesies and consideration possible in order to maintain the fraternal feelings that should always exist among colleagues." We can only imagine the state of affairs among rabbis that would have necessitated such a resolution. In any event nothing seems to have become of this resolution.

Joseph Stolz (1861–1941), the founding rabbi of Temple Isaiah in Chicago, was president of the CCAR in 1906. On July 2 of that year he delivered his president's message in Indianapolis and adumbrated his vision of the CCAR as a professional body. He argued that the Conference needed to find ways to prevent "unseemly rivalry and unbecoming commercialism in the filling of vacant pulpits." Concretizing Stolz's sentiments, Louis Witt (1878–1950) and Samuel H. Goldenson (1878–1962) called for the appointment of a committee that would bring back ideas "to relieve the present unregulated state of affairs with regard to candidating for pulpits."

The CCAR Executive Committee met during the January 1907 UAHC Convention in Atlanta and adopted a recommendation from the Committee on Candidating for Pulpits that requested the UAHC to appoint a committee to work with the CCAR on placement. By the time of the CCAR's Convention in Frankfort,

Michigan, in July 1907, the Conference seemed determined "to devise a plan to help congregations in the method of selecting Rabbis without advising which ones to select," as David Philipson's resolution put it. So the following year, on Wednesday morning, July 3, the CCAR agreed to establish a Pulpit Bureau "to aid congregations without Rabbis to secure them and Rabbis without positions or seeking other ones to be put in correspondence with such congregations." Nothing seems to have become of this resolution.

In 1910 Henry Cohen (1863–1952) was at the helm of the Pulpit Bureau, a committee of the CCAR whose first task was to collect information on the placement programs of other religious denominations. In the report he submitted in absentia he misunderstood his mandate and instead he surveyed eight CCAR members regarding the feasibility of a placement system that, besides placing rabbis in congregations, would work at resolving conflict and "weeding out of undesirables." But not only did Cohen misconstrue the charge, the responses he received were nearly unanimously discouraging, especially regarding the expulsion of members. By 1911 Cohen got it right, and learned that two placement systems predominate among the Christian groups: appointment by bishops and election by congregations. Cohen admitted that "there exists no satisfactory arrangement to bring together unemployed ministers and vacant pulpits." Nothing seems to have come of this survey.

Placement was back on the CCAR's agenda in 1915. Resolution E asked that a new committee be appointed to recommend "methods of pulpit candidating," because the members "strongly condemn all such methods of electing rabbis as tend to lower the high standard and dignity of the rabbinate, and we believe the present methods are on the whole of this tendency." Louis Witt, at that time the rabbi of Congregation B'nai Israel in Little Rock, Arkansas, assumed the chair of the Committee on Pulpit Candidating, and the next year his Committee acknowledged that placement had come before the CCAR at least a half-dozen times with nothing to show for it. "Our policy has hitherto been, in the main, one of evasion and procrastination."

The Committee denounced the use of the trial sermon as the sole criterion for selecting a rabbi, but it argued that if synagogues must use this method, it would be best to implement it by way of serial visits. That is, they imagined a placement system in which congregational representatives would visit a rabbi in his home congregation and vote up or down on that rabbi before considering the next candidate. The Committee called this system "right of way": "One man at a time and out of the way before another man is called." The CCAR printed a pamphlet with the plan and circulated it among the members, but only a handful replied. The CCAR summarily rejected the plan for a Bureau for Filling Pulpit Vacancies on July 1, 1917, without explanation. Nothing seems to have become of this effort.

The Depression Years

Little activity on placement occurred in the Roaring Twenties, but with the onset of the Great Depression (1929–1933), the need for a placement system grew urgent. Congregational membership dropped off dramatically, synagogues cut back on programs and staff, rabbis were let go, and the rabbinical students of Hebrew Union College faced uncertain futures. Family membership in the UAHC fell from 61,600 in 1930 to 52,300 in 1934. At the CCAR investments declined by 20 percent, and a large percentage of its members could not afford dues.[3]

With David Lefkowitz (1875–1955), rabbi of Temple Emanu-El of Dallas, Texas, in the presidency of the CCAR in 1931, the members convened at the Spink's Wawasee Hotel right on Lake Wawasee in Indiana. In his presidential address on Wednesday evening, June 17, he minced no words:

> We are meeting in our forty-second annual convention with chastened spirits and in a sober, if not somber, frame of mind. A considerable group of rabbis is now unable to find pulpits and it will be augmented I fear, through the ordinations this year . . . In addition, many congregations have felt the need of reducing the salaries of their rabbis, which in most cases were meagre enough.

Lefkowitz then asked the Conference to get serious about a placement system:

> The scene is being laid for an unholy scramble for pulpits far more undignified and disgraceful than it has ever been before in our American rabbinate. There will be bidding and under-bidding on the part of hard-driven colleagues, perhaps with families to support, and there will be all the playing of one rabbi against

another on the part of congregations, with wire-pulling and trial sermons thrown in for measure. Into the rabbinical profession will come the harsh competition and chaffer of the market-place with all the acerbities engendered in such unseemly dickering.

Within four days the Committee on the President's Message, chaired by no less than Julian Morgenstern, president of the Hebrew Union College, acted on Lefkowitz's remarks. It called for the CCAR Executive Committee to find a way to bring together for placement rabbis and congregations, especially ones in small, outlying communities. In addition, the Committee on Resolutions proposed, and the plenum adopted, a lengthy resolution on the economic conditions "that threaten with dire disaster many of our colleagues and their families, men without reproach who have served the rabbinate honorably and faithfully for many years and now in the prime of life find themselves sidetracked and shipwrecked." The resolution called for the setting of a minimum salary, establishing a code of conduct for the way CCAR members treated one another, and the reviving of the Pulpit Bureau effort "to protect the livelihood and welfare of its members as well as the dignity of the rabbinate." It looked like something would at last be done to mitigate "the unholy scramble for pulpits."

Yet in 1932, when the CCAR gathered at the Sinton Hotel in Cincinnati, all that happened was that the Committee on Resolutions asked that a Pulpit Placement Committee be appointed "to aid colleagues who are in need of proper placement." This Committee came into being and the renowned David Philipson, then in his seventies, chaired the group. On the morning of Sunday, June 25, 1933, Philipson reported that few pulpit vacancies had opened up, and in fact many congregations had closed, "thus throwing the rabbi out of a position . . . The unemployment which is so general has therefore also invaded the rabbinical field." He also noted that the UAHC had created its own Pulpit Placement Committee, and so he urged that the UAHC's and the CCAR's committees be merged. The plenum adopted the report, but nothing seems to have come of it.

Perhaps the rise of European fascism or the eruption of virulent anti-Semitism preoccupied the Conference. Perhaps the rebirth of the Jewish homeland or the chilling specter of another world war dominated the attention of the members. Or perhaps the CCAR stopped considering placement for several years in the mid-1930s because of the easing of the Depression. Indeed, in 1935 Barnett Brickner (1892–1958), reporting on aid to congregations and rabbis, claimed that "most of the unemployed rabbis had secured positions" though they were paid but subsistence wages.

Max Currick (1877–1947) was the longest serving rabbi in the history of Temple Anshe Hesed in Erie, Pennsylvania, and when he presided over the CCAR in 1938, he had already been with his congregation for thirty-seven years. Currick was president of the CCAR during Hitler's rise to international power, and his presidential address to the Conference at the Chelsea Hotel in Atlantic City, New Jersey, focused on efforts that the CCAR could undertake, along with other American Jewish organizations, to thwart Nazism and to support German Jewry. Still, he insisted that the Conference develop a code of ethics "in order, to put it mildly, to remove the embarrassments of unethical competition [in placement]." In this context he suggested "that the whole subject of placement be treated anew by the Conference." The Committee on the President's Message reiterated Currick's complaint, "The competition for pulpits which is now unfortunately prevalent had led to unethical practices which must be deeply deplored." The Committee proposed that the CCAR create a committee on placements with representatives from the UAHC.

In 1939 at the Mayflower Hotel in Washington, D.C., the CCAR celebrated its fiftieth anniversary. Although president Max Currick again asked the Conference to work with the UAHC on the issue of placement, the real activity resided with the Committee on the Code of Ethics chaired by past president David Lefkowitz. A good portion of the proposed Code dealt with placement. It forbade rabbis from applying for a still-occupied pulpit; it asked that searches proceed "in a dignified manner and with full reverence for the office of the rabbi"; and it demanded that rabbis be judged by their "whole record" and not just a "trial sermon."

When the Conference met in June 1940, at the Charlevoix Inn in Charlevoix, Michigan, the focus was on a continuation of the previous year's consideration of a code of ethics. CCAR President Emil Leipziger (1877–1963) of Touro Synagogue in New Orleans called for approval of the code to remedy "the chaotic and lamentable conditions which appear to exist in the rabbinate with regard to pulpit placement, rabbinical unemployment and inadequate income in small positions." The report of the Committee on a Code of Ethics was composed by David Lefkowitz and Abraham Feldman (1893–1977), then rabbi of Congregation Beth Israel of Hartford, Connecticut. In a postcard survey of the proposed 1939 Code of Ethics, the members of the CCAR by a slim margin had voted against this sentence: "No rabbi should make personal application to a congregation, even when a pulpit vacancy exists." The majority opposing this sentence believed that until the CCAR could devise an orderly and credible placement system, it would be unfair to prohibit direct application to congregations. Although the Committee wanted to keep the sentence, it was removed in the final code. Also Section II, Paragraph 5, the part asking congregations to visit rabbi candidates in their own congregations and not to make quick decisions based on the "trial sermon," was sent back to the Committee for rewording.

The World War II Years

Although World War II began in Asia in 1937 and in Europe in 1939, the United States did not formally enter the war until December 1941. With the nation's mobilization for war, 1,045 rabbis, over half of the American rabbinate, volunteered for military service. In fact Jewish chaplains had been attached to the American military since 1862 when, after considerable controversy, Rabbi Jacob Frankel of Philadelphia was commissioned as a hospital chaplain. By World War I, twenty-three Jewish chaplains were in uniform, sixteen of whom were Reform rabbis. During World War II, 311 rabbis received commissions as Jewish chaplains. Almost half of them, 147, came from the ranks of the CCAR. Both their departure to and return from war would create havoc for rabbinic placement. In June 1941, when the CCAR met at the Chelsea Hotel in Atlantic City, New Jersey, everyone knew that the United States was on the brink of war. Placement was low on the agenda, and resolving that the CCAR and the UAHC should work together on placement was all that could be mustered.

In 1942, however, James G. Heller sitting as both the president of the Conference and as the chairman of the Committee on Pulpit Placement and Ethics, offered a formal placement plan. He and his Committee presented it at an 11:20 P.M. special session of the Cincinnati Convention held at the chapel of HUC. The plan was fully formulated, and it provoked strong reactions from the rabbis. The plan envisioned dividing North America into ten or twelve placement regions with a group of three rabbis and three lay people on each regional pulpit placement committee. The whole arrangement was overseen by a Joint National Committee on Pulpit Placement of the CCAR and the UAHC. Congregations would write the National Committee about their need for a rabbi, and the National Committee would "recommend one man at a time." The Regional Committees would act as advisors and feeders to the National Committee.

The plenum hotly debated the plan. Some opposed the plan. For example, David Wice (1908–2002), then of Congregation B'nai Jeshurun of Newark, New Jersey, complained: "Tragic as have been the conditions in applying to congregations, I think you will multiply them a thousand fold by having these committees." But the plan had supporters, too, like David Polish (1910–1995): "It is surprising that so many members of the Conference who have been bitter against the anarchic situation in the rabbinate, are unready to accept a plan which is certainly better than the chaos in which we have been proceeding." Heller stepped out of his role as president and chair, asking for the privilege of the floor:

> The conditions in the rabbinate have been growing steadily worse and they have been growing worse for reasons that are not entirely the fault of the Conference. They have been growing worse, first, because the theological institutions have been pouring men into the rabbinate despite appeals that have been made to them, to limit the number who were to be graduated. We have had more men for years than there were positions for the men to occupy, and the natural result of that, added to the lack of government in the rabbinate, was to aggravate conditions that had existed before for many years.

After some parliamentary maneuvering the plan for Pulpit Placement was adopted in principle in a close 54 to 45 vote, but sent back to committee to rework the details.

By 1943 the CCAR was providing 55 percent to 60 percent of the Jewish chaplains to the American armed forces. In most instances congregations "recognized their patriotic duty both as Americans and as Jews" to grant their rabbis leaves of absence to enter the military chaplaincy. In fact, the yearbook of the CCAR of that year was dedicated to the first Jewish chaplain to lose his life in war, Alexander Goode (1911–1943), one of the famed four chaplains who died when the troop-transport ship *Dorchester* was torpedoed in the North Atlantic. A Committee on Placement and Ethics was appointed but appears not to have been active.

During these years the CCAR's Committee on Chaplains also had the burden of finding replacements for the rabbis who joined the chaplaincy. Because of the shortage of such rabbis, HUC and JIR accelerated their courses of study to provide rabbis for congregations in the absence of their regular rabbis. By 1944, 181 CCAR rabbis had volunteered for service, fully three-fifths of the available members. At the 1944 Convention that met over June 23 to 26 at the Hotel Gibson in Cincinnati, Ohio, the Committee released its "Principles on Replacement of Chaplains." The very first principle forbade rabbis from assuming the pulpit of a rabbi at war with the intention of holding it permanently; a rabbi could only replace another with

> the definite understanding that he shall relinquish the position, when the Chaplain returns to it from his service. Chaplains now serving should feel assured that everything possible will be done by both the Union and the Conference to protect their professional interests and to see that the services they are rendering will receive due consideration, and that on their return every possible assistance will be given them to recover their status.

Anticipating the demobilization of Jewish chaplains and their return to civilian life, President Solomon B. Freehof created an Emergency Placement Committee. "It would be intolerable if, when [the chaplains] return to this country, they should find no civilian position available to them."

The resolve of the Committee on Chaplaincy was tested by Hyman Judah Schachtel (1907–1990). When Henry Barnston (1868–1949) retired from Congregation Beth Israel in Houston, Texas, after a forty-four year rabbinate in 1943, Schachtel succeeded him without receiving clearance from the Committee, as required by the Conference. Beth Israel's associate rabbi, Robert Kahn (1910–2002), who had come to Houston as an assistant rabbi in 1935, was on a leave of absence serving in the Army chaplaincy, and many in the Conference and in the congregation felt that the pulpit should remain vacant until Rabbi Kahn returned. The CCAR's Executive Committee declared that Schachtel had "contravened the rules of the Committee on Chaplaincy," and it reaffirmed its intention to protect vacant pulpits so that returning chaplains might apply for them. (Beth Israel split over Schachtel's election, and the splinter group founded Congregation Emanu-El, naming Kahn the senior rabbi in absentia.)

A similar situation with a very different outcome arose in Hollywood, California. After being installed as rabbi of Temple Israel in March 1940, Morton Bauman (1912–1993) entered the Army chaplaincy in 1942. To replace him, in 1942 the congregation engaged a German refugee, Max Nussbaum (1908–1974), then with Congregation Beth Ahaba in Muskogee, Oklahoma. The CCAR intervened, reminding the leaders of the rule to keep open pulpits for the returning chaplains. By the time of Bauman's return to Temple Israel in 1945, the congregants had fallen in love with the charismatic and powerful Nussbaum and his wife Ruth. To solve the dilemma, Temple Israel engaged both Nussbaum and Bauman for four years until 1949 when Bauman left Temple Israel and began a twenty-eight-year tenure with Temple Beth Hillel in North Hollywood, California.[4]

When the CCAR gathered on June 25, 1945, at the Hotel Chelsea in Atlantic City, New Jersey, Hitler had committed suicide two months earlier, the German Armed Forces High Command had surrendered unconditionally, and the birth of the United Nations had begun. Franklin Delano Roosevelt had just died, and the horrors of the Holocaust were sinking in. The focus of placement was naturally on the returning chaplains. In his Report of the Committee on Chaplains, Barnett Brickner (1892–1958) described the continuing efforts "to prevent any replacement rabbis from taking the positions of those for whom they are substituting." But the real drama resided with Louis Egelson's Emergency Placement Committee. The Committee had adopted three principles that, if the Conference confirmed them, would guide the placement of the returning chaplains.

1. It should be the duty of chaplains to return to their former pulpits or positions from which they received leaves of absence.
2. Rabbis who are serving as replacements must relinquish their pulpits upon the return of the principals.

3. In filling pulpits for returning chaplains, married chaplains shall be given priority over single chaplains.

Then, as something of a throwaway, the Committee recommended the creation of a Central Committee for the Placement of Rabbis, which would permanently take over the placement of chaplains and all other rabbis.

The Conference softened principle 1 to refer to the moral obligation, rather than the duty, of the returning chaplain to go back to his original position. Principle 3 was altogether removed, because, as one rabbi argued, it "gives the impression that the single man in the chaplaincy is only to be placed after all the married chaplains are provided for. Our task is to place all the chaplains." The bulk of the rabbis' debate centered on the suggestion that the CCAR establish a permanent placement committee. Abba Hillel Silver (1893–1963) in particular railed against the idea:

> First of all, what is to be the life of this committee? How long is it to function? . . . Does this committee then remain the Rabbinical Placement Committee for civilian rabbis for this long a period of time? . . . I am also concerned about putting so much power in the hands of an executive director, a sort of rabbinical dictator, who will place men in the pulpits of this country.

In the end the plenum directed the Executive Committee of the CCAR to appoint a committee to study the problem of pulpit placement.

By late June 1946, Silver sat in the presidency of the CCAR. In his address to the CCAR Convention at the Sherman Hotel in Chicago, he claimed that the chaplain-rabbis returning from World War II "are being rapidly absorbed into their civilian ministries or into cognate professions." It was time to dissolve the Emergency Placement Committee, he argued. A few days later Brickner delivered the report of the combined Committee on Chaplains and Emergency Placement. He concurred with Silver that more pulpit vacancies existed than the number of chaplains returning, and he also concurred that the CCAR should sunset the Emergency Placement Committee. But he also insisted that chaplains receive preferential placement treatment: "When a pulpit became vacant, the secretary [of the Committee] wrote to that congregation enclosing a copy of the Statement of Principles and requested that preferential consideration be given to returning chaplains and to such men who had clearance [to serve as replacement rabbis]." This touched off a brouhaha. No one objected to encouraging congregations to give special consideration to veteran rabbis, but the colleagues believed the proposal was unfair to rabbis who did not serve in the armed forces. The fear was that the practice would create "a caste system made up of former military personnel," as Morton Berman (1900–1986) put it. True to his opposition to a placement system, Silver pointed out that since the Emergency Placement Committee no longer existed, Brickner was trying to legislate placement through the Committee on Chaplains. In the end the plenum voted to excise any reference to rabbis who received CCAR clearance or who had simply chosen not to enlist. The Conference simply urged congregations to give special attention to the chaplain rabbis.

The Post–World War II Years

In the years immediately following World War II, attempts to establish a placement system for Reform Judaism accelerated. In 1947 Brickner's Committee on Chaplains adopted a new mandate, that of procuring chaplains for the armed forces rather than placing them in civilian congregations. The Committee on Pulpit Placement and Ethics under the chairmanship of Louis Mann (1890–1966) was reconstituted and quickly ran afoul of the Executive Committee, which had only asked the Committee to meet with representatives of the UAHC to work out a placement plan. In addition to doing this, the Committee recommended many changes to the 1940 Code of Ethics. Also, the Committee wanted to put on hold the creation of a placement system until the merger of Hebrew Union College and the Jewish Institute of Religion was concluded. Mann helped to organize and to chair a newly created joint CCAR-UAHC Commission on Pulpit Placement and Ethics.

With Abraham Feldman (1893–1977) as president of the CCAR in 1948, Roland Gittelsohn was named the chair of the Committee on Placement. On Friday, June 26 of that year, the previous Committee chairman, Louis Mann, delivered a major address to the CCAR entitled "Pulpit Placement and Ethics." He cited the placement system of the Rabbinical Assembly (RA). "Our Conservative brethren have had a plan in operation almost two decades." Indeed, from the outset of the Conservative Movement in America, their rabbinic placement system was handled by the Jewish Theological Seminary, but beginning in the 1930s the RA demanded a central voice in the placement process.[5] Until the mid-1940s the RA's Placement Committee was staffed by volunteers, but in 1944, under the pressures of World War II, Norman Salit, a rabbi and a lawyer, was hired to work with rabbis, chaplains, and congregations. When Salit left the position after the war, Bernard Segal (1907–1984) was appointed the RA's first full-time executive director, serving also as director of the Joint Placement Commission of the Rabbinical Assembly and the Jewish Theological Seminary. Segal, in turn, was succeeded by Wolfe Kelman (1923–1980) in 1951, who also devoted a large portion of his work to placement.[6]

Mann bemoaned the "old boys" network of rabbinic placement, as well as the "trial sermon" criterion. Mann employed words like "anarchy," "chaos," and "free-for-all" to describe the contemporary situation. Self-effacing and humble rabbis were at a disadvantage as compared to ambitious, forceful rabbis:

> A practice that often penalizes virtue and rewards an aggressive disregard for the highest form of professional ethics is unwholesome. It breaks down morale and causes dissatisfaction that is both consuming and corrosive.

Acknowledging that no placement plan would satisfy everyone, Mann laid out the tenets of a successful plan:

> a) a full-time director with many special gifts and qualifications; b) a staff to carry out the plan; c) full cooperation with a policy-making body; d) criteria for evaluation plus a means of keeping information up-to-date; e) the realization that it must be and remain tentative and experimental subject to constant modifications as the accumulated wisdom through trial and error dictates; f) the knowledge that the success of the plan will depend upon its being not too strong to preclude elasticity and resiliency, and not too weak to be without sanctions and significance.

He also called for the creation of a new kind of Joint Commission on Placement, one with representatives from the CCAR, the UAHC, HUC, and JIR (whose merger was in progress at this time). The Commission would assess rabbis, partly, but not exclusively, on the basis of seniority, and it would likewise assess congregations.

It would then recommend candidates and congregations to one another, rewarding "the modest, capable and conscientious rabbi." It would prohibit rabbis from applying directly to congregations and from soliciting other rabbis to lobby on their behalf for positions. The Commission would have the power to sanction, even to expel, rabbis for violating its rules and policies. "Congregations also must be subject to discipline and standards when they fall below accepted standards." Many of Mann's ideas eventually found their way into the Reform Movement's existing placement system.

Still the president of the Conference in June 1949, Abraham Feldman alluded to the "serious dislocation" that the war years had wrought on the effort to establish a placement system. With the presentation of Gittelsohn's plan he made this observation to the plenum: "To be fully effective any plan of placement must be *yours*." [Feldman's emphasis] He warned the Conference that if the members wanted a placement plan, this was the moment for a decision.

Indeed, the moment had arrived. The CCAR's congregational partner, the UAHC, had concurred. As far back as 1939 the UAHC's 36th Biennial Council resolved to appoint a joint committee with the CCAR to "consider the proper procedure for filling pulpit vacancies."[7] For years the Union had taken up the issue in roundtable discussions, administrative meetings, and executive board proceedings. Gittelsohn's plan went before the UAHC's Administrative Committee in September 1949, which sent it on favorably to the UAHC's Executive Board for approval. In December, UAHC President Eisendrath explained the plan to the Executive Board, calling it "long overdue" and expressing his hope "that this Board will recommend" the plan to the General Assembly.[8] By a vote of 28 to 5 the UAHC's Executive Board agreed to submit the plan to the November 1950 General Assembly to be held in Cleveland, Ohio.[9]

Gittelsohn was well aware that the New York Federation of Reform Synagogues ferociously opposed the plan. He had presented it to the group in June 1950. He described the "almost frantic fear evident regarding congregational autonomy and sanctions."[10] To him it seemed that the congregations saw no problem and no chaos in the current placement situation. After that meeting he admitted that the "prognosis is not good" for the needed two-thirds approval of the UAHC's General Assembly. In his notes he worried that the "opposition of Morgy [Julian Morgenstern], [Abba Hillel] Silver, [Solomon B.] Freehof [is] having an effect."[11] He crossed out this line so as not to state it publically. Gittelsohn hoped that the rabbis of CCAR would speak to their lay leaders to enlist their support and avoid a "rabbis vs. laymen fight" on the Assembly's floor. Gittelsohn felt that with that support the plan would have a chance, but he was not optimistic.

In late October 1950, two weeks before the UAHC's General Assembly, a Special Committee Representing Congregations in the Metropolitan District of New York circulated a pamphlet entitled "Second Statement in Opposition to the Plan of the Joint Placement (Rabbinical) Commission of the Union of American Hebrew Congregations":

> No Congregational activity of a constituent congregation is superior to the selection of a rabbi. Independence and autonomy in the selection of a rabbi is the first and foremost right of a congregation in Judaism . . . Our congregations, since their introduction in America, have been entirely independent and autonomous—free from all ecclesiastical control—and yet the admission is made that there must be surrender of some of this autonomy.[12]

The pamphlet, signed by lay leaders H. M. Stein and Henry Fruhauf (1923–2010), concluded by calling for the establishment of a voluntary Placement Bureau to "serve the congregations when they seek its advice and be ready to be helpful when called upon."[13] What's more, the pamphlet included an appended "Exhibit 1: Silver-Freehof Statement," in which the two past presidents of the CCAR labeled the placement plan "undesirable from nearly every point of view."[14]

When Gittelsohn's placement plan came before the General Assembly on Tuesday morning, November 14, Colonel Frederick F. Greenman (1892–1961) moved to amend the resolution in order to allow congregations to opt out of the plan and also to go into search before a pulpit was actually vacated. Greenman, a prominent Manhattan attorney and Republican party activist, was the honorary president of the New York Federation of Reform Synagogues and a trustee and a vice-president of Temple Emanu-El. His amendment was seconded by Judge Meier Steinbrink (1880–1967), a New York Supreme Court justice from Brooklyn and a past president of Congregation Beth Elohim, who also feared that the plan impinged upon the autonomy and independence of congregations. The debate lasted so long that the luncheon session scheduled to follow had to be canceled. Rabbi James G. Heller delivered the summation in favor of the plan; Rabbi Abba Hillel Silver delivered the summation in opposition to the plan. The motion to amend was carried, and the now amended motion passed[15]—and proved to be unacceptable to CCAR.

So it was at the June 1951 CCAR Convention that President Philip Bernstein (1901–1985) conceded that he "profoundly regrets that this plan was rejected by the Union of American Hebrew Congregations at its meeting in Cleveland in November 1950." Nonetheless, Bernstein urged the Conference to try again to create a placement system despite "only a temporary setback." He thanked Gittelsohn and his Committee profusely, expressing his belief that "ultimately there will be a just and workable Placement plan." The next day after delivering his final report to the Convention, Gittelsohn resigned as chairman.

The 1950s

When the CCAR met at the Statler Hotel in Buffalo, New York, in June 1952, its membership had grown to 625, a 50 percent increase since World War II. After the defeat of the Gittelsohn plan, a provisional placement plan was in operation and overseen by a Provisional Placement Committee (PPC). But as President Philip Bernstein noted, "It falls far short of the original Placement Plan in provisions for orderly and safeguarded pulpit changes." Jacob Rudin (1902–1982) chaired the CCAR's Committee on Placement and represented the CCAR on the PPC. He described the workings of the PPC. One volunteer from the CCAR, the UAHC, and HUC-JIR sat on the PPC, and the PPC received congregations' requests for rabbis. The PPC then sent the congregations small panels consisting of the names of about six rabbis along with a completed but brief biographical questionnaire and a one-page autobiography on each candidate. After that, the PPC's job was finished and the remainder of the process rested in the hands of the congregations.

Rudin also complained about the workload of the PPC. The PPC had written three hundred letters in the course of one year, not to mention the phone calls and the monthly in-person meetings.

Furthermore, 125 to 150 rabbis were in constant placement for fewer and fewer positions. "This is the basic problem: Too many men, not enough congregations." Even by giving the PPC as much as an hour a day, "this machinery is cumbersome." It was, however, cheap; Rudin estimated the cost to the CCAR of the first year of the PPC to be $30. At the same time the CCAR was discussing the possibility of hiring its first executive director, and one of the arguments for doing so was that he could assist with the placement efforts like the RA's Wolfe Kelman.

In 1953 at the Stanley Hotel in Estes Park, Colorado, the conversation about a full-time CCAR executive director continued, though the hiring and installation of this man would await the 1954 Convention. Meanwhile the PPC soldiered on with its work, even though both rabbis and congregations were not obligated to make use of it. Still, virtually every congregation in search and every rabbi in placement sought its help. In two years' time the PPC played a role in filling no less than sixty pulpits. For Jacob Rudin, still the CCAR's representative on PPC, the Committee had proven the viability of a permanent placement plan. "None of the fears voiced by the opponents to the plan has materialized." The main problem: the workload had grown increasingly onerous. The Committee had written nearly one thousand letters in two years and had dealt with two hundred members of the Conference. The Committee still met monthly and was in constant telephonic contact with one another.

Sidney Regner (1904–1993) had been the rabbi of Temple Oheb Sholom in Reading, Pennsylvania, since 1927 and an active member of the CCAR, sitting on numerous committees and boards. At the CCAR's 1954 Convention in Pike, New Hampshire, Regner was elected and installed as the CCAR's first executive director. The CCAR also decided to establish its headquarters in New York City following the UAHC's move there in 1951. In the realm of placement a new chair for the Provisional Placement Committee was appointed. Nathan A. Perilman (1905–1991), whose rabbinate at Emanu-El of New York spanned 1932 to 1973, assumed the chair perhaps as a foil to the Emanu-El–based opponents of the Gittelsohn plan. Reminding the members that the Provisional Placement Committee was purely advisory and voluntary, he also complained about the hundreds of letters, phone calls, and personal interviews that went into the thirty-six placements for that year.

Over the course of the next year Regner gradually took over the CCAR role on the Provisional Placement Committee. Though the Committee had placed some fifty colleagues, Perilman, still the chair of the CCAR's Advisory Placement Committee, had grown all the more convinced "that we should soon look to the time when the provisional character of this committee can be changed into permanent status." Barnett Brickner ascended to the CCAR presidency in 1955, and he too called for another study of the need for a permanent placement bureau run jointly by the Conference, the UAHC, and HUC-JIR.

By 1956 Regner was staffing the Provisional Placement Committee for the CCAR, while Perilman was still chairing the Advisory Placement Committee. After a full year on the PPC Regner was lamenting the maldistribution of positions: a great many small congregations but few large and attractive congregations. Consequently the panels of rabbis sent to the large congregations necessarily omitted many deserving, qualified rabbis. Moreover, because the placement system was working as well as it might, Regner was ready to jettison the word "provisional" from the Committee's title. Perilman, on the other hand, was convinced that the growing complexity of the PPC's operation required at the very least the hiring of an executive assistant, "who would devote full time to the business of the Committee . . . [and would] visit congregations and rabbis to personalize the work that is presently done almost entirely by mail."

Regner continued to complain about the workload of placement. In 1957, a year in which there were about eighty-five placements, he wrote:

> The work of placement requires my continual attention. Each placement is a laborious process involving drawing up a list of rabbis to whom to write, correspondence with the congregation, and sometimes, either when no rabbis to whom we have written evince an interest in the congregation or when the congregation is not inclined to act favorably on any on the list, the process has to begin anew.

So in 1957 the president appointed a committee to explore the hiring of a full-time executive assistant to assist with placement.

In 1958 Abram Goodman (1903–2002) took over the Advisory Placement Committee from Nathan A. Perilman for just one year.

Regner complained again about the burdensome work; in this year ninety-five placements were made, a 10 percent increase over the previous year. In addition, the UAHC had taken close notice of the Provisional Placement Committee and passed a resolution insisting that PPC refrain from recommending rabbis to congregations not affiliated with the UAHC and student-rabbis to similar synagogues. Although the CCAR's Executive Board endorsed the UAHC resolution, it reserved the right to dissent under special circumstances.

The CCAR Convention of 1959 proved to be the tipping point for rabbinical placement. Ironically the Convention met at the Mt. Washington Hotel in Bretton Woods, New Hampshire, the site of the 1949 Convention that had so hopefully approved the Gittelsohn plan. Jerome Malino (1911–2002), the rabbi of the United Jewish Congregation of Danbury, Connecticut, for sixty-seven years, took over the Advisory Placement Committee. Jacob Rudin, the CCAR representative to the Provisional Placement Commission and chair of the Placement Committee in 1952 and 1953, assumed the presidency. In his presidential address he pushed hard for the engagement of a placement director. "The right kind of man, understanding, sympathetic, would be counselor and friend as well as Director of Placement." What's more, Regner delivered a lengthy report on placement that provoked a full discussion among the colleagues. Regner described the process of putting together the panels. "We have no IBM machines to determine a man's qualifications," so the members of the PPC used their judgment, their knowledge of the rabbis, and their intuition regarding best matches. He again lamented the maldistribution of jobs and rabbis so that positions in small congregations remained unfilled even while some rabbis were unemployed. He also regretted that some rabbis circumvented the PPC, depriving other, often more deserving colleagues of the opportunity for advancement.

In the ensuing discussion Samuel Sandmel (1911–1979), a member of the PPC, opposed the idea of a single placement director, fearing the concentration of power in one person. But Eugene Lipman (1920–1994) seemed to have caught the majority sentiment: "From my standpoint, as a rabbi, I feel a real sense of urgency for us as rabbis to want to change the system as soon as possible to one which will accord us more dignity and more discipline." James G. Heller recalled the bitterness of the 1950 defeat of the placement proposal by the UAHC's General Assembly, but he contended that since the CCAR had learned much from the experiment with the PPC, the CCAR should consider establishing its own placement system even without its Reform Movement partners. H. Bruce Ehrmann (1918–) suggested that the CCAR mail a monthly list of congregational openings to all the members and allow members a brief period of time to signify their interest, an idea that eventually made its way into the current placement system. Given the prominence of the players and the depth of the conversation, the CCAR was now primed to launch another placement initiative.

The following year, 1960, with Bernard Bamberger (1904–1980) in the presidency, the effort to construct a placement system gained momentum. Bamberger made the creation of a placement system the centerpiece of his presidency. "I argued that to achieve any significant improvement we must not merely make some procedural changes, but adopt a mandatory system with provisions for enforcement," he said. He called for, and the Conference concurred, a special committee to draw up a comprehensive plan for placement including "such measures to insure compliance as it deems proper." Regner continued kvetching about how much of his time the Provisional Placement Committee occupied. "What this involves, sheerly in the mechanics of the job, in meetings, in correspondence with rabbis and congregations, in memos to the other members of the committee, in telephone calls, consumes, as you can well imagine, a great deal of time." And still the maldistribution of rabbis obtains: too many rabbis clamoring for large congregations, too few rabbis interested in smaller ones. He concluded, "We cannot do a proper job of placement unless we have a man working full time on it, under the direction of a committee which will devote considerable time to it."

Bamberger entrusted the design of a new placement system to a Special Committee on Placement chaired by Jacob Rothschild (1911–1973), the rabbi for the Hebrew Benevolent Congregation ("The Temple") in Atlanta. An outspoken opponent of racial injustice in the deep South, Rothschild received international attention when fifty sticks of dynamite exploded at The Temple on October 12, 1958, probably in retaliation for his unequivocal support of civil rights. Rothschild's Special Committee met in New York first on December 28, 1960, and for a second time on March 2, 1961, to hammer out the placement plan. Nearly all the Committee members attended the second meeting, though notably Beryl Cohon (1889–1976) was absent.

Three months later at the New Yorker Hotel on Thursday morning, June 22, 1961, he stood before more than 450 colleagues at the CCAR Convention: "The appointment of this Special Committee on Placement represents a fourth attempt made by our Conference in the last twenty years to devise a satisfactory system of rabbinical placement." The plan itself called for the CCAR to assume all costs for placement with the greatest expense being the hiring of a director of placement who would therefore be a member of the CCAR staff. (In a letter dated March 27, 1961, to Bertram Korn, Rothschild was still undecided if the placement director worked under—or independent of—the CCAR executive director.)[16] Placement would be overseen by a Rabbinical Placement Commission which was to be composed of eleven members, seven of whom would be appointed by the CCAR. The plan would be mandatory for members of the Conference, requiring them to only seek pulpits through the Placement Commission. The Placement Commission would compile information on rabbis and congregations and use the information to match rabbis and congregations. The plan called for disciplinary action against any CCAR member found to be in willful violation of the Placement Commission. Finally, the plan would be given a three-year trial, after which it would be evaluated for continuation.

Beryl D. Cohon wrote a minority report that only he signed. His disagreement with the plan's compulsory provisions was expressed in writing to the March 2 meeting and in subsequent correspondence with Rothschild.[17] Cohon suggested to Rothschild that he (Cohon) might put his concerns in a minority report, and Rothschild consented. In his report Cohon objected strenuously to the mandatory nature of the plan. His dissent set the tone for subsequent discussion of the plan. As correspondence with Regner shows, the plan itself deliberately avoided using the word "sanctions," speaking instead of disciplinary actions.[18] Still, most of the criticism of the plan centered on this issue. Allan Tarshish (1907–1982) asked why the plan did not include sanctions on congregations. "Because this is a plan which puts placement into the hands of the CCAR," explained Rothschild. So long as the rabbis subscribe to the plan, there is no need for the congregations to subscribe to it. After James G. Heller gave a passionate defense of the need for disciplinary action in the plan, Roland Gittelsohn, the author of the doomed 1949 plan, rose to support it vigorously. He reiterated his previous position: a placement plan will only work if it is mandatory. Eugene Mihaly (1918–2002) moved to strike the section on disciplinary action (i.e., sanctions). Finally, Bamberger, at the urging of the members, spoke. He challenged Mihaly's motion, asking, "What does it mean if you say a plan is mandatory and then cut out the provision for enforcement? . . . Do you want a mandatory plan or not?" In the end, Mihaly's motion was defeated, as was a motion to table, and the report was adopted.

Conclusion

The 1961 Rothschild plan was similar to the 1949 Gittelsohn plan in many respects. Both plans contemplated the creation of an oversight body, the hiring of a full-time director, and a three-year trial period. The plans differed on important points also. Gittelsohn's plan required the UAHC, CCAR, and HUC-JIR to share the costs of placement; Rothschild's plan only expected the CCAR to pick up the expenses. Moreover, in the Gittelsohn plan all placement-related matters such as contracts, negotiations, and recommendations, had to be directed by the placement bureau. In Rothschild's plan the mandatory aspects of placement pertained to only rabbis, not to congregations. The most important difference turned on sanctions. Gittelsohn's plan imagined an ascending scale of punishments that could be levied against recalcitrant CCAR members and refractory UAHC congregations, while Rothschild's plan anticipated vague disciplinary actions aimed at CCAR members only, not congregations. Clearly the CCAR had learned much in the decade following the defeat of the Gittelsohn plan. Rothschild's plan made few demands on the congregations but held the rabbis to a very high standard.

In addition, much had changed in the world of American Jewry between the 1940s and the 1960s. Most important was the suburbanization of American Jews that took place in the 1950s and 1960s. With the proscription of restrictive residential covenants, the educational benefits of the GI Bill, a shortage of housing in cities, and government programs to encourage home ownership, Jews flocked to the new mass-produced suburbs like Levittown on New York's Long Island. Historian Arthur Hertzberg once estimated that one-third of urban Jews moved to the suburbs between 1945 and 1965.[19] This engendered an explosion of synagogue construction with over a thousand synagogues built or rebuilt, mostly in suburbia. This out-migration from urban centers, especially New York, where the suburbs grew by hundreds of thousands of Jews, had the effect of diminishing the influence of the New York City opponents to placement.

Related to this phenomenon was the national redistribution of the Jewish population from the Northeast to the Sun Belt. Miami's Jewish population grew tenfold between 1945 and 1965, from 13,500 to 140,000, and during these same years Los Angeles's Jewish population expanded from 160,000 to 500,000.[20] In the Reform Movement the UAHC's Pacific Southwest Council, which included Southern California, Arizona, and adjacent areas, added fifty-two new congregations during this period. This shift to the Sun Belt, along with the move to suburbia, caused American Jewry to become more diverse and less monolithic, further diluting the power of the New York City congregations over the North American Reform Movement.

The seventy-year struggle to devise a rabbinical placement system was only partly about crafting a dignified and orderly method of employing rabbis. During the discussion of the Rothschild plan, Harry Essrig (1912–2003) asked, "Is this, or any placement plan, meant to advance the so-called trade-union aspects of the rabbinate, or is it meant to advance the professional interests of the rabbinate?" He identified the core issue of rabbinical placement. Placement is not the goal in and of itself; it is instrumental to a much larger end. Placing the right rabbis in the right synagogues enhances both rabbinic fulfillment and congregational Jewish growth. It leads to a deepening of Jewish life and observance. The result of the congenial fit between rabbi and synagogue is the living out of the covenant made between God and Abraham and Sarah thousands of years ago. In rabbinic placement, much more is at stake than merely whether a rabbi has a job or whether a congregation has a rabbi; it is the nurturing of the words of the living God.

Notes

1. Unless otherwise indicated, all discussions are drawn from the pages of the CCAR yearbooks of the year under consideration.

2. "Temple Beth-El," *New York Architecture,* July 24, 1998, http://nyc-architecture.com.
3. Michael A. Meyer, *Response to Modernity* (New York: Oxford University Press, 1988), 307–9.
4. Rabbi John Rosove and Enid Sperber, e-mail correspondence, April 15 and 16, 2012.
5. Herbert Rosenblum, "Emerging Self-Awareness: The Rabbinical Assembly in the 1920s and 1930s," in *A Century of Commitment: One Hundred Years of the Rabbinical Assembly*, ed. Robert E. Fierstein (New York: The Rabbinical Assembly, 2000), 55.
6. Pamela Nadell, "New and Expanding Horizons: The Rabbinical Assembly 1940–1970," in *A Century of Commitment*, 72–74.
7. "Resolutions Adopted by the 36th Biennial Council," *Proceedings of the UAHC—65th Annual Report*, September 1939, 201.
8. "President's Report to the Executive Board," *Proceedings of the UAHC*, December 3, 1949, 207.
9. "Executive Board Resolutions," *Proceedings of the UAHC*, December 2–4, 1949, 184–85.
10. Roland Gittelsohn, "Notes of Report of Committee on Placement," American Jewish Archives—*Roland Gittelsohn Papers*, box 55, folder 7, June 8, 1950, 3.
11. Ibid.
12. H. M. Stein and Henry Fruhauf, *Second Statement in Opposition to the Plan of the Joint Placement (Rabbinical) Commission of the Union of American Hebrew Congregations* (New York: n.p., October 30, 1950), 3, 4. Thanks to the American Jewish Archives for discovering this document.
13. Ibid., 5.
14. Ibid., 7.
15. "Placement Plan," *Proceedings of the UAHC—41st General Assembly* (Cleveland, Ohio, November 12–15, 1950), 482.
16. "Jacob Rothschild Papers," Manuscript, Archives, and Rare Books Library, Emory University, box 5, folder 8.
17. Ibid.
18. Letter to Sidney Regner, March 27, 1961. Ibid.
19. Quoted in Edward S. Shapiro, "Jews in the Suburbs," *My Jewish Learning*, http://www.myjewishlearning.com/history/Modern_History/1948–1980/America/Suburbanization.
20. Jonathan Sarna, *American Judaism, A History* (New Haven: Yale University Press, 2005), 292.

Kaskel's Chutzpah

Gary Stein

"Your people must leave all the villages," the government official barked. "The district must be emptied. I have an order here!"[1] With that command begins the expulsion of the Jews from the town of Anatevka in *Fiddler on the Roof*. This fictional scene of Old World anti-Semitism is instantly recognizable to millions of Americans and, especially, American Jews.

Yet not many Americans, and probably not many American Jews, are aware of a strikingly similar real-life instance of anti-Semitism that took place on American soil. During the Civil War, Union General—and future President—Ulysses S. Grant issued General Orders No. 11, expelling "[t]he Jews, as a class" from a military district comprising portions of Kentucky, Tennessee, and Mississippi. Like the expulsion order in *Fiddler on the Roof*, General Orders No. 11 was directed at all Jews indiscriminately, solely because they were Jews. There is one notable difference: The Jews of Anatevka were given three days to gather their belongings and leave. General Grant gave the Jews of the Department of the Tennessee only twenty-four hours to comply with his order.[2]

In *When General Grant Expelled the Jews*, Brandeis University Professor Jonathan D. Sarna popularized the little-known story of General Grant's infamous 1862 order, just in time for its sesquicentennial anniversary.[3] Oddly enough for a chronicle of "the most notorious anti-Jewish order by a government official in American history,"[4] this is an inspiring story with a feel-good ending. The reason Grant's order has garnered so little historical attention is

---

GARY STEIN is a partner in the law firm of Schulte Roth & Zabel LLP in New York City. He writes frequently about American law and history.

An earlier version of this article appeared online as "The Most Notorious Anti-Jewish Official in American History: Kaskel's Chutzpah," *momentmag.com*, February 20, 2013, http://www.momentmag.com/the-most-notorious-anti-jewish-official-in-american-history/.

that it had so little effect. The order was rescinded almost immediately by President Lincoln; it was resisted by many Union officers in the field during its brief existence; and it was generally reviled by the press and politicians.[5] For years General Orders No. 11 hung like a political albatross around General Grant's neck, undermining his presidential ambitions.[6] Grant himself later condemned it, describing it as "a source of great regret" and rationalizing it as having been issued "without any reflection."[7]

As President, Sarna writes, Grant "sought to atone for General Orders No. 11," for instance by appointing Jews "to government positions they could never have aspired to before."[8] When Russia sought to expel thousands of Jews from their homes in 1869, President Grant lent a sympathetic ear to protests from American Jewish leaders and publicly denounced the Russian action. The author of General Orders No. 11 now exclaimed that "it is too late, in this age of enlightenment, to persecute any one on account of race, color or religion."[9] Thus, instead of tainting the American tradition of religious liberty, Grant's clumsy bigotry wound up confirming it, and solidifying the position of American Jews within it.

As Professor Sarna recounts, the short shelf life of General Orders No. 11 is due in no small measure to the vociferous protests made by the American Jewish community and, in particular, by a Paducah, Kentucky, merchant named Cesar Kaskel. A 30-year-old Jewish immigrant, Kaskel had faith that America was different from his native Prussia. When summoned by Paducah's Provost Marshal on December 28, 1862, to receive news of his banishment, Kaskel "instantly decided to fight."[10] That same day—within a few hours of being served with the expulsion order—Kaskel, together with his brother and three brothers from another Jewish family, fired off a telegram to President Lincoln. Far from a diplomatically worded plea for mercy, the telegram forcefully proclaimed the Jews of Paducah "greatly insulted and outraged by this inhuman order, the carrying out of which would be the grossest violation of the Constitution, and our rights as good citizens under it."[11] The telegram asked Lincoln to take "immediate" action to countermand General Orders No. 11. In fact, as Sarna notes, the telegram repeated the word "immediate" three times in three sentences.[12]

Failing to get an immediate response to his telegram, Kaskel set off for Washington in a steamship and distributed a broadside against General Orders No. 11 to the press, urging them to lend their aid "to blot out as quick as possible this stain on our national honor."[13] Arriving in Washington on January 3, 1863, Kaskel, with the assistance of a Republican congressman, sought and received an immediate audience with President Lincoln (who had remained blissfully unaware of Grant's order). Kaskel got what he came for. Lincoln immediately instructed General Henry Halleck, in charge of the Union Army, to revoke General Orders No. 11.[14] Victorious, Kaskel went back home to Paducah (only to move, during the war, to New York City, where he opened a haberdashery shop).[15]

The reaction of Kaskel and other American Jews contrasts sharply with that of the fictional inhabitants of Anatevka and the countless real Russian Jews who were the victims of actual expulsion orders in the nineteenth and early twentieth centuries.[16] In *Fiddler on the Roof*, Tevye and his neighbors initially contemplate resisting the expulsion order; calls ring out to "defend ourselves," "refuse to leave," "fight!" But this talk quickly fizzles out into resigned acquiescence, after the sympathetic Russian official who delivers the order reminds them of the power of the Russian militia and army. The rabbi counsels that they will have to wait for the Messiah someplace else, and the Jews of Anatevka console themselves by reflecting that "Anatevka hasn't exactly been the Garden of Eden" anyway.[17] An actual Russian rabbi of the time advised Jews to be "as quiet as water and lower than the grass."[18] Such submissiveness came under withering attack from within the Russian Jewish community in the early twentieth century, most famously in Chaim Nachman Bialik's poem, "In the City of Slaughter," condemning the failure of the Jews of Kishinev to resist a particularly brutal pogrom in 1903.[19]

Jewish passivity in the face of persecution has been called, derisively, the "*galut* mentality"—the feeling of powerlessness that comes with being a people in exile (*galut*) who are strangers in the nation in which they live.[20] The nineteenth-century Jews who resisted General Orders No. 11 were also in *galut*, in the Diaspora. Measured in temporal terms, they were less at "home" in America than the Russian Jews who had populated towns like Anatevka for generations. Learning of the expulsion decree, an uncomprehending Tevye protests that Anatevka "has always been our home."[21] By contrast, Kaskel, who had emigrated to the United States in 1858, was a relative newcomer—Paducah, Kentucky, had been his home for only four years.[22]

Moreover, the conditions for resistance were far from optimal. American Jews at the time represented a tiny minority and did not possess significant political influence. Although swelled by waves of immigration during the 1840s and 1850s, the ranks of American Jews still numbered only about 150,000 persons in 1860, about one-half of one percent of the total population.[23] There were no high-level Jewish officials in the Lincoln Administration, no Jewish federal judges, and only one Jewish member of Congress (out of more than 230).[24] Further, the United States was in the midst of a bloody Civil War, its future hanging in the balance. Already known as one of Lincoln's few generals who could actually win a battle, Grant claimed the expulsion was necessary to clamp down on smuggling that was hampering the war effort. He was about to launch the Vicksburg campaign, which would cost the lives of tens of thousands of Union soldiers.[25] The Department of the Tennessee was under martial law. If there ever was a time for Jews to not rock the boat and to submit to an odious decree under the influence, or the excuse, of the *galut* mentality, this would appear to have been it.

The intriguing question that Sarna's book raises is, why didn't they? Their actions cannot be viewed, in the American context, as aberrational. In an eerie historical parallel not mentioned by Sarna, a very similar scene had played out just a few months before in Confederate territory. On August 30, 1862, the town of Thomasville, Georgia, gripped by fear of an economic crisis and a Union attack, issued a resolution directed at the "class of German Jews, located among us" who were allegedly issuing counterfeit currency and extorting high prices for scarce goods. The Jews were ordered to leave Thomasville within ten days, and no other Jews were allowed to settle in the town. A Committee of Vigilance was appointed to oversee the expulsion.[26]

As with General Orders No. 11, the Thomasville resolution was met with furious and organized Jewish resistance. The German Jewish community of nearby Savannah, as well as the German Jewish members of two Georgia infantry regiments, issued angrily worded public denunciations and advised Jews to cut their ties to Thomasville and supporters of the expulsion.[27] In the end, the Thomasville anti-Semites backed down: the Jews were not expelled, and there were no lasting consequences for Jewish economic success or social integration in the town.[28] The experience confirmed for one of the protest leaders, twenty-three-year-old

Charles Wessolowsky—who, like Cesar Kaskel, had emigrated to the United States from Prussia four years earlier—that "the Jews in America could combat hatred whenever and wherever it reared its ugly head."[29]

If American Jews were rejecting the accommodationist policies inherent in the *galut* mentality, it may be because they were reinventing the concept of *galut* itself. As Israeli Professor Ofer Shiff has explained, American Jewish leaders of the mid-nineteenth century, particularly in the emerging Reform Judaism Movement, rejected "the inherent incompleteness of life in *galut*" as traditionally understood, with its hope of ending the Jews' "alien status" by returning to the "Old Zion," a Jewish state in Palestine. Instead, these Jews heralded America as a "New Zion," where Jews not only could freely practice their religion without interference, but also could shed their alien status.[30] Not all felt this way; traditionalists like the Philadelphia Orthodox Jewish leader Isaac Leeser felt that Grant's order made clear that American Jews "were still in exile, subjected, like all other Diaspora Jews, to the 'decrees of those in power, who are not restrained by any feeling of humanity and justice from inflicting injury on us.'"[31] Leeser seems to have missed the larger lesson—that "those in power," supported by popular opinion, had *stopped* Grant's decree before it could inflict great injury.

More attuned to the new American realities, Reform Judaism even advanced "a new definition of *galut* as a means to propagate the universal truths of Judaism to the rest of humanity."[32] The idea that God dispersed the Jews to all parts of the world as a "punishment for the sinfulness of Israel"[33] was incorrect, explained Rabbi Isaac Mayer Wise of Cincinnati, the nation's leading voice of Reform Judaism, in 1868; instead God saw it as an opportunity "for the realization of [Judaism's] high priestly mission, to lead the nations to the true knowledge and worship of God."[34] Chicago Rabbi Bernhard Felsenthal echoed this sentiment four years later in explaining to Christians: "We do not look upon the dispersion as a curse; on the contrary, we regard it as a blessing—a blessing for you and all mankind."[35] In America, Jews even converted Christians to Judaism. As Professor Sarna described in an earlier work, this was nothing short of "remarkable" and alarmed Jews in Old World nations such as England, who refused to accept converts out of fear they would provoke reprisals.[36]

Thus, the more fundamental question raised by the failure of General Grant's expulsion order is, why did the *galut* mentality never take hold in America the way it did in Europe? Granted, the Jews who led the fight against expulsion in 1862 appear to have been relatively well-off, well-educated, and well-integrated into mainstream society, certainly in comparison to the shtetl Jews of Eastern Europe. But the history of Germany Jewry in the nineteenth century belies any argument that affluence and assimilation guarantee acceptance. While striving towards greater civil rights and, ultimately, emancipation, German Jews were well aware of their outsider status, that "the Jew was always a *Fremdkörper*, an alien body within Germany."[37] Their reaction to outbursts of anti-Semitism during the nineteenth century can generally (if over-simplistically) be characterized as hunkering down and waiting for the storm clouds to pass.[38]

It thus would be difficult, if not impossible, to attribute Cesar Kaskel's courageous resistance to General Orders No. 11 to a mind-set shaped by his prior Prussian experience. After all, Kaskel had fled Prussia partly because of, according to Sarna, its "severe legal limitations on where [Jews] could live and what kinds of occupations they could pursue."[39] Rather, Kaskel's anti-*galut* mentality seems inescapably the product of the political and social conditions of America, which nurtured it and allowed it to bloom into an open, direct, and unapologetic assertion of basic human rights in the face of official oppression. Kaskel felt strongly, writes Sarna, that "in America opportunity was unlimited and freedom guaranteed to people of all faiths—Jews included."[40]

Our culture—especially our legal culture—instinctively credits the Constitution as the wellspring emboldening aggrieved minorities to speak up for themselves. And indeed, as noted above, Kaskel's telegram to Lincoln specifically characterized General Orders No. 11 as a gross "violation of the Constitution, and our rights as good citizens under it." Other opponents likewise denounced General Orders No. 11 not only as an affront to principles of humanity and religious liberty, but as a violation of law. Rabbi Wise of Cincinnati, who played a central role in organizing protest to Grant's order, demanded that the order be rescinded based on the President's oath "to enforce the laws"—meaning, presumably, the Constitution.[41] A petition from the Missouri branch of B'nai B'rith called upon President Lincoln, as "the Defender and Protector of the Constitution," to annul the order and thus "protect the liberties even of your humblest constituents."[42]

Certainly the Constitution gave American Jews an important argument not available to those who had been, and would be, the victims of expulsion orders in Europe and elsewhere. Those in *galut* traditionally sought salvation in prayer, in an appeal to God to bring forth the Messiah and restore the land of Israel. In America, however, they could seek salvation in the nation's founding document, which stood foursquare against religious discrimination. Despite his later claim that American Jews had not escaped exile, Isaac Leeser reveled in 1845 that in America "it matters not whether the majority be Christian or Jewish; the constitution knows nothing of either"; "in the fundamental charter of the United States, neither Christianity nor Judaism is mentioned by name"; "[b]oth Jews and Christians . . . were placed upon such an equality that a preference was given to neither."[43] Anchoring assertions of Jewish equality in the Constitution, universally embraced throughout American society as the definitive expression of the nation's most sacred political values, gave those assertions unquestionable legitimacy.

And yet constitutional *law* played essentially no role in the fight against General Grant's expulsion order. From the perspective of the early twenty-first century, what is perhaps most striking about that fight is the weapon that was not used. If something similar were to happen today, opposition to it surely would not rely simply on supplication to presidential authority. The principal means of resistance would be a lawsuit in federal court, seeking first an emergency restraining order and then a permanent injunction adjudging the order unconstitutional and barring its enforcement. No similar legal strategy was employed in 1862. No legal strategy was even contemplated, so far as appears from the historical record. Notably, while the appeals to President Lincoln invoked the Constitution in a general way, none of them specifically cited the First Amendment guarantee of religious liberty or the Fifth Amendment right to due process, or articulated any recognizably legal argument. For his part, Lincoln did not seek the advice of government lawyers before deciding whether to sustain Grant's order. His attorney general, Edward Bates, upon forwarding the B'nai B'rith petition to the President, expressed "no particular interest in the subject."[44]

Of course, President Lincoln's swift reversal of General Grant's order obviated any need for litigation. But assume that Lincoln had instead backed Grant, and the Jews had mounted a legal challenge to General Orders No. 11. Would it have succeeded? There is little reason to believe that it would have. The order was a military measure, whose justification was the need to inhibit the flow of smuggled goods into the Confederacy, which was undermining the Union's efforts to suppress the rebellion. As such, had it come before a federal court, it would have been reviewed with great deference. Antithetical to our core constitutional values as the forced expulsion of an entire religious group may seem, the federal judiciary's track record during the Civil War was far from stellar in safeguarding even core constitutional rights from Executive Branch intrusions justified on the basis of military necessity.

For example, in April 1863, Union General Ambrose Burnside, the commander of the Department of the Ohio, issued General Orders No. 38, specifically targeting political speech in opposition to the war. It announced that "the habit of declaring sympathies for the enemy will not be allowed in this Department" and that violators "will be at once arrested."[45] After giving a speech the following month describing the war as "wicked, cruel, and unnecessary" (and attacking General Orders No. 38 as a "base usurpation of arbitrary authority"), antiwar Democrat Clement Vallandigham, a former congressman, was arrested on Burnside's orders, and tried and convicted by a military tribunal.[46] Applying for a writ of habeas corpus, Vallandigham's lawyers argued that his arrest and prosecution violated bedrock constitutional guarantees to, among other things, due process of law, the right to indictment by a grand jury, and the right to a public trial by an impartial jury. They also argued that Vallandigham's conduct was constitutionally protected speech under the First Amendment.[47]

These arguments, impressive as they may seem, got Vallandigham exactly nowhere. The federal court denied his application, holding that it lacked authority to issue a writ of habeas corpus for a person in military custody, that it was inexpedient to interfere with the exercise of military power, and that constitutional rights normally inviolable must yield during wartime. Unable to "shut its eyes to the grave fact that war exists," the court found in the Constitution "such a capacity of adaptation to circumstances as may be necessary to meet a great emergency," adding that it was "not a time when any one connected with the judicial department" should "embarrass or thwart the executive in his actions to deliver the country from the dangers which press so heavily upon it."[48]

An even more extreme viewpoint was expressed in 1866 by a different federal judge, who wrote that it was "useless to speak of law—meaning thereby the laws of peace—when [a] state of war actually exists."[49] In a state of war the law "refrains from speaking, and is, of its own accord, silent and unenforced."[50] Even the Constitution, the supreme law, is "still law," and thus powerless to protect even religious liberty during a state of war: "The Constitution guarantees to every citizen 'the free exercise of religion'; but the state of war prevails, and the free exercise of religion is gone."[51]

Nor should such judicial diffidence be deemed a product of the uniquely existential threat posed by the Civil War. During World War II, the federal government issued an expulsion order of a similar nature to General Orders No. 11 but on a much larger scale—the forced resettlement and internment of more than one hundred thousand Japanese Americans solely because of their race. The Supreme Court, in *Korematsu v. United States*,[52] nevertheless upheld the measure as constitutional. Projecting *Korematsu*'s reasoning back in time, it is easy to imagine how the Supreme Court would have made short work of a lawsuit by Cesar Kaskel challenging the constitutionality of General Orders No. 11. Just substitute the name Kaskel for Korematsu, and other relevant circumstances from the 1860s for those of the 1940s, in this key passage from the *Korematsu* opinion:

> [Kaskel] was not excluded from the Military Area because of hostility to him or his race. He was excluded because we are at war with [the Confederate States], because the properly constituted military authorities . . . felt constrained to take proper security measures, because they decided that the military urgency of the situation demanded that all citizens of [Jewish] ancestry be segregated from [the Department of the Tennessee] . . . There was evidence of disloyalty on the part of some, the military authorities considered that the need for action was great, and time was short.[53]

This is all the more true considering that Kaskel's lawyers would not even have had at their disposal arguments based on the Equal Protection Clause—which was not adopted until 1868—and the doctrine of strict judicial scrutiny, inspired by that Clause, for laws discriminating on the basis of race, religion or nationality.[54]

When we search for reasons why Cesar Kaskel and the American Jewish community were able to free themselves of the *galut* mentality, we must look beyond the shibboleth that America is a nation governed by the rule of law and beyond any sense of empowerment that American Jews may derive from their ability to assert legally enforceable rights *against* the state. Far more fundamental was their conviction that American Jews, just as much as every other American, were *part* of the state. Kaskel's letter to the press denounced Grant's order as a "stain on *our* national honor," a revealing choice of words suggesting that, in Kaskel's view, America belonged to Jews as well as to Christians. That sense of belonging is something that Jews in Kaskel's native Germany, despite their yearnings, could never truly attain, unless they stopped being Jews and converted to Christianity, as thousands of them did in the nineteenth century (only to discover that even then, they still stood apart).[55]

To be sure, German Jews, in 1871, eventually achieved full emancipation under the unified Germany's new constitutional charter. But that fact highlights the limits of law, even constitutional law. Emancipation in Germany did not flow from a doctrine of natural rights that recognized Jews' innate humanity as entitling them to legal equality. It was, instead, based on a "quid pro quo" that demanded Jews abandon their supposedly degenerate culture and economic practices and imitate German manners.[56] Moreover, vast segments of Christian society in Germany bitterly opposed emancipation, continuing to view the Jews in medieval terms as irredeemably parasitical and inhuman, as was also true in France, despite the granting of full legal equality to Jews in the French Revolution.[57] Formal legal emancipation proved woefully insufficient to forestall the tragic tsunamis of anti-Semitism that swept Germany and France in the late nineteenth and twentieth centuries.

A comparable point can, of course, be made about the experience of American blacks. After the Civil War, the former slaves attained full legal equality under the Constitution with the adoption of the Thirteenth, Fourteenth, and Fifteenth Amendments. But that did not stop Southern whites from inflicting horrific acts of violence upon them.[58] As this history underscores, there is a dialectic between majority antipathy and minority assertiveness. It is not easy for the minority to resist when resistance may awaken murderous impulses on the part of the majority. Whatever hesitations American Jews may have had about challenging General Orders No. 11, concern for their physical safety does not appear to have been one of them. Anti-Semitism has a lengthy, ugly, and even occasionally deadly history in America, especially in times of stress such as the Civil War.[59] But it has been different in kind from the virulent strains of eliminationist anti-Semitism found in Europe, where "everybody had the disappearance of the Jews on the agenda," whether through expulsion, assimilation, conversion, or extermination.[60]

European anti-Semitism was molded by medieval corporatism. Jews were viewed as a corporate body "'placed outside the framework of general society,'" which "encouraged Christian ruling authorities to assign collective responsibility, and even collective punishment, to an entire Jewish community for the real or imagined hostile acts of individuals."[61] Outbreaks of anti-Semitism in Europe were often fueled by this belief that Jews bore collective responsibility for the misdeeds of its members (a belief ultimately traceable to the charge of collective Jewish guilt for the crucifixion of Christ). Fertile conditions existed for this perverse logic to sprout in the Department of the Tennessee in 1862; some Jewish merchants unquestionably *were* involved in illicit smuggling activities (as were some Christian merchants).[62] As Professor Sarna notes, General Orders No. 11 hearkened back to the "older, corporate view of the Jew common in the Middle Ages," treating Jews "as a class" rather than as individuals.[63] Yet in the highly individualistic and decidedly non-corporatist culture of America, this concept of collective responsibility could not gain traction. President Lincoln himself reportedly explained that he had revoked Grant's order because "I do not like to hear a class or nationality condemned on account of a few sinners."[64]

America, "the first nation in the world to base its nationhood solely on Enlightenment values,"[65] never passed through a medieval or feudal phase.[66] Therein, perhaps, lies the answer to why American Jews were able to view themselves—and assert themselves—as full-fledged members of American society. "The great advantage of the Americans," Alexis de Tocqueville famously observed, "is that they have arrived at a state of democracy without having to endure a democratic revolution; and that they are born equal, instead of becoming so." Less familiar, but arguably equally insightful, is de Tocqueville's observation in his immediately preceding sentence: "Democracy leads men not to draw near their fellow-creatures; but democratic revolutions lead them to shun each other, and perpetuate in a state of equality the animosities which the state of inequality engendered."[67]

To paraphrase de Tocqueville, the great advantage of American Jews is that they were born equal—or arrived equal, in the case of immigrants like Cesar Kaskel, Charles Wessolowsky, and the real-life Tevyes driven away from their Old World homes by official edict. As a result, the anti-Jewish animosities engendered by centuries of bigotry and butchery, which continued to afflict European nations even after their democratic revolutions, simply never took root in the same way in the United States. Secure psychologically that the logic of American liberty and equality extended to them—and secure physically that they would not thereby precipitate a pogrom or an outbreak of mob violence—American Jews could feel free to fight back against anti-Semitism, even if that meant standing up to a prominent military commander in the nation's darkest hour.

Notes

1. Script for *Fiddler on the Roof* (movie version), available at http://www.script-o-rama.com/movie_scripts/f/fiddler-on-the-roof-script.html.
2. John Y. Simon, ed., *The Papers of Ulysses S. Grant*, vol. 7 (Carbondale: Southern Illinois University Press, 1979), 50.
3. Jonathan D. Sarna, *When Grant Expelled the Jews* (New York: Schocken Books, 2012).
4. Ibid. (book jacket).
5. Ibid., 18–22, 24–27. Some Jews were expelled before the order was countermanded. Sarna estimates that fewer than one hundred Jews were affected. Ibid., 17.
6. Ibid., 50–79.
7. Ibid., 77–78.
8. Ibid., 83.
9. Ibid., 98–102.
10. Ibid., 8.
11. Ibid., 9–11.
12. Ibid., 11.
13. Ibid., 12.

14. Ibid., 21–22.
15. Isaac W. Bernheim, *History of the Settlement of Jews in Paducah and the Lower Ohio Valley* (Paducah, KY: Temple Israel, 1912), 23.
16. Expulsions of Jews from cities, villages, and border areas were commonplace in nineteenth-century Russia and uprooted hundreds of thousands of people. See, e.g., Simon M. Dubnow, *History of the Jews in Russia and Poland*, vol. 2 (Philadelphia: Jewish Publication Society, 1918), 30–34, 265–66, 343–46, 384–85, 399–406, 428–29; Hans Rogger, "Government, Jews, Peasants, and Land in Post-Emancipation Russia," *Cahiers du Monde Russe et Sovietique* 17 (January–March 1976): 5, 7–8, 9–10, 14; Bella Lowy, "The Russian Jews: Extermination or Emancipation," *Jewish Quarterly Review* 6 (1894): 537.
17. Script for *Fiddler on the Roof*. While a product of post–World War II American culture, *Fiddler's* depiction is faithful to the 1913 Sholem Aleichem story on which it is based, in which Tevye laments that "these things come from God, a man can't do anything about them." Sholem Aleichem, *Tevye the Dairyman and the Railroad Stories*, trans. Hillel Halkin (New York: Schocken Books, 2011). *See also* Shlomo Lambroza, "Jewish Self-Defence During the Russian Pogroms of 1903–1906," *The Jewish Journal of Sociology* 23 (1981): 124 (citing views of religiously orthodox Russian Jews that "pogroms were a manifestation of the will of God, and therefore one had to endure them").
18. Lambroza, "Jewish Self-Defence," 124.
19. See, e.g., Monty Noam Penkower, "The Kishinev Pogrom of 1903: A Turning Point in Jewish History," *Modern Judaism* 24 (October 2004): 187–225.
20. See, e.g., Michael Barnett, "Cosmopolitanism: Good for Israel? Or Bad for Israel?," in *Israel in the World: Legitimacy and Exceptionalism*, ed. Emanuel Adler (New York: Routledge, 2013), 39–40 (according to Zionists, "Jews in the *galut* had a victim mentality, cowardly, cowering, and passive"). The subject of European Jewish resistance to anti-Semitism is highly controversial, particularly as it relates to the Holocaust. Modern scholarship has undermined the accuracy of works written in the shadow of the Holocaust, such as Raul Hilberg, *The Destruction of the European Jews* (London: WH Allen, 1961), which portrayed an ingrained culture of Jewish passivity. See, e.g., David Biale, *Power and Powerlessness in Jewish History* (New York: Schocken Books, 1986), 4–5 (acknowledging "a consensus on the powerless and apolitical nature of Diaspora Jewish history," but arguing against this interpretation). Certainly the assertiveness of American Jews tends to refute any suggestion that the *galut* mentality was an inevitable by-product of Jewish life in the Diaspora.

21. Script for *Fiddler on the Roof*, op. cit.
22. Sarna, *Grant*, 151.
23. Ibid., xii; Ira Sheskin and Arnold Dashefsky, eds., *Jewish Population in the United States, 2010*, 3, available at http://www.jewishdatabank.org/Reports/Jewish_Population_in_the_United_States_2010.pdf.
24. The first Jewish Cabinet member was Oscar Strauss, appointed Secretary of Commerce and Labor in 1906. The first Jewish federal judge was Jacob Treiber, appointed to the bench in Arkansas in 1900. Michael Hahn, a member of the Unionist Party from Louisiana elected in 1862, was the only Jewish congressman at the time of Grant's order.
25. Sarna, *Grant*, 37–38, 44–45.
26. Louis Schmier, "Notes and Documents on the 1862 Expulsion of Jews from Thomasville, Georgia," *American Jewish Archives* 32 (April 1980): 10, 13–14; Mark I. Greenberg, "Ambivalent Relations: Acceptance and Anti-Semitism in Confederate Thomasville," *American Jewish Archives* 45 (Summer 1993): 14–15.
27. Schmier, "Expulsion of Jews," 11–12, 15–22.
28. Greenberg, "Ambivalent Relations," 15, 24–25.
29. Louis Schmier, ed., *Reflections of Southern Jewry: The Letters of Charles Wessolowsky, 1878–1879* (Macon, GA: Mercer University Press, 1982), 5.
30. Ofer Shiff, "At the Crossroad between Traditionalism and Americanism: Nineteenth-Century Philanthropic Attitudes of American Jews toward Palestine," *Jewish History* 9 (Spring 1995): 38–42.
31. Sarna, *Grant*, 28 (quoting Isaac Leeser, "On Persecution," *The Occident* 20 [February–March 1863]).
32. Shiff, "At the Crossroad," 41.
33. In the words of Jewish liturgy: "Because of our sins we were exiled from our land and removed from our soil."
34. Schiff, "At the Crossroad," 41–42 (quoting James G. Heller, *Isaac Mayer Wise* (New York: Union of American Hebrew Congregations, 1965), 536).
35. Bernhard Felsenthal, *The Wandering Jew: A Statement to a Christian Audience, of the Jewish View of Judaism* (Chicago: Carpenter and Sheldon, 1872), 5.
36. Jonathan D. Sarna, "The American Jewish Response to Nineteenth-Century Christian Missions," *Journal of American History* 68 (June 1981): 45–46.
37. Daniel Jonah Goldhagen, *Hitler's Willing Executioners* (New York: Alfred A. Knopf, 1996), 55.
38. See, e.g., Amos Elon, *The Pity of It All: A History of Jews in Germany, 1743–1933* (New York: Henry Holt and Co., 2002), 101–106

(describing as "remarkably restrained" Jewish reactions to widespread rioting in Bavarian cities in 1819, in which angry mobs raced through the streets demolishing Jewish property and screaming *"Hep! Hep! Jude verreck!"* [Death to all Jews!]); Peter G. J. Pulzer, *Jews and the German State: The Political History of a Minority, 1848–1933* (Detroit: Wayne State University Press, 2003), 37 (general tendency of Jewish leaders to revival of anti-Semitism in the 1870s was "to play it down, to let it blow over").

39. Sarna, *Grant*, 3.
40. Ibid., 3.
41. Isaac Markens, "Lincoln and the Jews," *American Jewish Historical Quarterly* 17 (1909): 117.
42. Sarna, *Grant*, 16.
43. Shiff, "At the Crossroad," 39.
44. Sarna, *Grant*, 17.
45. Michael Kent Curtis, "Lincoln, Vallandigham, and Anti-War Speech in the Civil War," *William & Mary Bill of Rights Journal* 7 (December 1998): 119 (quoting General Orders No. 38).
46. Ibid., 121–25.
47. Ibid., 125–29; see also Geoffrey R. Stone, "Abraham Lincoln's First Amendment," *New York University Law Review* 78 (April 2003): 3–6.
48. *Ex parte Vallandigham*, 28 F. Cas. 874, 921–22 (C.C.D. Ohio 1863).
49. *Reeside v. United States*, 2 Ct. Cl. 1, 17 (1866).
50. Ibid., 18.
51. Ibid., 17–18.
52. 323 U.S. 214 (1944).
53. Ibid., 223–24.
54. Eric L. Muller, "All the Themes But One," *University of Chicago Law Review* 66 (Fall 1999): 1423–24.
55. Deborah Hertz, *How Jews Became Germans: The History of Conversion and Assimilation in Berlin* (New Haven: Yale University Press, 2007).
56. David Sorkin, "Emancipation and Assimilation: Two Concepts and their Application to German-Jewish History," *Leo Baeck Institute Yearbook* 35 (January 1990): 17–34; Goldhagen, *Willing Executioners*, 56–58.
57. The depth and intensity of post-revolutionary French anti-Semitism, particularly as reflected in the Dreyfus Affair and the Vichy regime, is now well-documented. See, e.g., Paula E. Hyman, "New Perspectives on the Dreyfus Affair," *Reflexions Historiques* 31 (Fall 2005): 335–49 (summarizing literature). As elsewhere in Europe, the reaction of French Jews to these anti-Semitic outbursts

has often been criticized as overly passive (most famously by Leon Blum and Hannah Arendt), but more modern scholarship has brought to light a counter-narrative of Jewish resistance as well. Ibid., 345–49. Compare, e.g., Michael Marrus, *The Politics of Assimilation: A Study of the French Jewish Community at the Time of The Dreyfus Affair* (Oxford: Clarendon Press, 1971), 205 ("The weight of evidence seems to lie with those who believed that the predominant Jewish response [to the Dreyfus Affair] was a passive one, and that Jews tended to refrain from any involvement at all.") with Pierre Birnbaum, *The Anti-Semitic Moment: A Tour of France in 1898*, trans. Jane Marie Todd (New York: Hill and Wang, 2003), 315–16 (arguing that the passivity thesis "does not hold" and citing instances of resistance by "countless Jews" during the Affair).

58. See, e.g., Nicolas Lemann, *Redemption* (New York: Farrar, Straus and Giroux, 2006) (detailing massacres and wanton murder of blacks in the South in the 1870s).
59. See, e.g., Leonard Dinnerstein, *Anti-Semitism in America* (New York: Oxford University Press, 1994). But as Professor Dinnerstein concluded, "while antisemitism has always been a problem for Jews in a Christian society it has always been weaker in the United States than in European nations." Ibid., 250.
60. William Safran, "The Jewish Diaspora in a Comparative and Theoretical Perspective," *Israel Studies* 10 (March 2005): 43. *See also* Steven T. Katz, "In Place of an Introduction: Some Thoughts on American Jewish Exceptionalism," in *Why Is America Different? American Jewry on Its 350th Anniversary*, ed. Steven T. Katz (Lanham, MD: University Press of America, 2010), 11 (noting that "the sort of ferocious, paranoid, collective anti-Judaism—and the deadly violence that it spawned—that was, and had been for centuries, entrenched in Europe was largely absent from the American scene").
61. Mark R. Cohen, *Under Crescent and Cross: The Jews in the Middle Ages* (Princeton, NJ: Princeton University Press, 1994), 124 (quoting Salo Wittmayer Baron, *A Social and Religious History of the Jews*, vol. 11 [New York: Columbia University Press, 1967], 76) (emphasis omitted).
62. Sarna, *Grant*, 40–44.
63. Ibid., 32.
64. Ibid., 23.
65. Gordon S. Wood, *The Idea of America: Reflections on the Birth of the United States* (New York: Penguin Press, 2011), 274–75.
66. Louis Hartz, *The Liberal Tradition in America* (New York: Harcourt Brace Jovanovich, 1955).
67. Alexis de Tocqueville, *Democracy in America*, ed. Harvey C. Mansfield and Delba Winthrop (Chicago: University of Chicago Press, 2000), 485.

The Sigd: From Ethiopia to Israel

Shai Afsai

Until the middle of twentieth century, the Jews of Ethiopia—the Beta Israel (House of Israel), as they referred to themselves—lived in almost complete isolation from other Jewish communities around the globe.[1] During this prolonged separation, they developed and preserved distinct religious traditions not found in the rest of the Jewish world.[2] One such tradition is the annual Sigd holiday, which **ordinarily** occurs fifty days after Yom Kippur. On this day thousands of Ethiopian Jews from across Israel ascend to Jerusalem, primarily to the Armon Hanatziv Promenade that overlooks the Old City. Since 2008, the Sigd has been an official Israeli state holiday, though it continues to be celebrated mainly by the country's Jewish community from Ethiopia, which now numbers about 130,000.[3]

In November 2012, and again in late October and early November of 2013, I travelled to Israel for the purpose of celebrating this unique holiday.[4] I met with qessotch—i.e., *kohanim* or priests, the traditional religious leaders of Jews from Ethiopia—rabbis, and community members who shared their understanding and experience of the holiday.[5] They were pleased at the opportunity to convey their traditions and regretted that most Jews remain unfamiliar with the Sigd.

On the morning preceding the 2012 holiday, I visited the apartment of Qes Emaha Negat who, being close to eighty, is among the oldest qessotch in Israel—to learn about the Sigd's origins and customs. Born in the Gondar district of Ethiopia, Qes Emaha moved to Israel in 1991, and now lives in the sea-side city of Netanya.

SHAI AFSAI is a writer living in Providence, Rhode Island. Much of his recent work has focused on the religious traditions of Jews from Ethiopia and on the Igbo practicing Judaism in Nigeria.

I wish to thank Shoshana Ben-Dor and the anonymous reviewer of this article for their encouragement and comments, as well as **filmmaker** Tezeta Germay and the Council of Kohanim of Ethiopian Jews in Israel.

A large photograph of the synagogue constructed in the Gondar district by his father, a qes and scribe, hangs in the living room. Clothed entirely in white, his head wrapped in a white turban, and speaking Hebrew and Amharic, Qes Emaha recounted the biblical events in which the Sigd is rooted.

Sigd means "prostration" or "bowing down" in Ge'ez, the ancient Ethiopian liturgical language, and is akin to the Aramaic word *seged*. The holiday commemorates and is patterned after events described in the Book of Nehemiah, chapters 8–10, which relates that after the Jews returned from the Babylonian exile to the Land of Israel in the sixth century B.C.E, they gathered in Jerusalem on the first day of the Hebrew month of Tishrei (Rosh HaShanah)[6] and requested that Ezra the Scribe read to them from the Torah:

> So on the first day of the seventh month, Ezra the priest brought the Torah before the assembly, which was made up of men and women and all who were able to understand . . . Ezra praised the Lord, the great God, and all the people lifted their hands and responded, "Amen! Amen!" Then they bowed down and worshiped the Lord with their faces to the ground . . . The Levites . . . instructed the people in the Torah while the people were standing there. They read from the Book of the Torah of the Lord, making it clear and giving the meaning so that the people understood what was being read. (Neh. 8:2–8)

In addition to that Rosh HaShanah gathering, the Book of Nehemiah recounts another Jerusalem assembly that took place about three weeks later, on the twenty-fourth of Tishrei. That second assembly culminated in the Judean community publically recommitting itself to the covenant between God and the Jewish people:

> On the twenty-fourth day of the same month, the Israelites gathered together, fasting and wearing sackcloth and putting dust on their heads. Those of Israelite descent had separated themselves from all foreigners. They stood in their places and confessed their sins and the sins of their ancestors. They stood where they were and read from the Book of the Torah of the Lord their God for a quarter of the day, and spent another quarter in confession and in worshiping the Lord their God. (Neh. 9:1–3)

Those two ancient Jerusalem assemblies, on Rosh HaShanah and on the twenty-fourth of Tishrei, are the Sigd's blueprint.

Accordingly, reading, translating, and expounding upon portions of Scripture, as well as the lifting of hands in prayer, and prostration, are features of the day. As on that twenty-fourth of Tishrei gathering, the Sigd also involves separation from the gentiles, fasting and a communal confessing of sins, as well as repentance and a renewal of the Israelite covenant with God. In addition, among its central themes is the Jewish longing to return from the exile to Jerusalem. Although based on historical events that occurred in the month of Tishrei, the Sigd is now celebrated on the twenty-ninth of the Hebrew month of Cheshvan, fifty days after Yom Kippur.

How did the Beta Israel come to celebrate this Nehemiah-based holiday, which is not found in any other Jewish community? One traditional view, espoused by certain qessotch and rabbis, holds that in the past all Jews observed the annual holiday, but over time the practice was lost by Jews outside of Ethiopia. This is the position taken by Rabbi Sharon Shalom in his recently-published Hebrew work on the halachic and ideological world of Ethiopian Jewry, *From Sinai to Ethiopia* (2012): "In my assessment, in earlier times the Sigd holiday was known in the entire nation of Israel, but the historical circumstances caused this holiday to be forgotten, though in Ethiopia this tradition was preserved."[7]

According to that perspective, the original date of the holiday, maintained since the days of Ezra and Nehemiah, was eventually moved from the twenty-fourth of Tishrei. "Our forefathers who went down to Ethiopia," said Qes Emaha, "decided to hold this holiday at the end of Cheshvan, fifty days after Yom Kippur." In its current place on the Jewish calendar, writes Rabbi Shalom, "[t]he Sigd holiday bridges between the individual's soul-searching, whose time is Yom Kippur, and the source of the central tragedy of the nation of Israel—the exile, which came about because of a lack of proper interpersonal relationships."[8] Hence, prior to the Sigd there is a special emphasis on resolving quarrels and disputes among community members, and maintaining peaceful interactions.[9]

However, a different tradition holds that the Sigd was developed within Ethiopia by qessotch and monks, perhaps in the fifteenth century, in response to the circumstances in which the Beta Israel community found itself there.[10] As noted by Shoshana Ben-Dor, the Beta Israel's "collective memory is of religiously based conflict" with its Christian neighbors and persecution at their hands.[11] The holiday, she suggests in "The Sigd of Beta Israel: Testimony to a Community in Transition" (1987), emerged in Ethiopia from those conditions. Ben-Dor proposes that "the creation of the Sigd should be viewed as a reaction to and a reflection of the way in which the community perceived itself to be threatened with loss of its identity, as a result of both wars and assimilation."[12] The Jerusalem assemblies in the days of Ezra and Nehemiah, during which the Jews publicly reasserted their national identity and loyalty to God, were especially inspiring to the isolated community in Ethiopia and supplied the framework for the holiday.[13] This approach is also taken by Rabbi Mabrato Solomon, currently the coordinator of an Israeli rabbinic leadership program for Ethiopian Jews:

> It seems appropriate to say that indeed the source and content of the Sigd day derive from the verses' description in Nehemiah, but something that happened in the lives of the Jews of Ethiopia over the course of the generations is what compelled them to establish this special day. This is perhaps also the reason for why a similar day does not exist among the other communities of Israel. Indeed, the verses in Nehemiah are the source of the inspiration, but I contend that in their time the Ethiopian sages saw fit to establish a special holiday because of a great tragedy that befell them, such as assimilation, lack of conscientiousness about guarding Jewish identity, lack of full conscientiousness about the mitzvot, and the like.[14]

Though the qessotch are pleased that the Sigd became an official Israeli state holiday in 2008, they remain concerned about its future. Qes Emaha worries that the Sigd has been losing its religious significance in Israel, and is being reduced to a cultural event. October or November serve up an array of activities and programs connected with Ethiopian Jewry in the lead up to the holiday, but many of them lack a religious framework. "It would be better if there were more religious study in the days before the holiday, and less entertainment, performances, folklore, and music," said Qes Emaha. "These past days have taken the holiday out of its context, which is introspection. Whoever goes to Jerusalem tomorrow with pure thoughts, candidly, will celebrate the holiday as it should be. One must come to serve God and to pray. It is not just a social gathering."

One of the many educational and cultural events occurring across Israel prior to the 2012 holiday took place at Ramat Gan's Bar-Ilan University on the eve of the Sigd. There, Mula Zerihoon, an Ethiopian-born qes in his early forties who was ordained in Israel and serves as the spiritual leader of the Beta Israel community in the town of Kiryat Ekron, discussed the Sigd with an audience comprised mostly of high school and college students, as well as soldiers. Accompanying himself by turns with a drum and a small gong, he also chanted verses from the holiday's prayers. "We took this holiday from the Land of Israel and guarded it through the generations," Qes Mula told the audience.

Among the Sigd's central themes, Qes Mula emphasized, is the Jewish longing to return to Jerusalem. In Ethiopia, he recalled, the Sigd was celebrated atop mountains. "When we climbed the mountain, we felt Jerusalem in our heart of hearts. This deeply impacted our Judaism," he said. "Jews came from afar, two or three days on foot, on horses, and on mules, in order to have the chance to hear Torah from the qessotch. The people learned and were strengthened." In Ethiopia, the holiday also entailed the emblematic separation of the Beta Israel from the neighbouring Christians, as well as the public display of Jewish unity. The intensive Christian missionizing directed at the Jews of Ethiopia in the nineteenth and twentieth centuries by Europeans and their local agents[15] added weight to that aspect of the holiday.[16] "On this day," explained Qes Mula, "we said to the Christians surrounding us: We are Jews, resolute, believers in the Torah. You cannot sway us and convert us to Christianity, and cannot draw us to your religion."

In Israel, the Sigd's theme of Jewish unity continues, with Jews from other communities being welcomed to celebrate the holiday. "I am delighted to see Jews of so many colours, of so many shades, from so many countries. This is the Redemption," Qes Mula declared to the Bar-Ilan audience. "Just as this holiday guarded us in Ethiopia, we will continue to guard it in Israel, where there is no religious persecution and each person follows his religion.[17] Tell everyone—the non-Ethiopians and the Ethiopians—about the holiday . . . The Sigd should be a holiday of the entire nation of Israel."

That the holiday should be embraced by more Jews is a theme I heard repeatedly. The increased contact between the Jews of Ethiopia and the wider Jewish world that began in the twentieth century resulted in Ethiopian Jewry gradually bringing its religious traditions and practices more in line with Rabbinic Judaism. Thus, for example, Ethiopian Jews began celebrating Chanukah, wearing tallitot, and donning *t'fillin*. This process of adaptation, already begun in Ethiopia, continued and intensified in Israel.[18] World Jewry, however, did not in turn take on any of Ethiopian Jewry's unique traditions. It was an entirely one-sided affair.[19] And while Ethiopian Jewry increasingly accepted rabbinic authority, the religious authority of its own traditional spiritual and ritual leaders, the qessotch, was not reciprocally recognized.[20] (The qessotch's continued inability to officiate at state-recognized marriages in Israel is but one example of this.)[21] The importance that the qessotch and community leaders placed in recent years on making the Sigd an official Israeli state holiday indicates that they have become less amenable to this imbalance in religious exchange, with its attendant implication that Ethiopian Jewry has nothing to offer the wider Jewish world in the way of religion.

Their current approach extends beyond what was observed by Monika Edelstein in 2002. She noted then that "[t]he fact that the Etiopi community has chosen to continue to distinguish itself through unique religious holidays in Israel speaks to their desire to be recognized as a distinct subculture with long-standing, valid traditions and to the perseverance of beliefs and practices developed in Ethiopia, despite pressures to assimilate in Israel."[22] From the perspective of the religious leaders of Ethiopian Jewry with whom I met, however, state recognition of the holiday, which was granted in 2008, is but a good start. They would also like to have the celebration become an integral part of the yearly Jewish holiday cycle, at least in Israel. "Let more Jews join in its celebration—but without changing its traditions," Qes Mula said to me. If this were to occur—if more Jews were to celebrate the Sigd—it might help mitigate the long-standing imbalance of Jews from Ethiopia taking on the practices of Rabbinic Judaism while not being able to offer any of their own unique traditional practices in return. In addition, since (as will be seen below) the qessotch are central to the holiday in a way that rabbis presently are not,[23] the Sigd's integration into the Hebrew calendar would carry the message that qessotch are significant Jewish religious figures, and that their treatment by the Israeli government and rabbinate should not fall short of that accorded to rabbis.

One of the first worshipers I encountered in Jerusalem on the morning of the 2012 Sigd celebration was Adgo Salehu. Dressed in white and draped in a red, yellow, and green sash, Salehu arrived early at the Armon Hanatziv Promenade, where he located a prime spot to situate his tripod-mounted video camera and record the celebration. He began his conversation with me by underscoring the Sigd's role in sustaining Ethiopian Jewry throughout its long exile and then quickly moved to advocating that all Jews embrace the holiday. "By virtue of keeping the Sigd and the Torah in Ethiopia, and of our prayers, we were finally able to reach Jerusalem," Salehu said. "One must hear the reason for why the Sigd holiday was formed. The message of the holiday is that we are all brothers and that all Jews are accountable for one another. This day of prayer must be not only for the Jews from Ethiopia, but for the whole nation. It is important that the Sigd holiday develops and expands, and that more people join in its celebration."[24]

This notion was more forcefully expressed to me by Qes Emaha a few days after the 2013 Sigd celebration. The intrinsic importance of the holiday to the qessotch, as well as its emblematic significance, was apparent:

> Preserving and passing on the [Beta Israel] heritage to the next generation is the most important matter for us today . . . You interviewed me last year about the Sigd. The Sigd is not something that the community created there [i.e., in Ethiopia]. It was observed here, in Jerusalem, after the return from Babylon. And so our community safeguarded it, in order to strengthen Judaism, and we kept it for twenty-five hundred years. Why the rest of the nation of Israel did not keep it, we do not understand. We now want the entire nation of Israel to preserve this heritage—that it be a *yom shabbaton* for the entire nation of Israel. The heritage of the Beta Israel comes from the Torah and Judaism, and it is important to us that it will not vanish at some point. Just as the Sigd was not forgotten, so too the rest of the traditions of the Beta Israel must not be forgotten.

During the Sigd, dozens of qessotch assemble at Jerusalem's Armon Hanatziv Promenade, where they lead the religious ceremony from atop a platform adorned with the flags of Israel and Jerusalem. Some are dressed all in white; others wear cloaks of embroidered gold, blue, purple, or black, adorned with large Stars of

David. In addition to multi-colored parasols, the qessotch carry fly whisks and walking sticks, all three items representing their honoured position. Beneath a blue and white "Welcome to the Sigd Holiday" banner written in Hebrew and Amharic, the qessotch chant prayers in Ge'ez and Agaw, praising God and beseeching forgiveness and blessings for the Jewish people. Biblical passages, including those describing the giving of the Ten Commandments on Mount Sinai (Exodus 20) and the renewal of the covenant by the Jews who returned from the Babylonian exile (Nehemiah 9) are read to the congregation in Ge'ez, and then translated into Amharic, the first language of many members of the Jewish community from Ethiopia.

Around noon, however, the religious ceremony is suddenly interrupted in order for an array of politicians, government spokespeople, and community organizers to deliver speeches. Whereas in Ethiopia the Sigd ceremonies were traditionally directed by the qessotch,[25] in Israel there are other Masters of Ceremonies at the Armon Hanatziv Promenade, where the main celebrations of the holiday have been taking place since 1984. Often these MCs do not consider the qessotch's prayers and Torah teaching to be the central purpose of the gathering, but rather the speeches delivered by the various officials and dignitaries in attendance,[26] which are frequently devoid of any religious content. Thus, even when heaping praise on the Ethiopian Jewish community in the midst of its holiday, these speakers represent a disturbance of the religious proceedings. "The holiday here [in Israel] is not celebrated at all the way it was there [in Ethiopia]," said Qes Emaha, "because here we begin to pray and translate the scriptures for the people, and then the politicians arrive and interrupt." Likewise, pointing to some of the difficulties that the Beta Israel community currently faces in celebrating the Sigd, Qes Mula told the Bar-Ilan audience, "Here the holiday is quite different. Though they do not mean to do so, the government ministers and politicians unintentionally disrupt the prayers."

Ethiopian rabbis have expressed similar views and been very critical of that feature of Sigd celebrations in Israel. "This day is largely run by community activists, who bring into it extraneous matters, such as politics and the like," writes Rabbi Mabrato Solomon. "Therefore, the character of the day is greatly undermined, and it is losing its original religious aspect. It is to be feared that in a number of years the true aspect of the holiday will disappear." As part of countering this trend, Rabbi Solomon recommends relocating the main celebration of the holiday from the Armon Hanatziv Promenade (*tayelet*) to the Western Wall (*kotel*) plaza, where a minority of Ethiopian Jews have preferred to celebrate the Sigd. In addition to reinstating an atmosphere of holiness around the day, such a move is appropriate, in Rabbi Solomon's opinion, because for centuries Ethiopian Jewry longed to reach the Temple Mount and today the closest adjacent prayer area is by the Western Wall. In addition, since he believes that "much of the content of the day is appropriate for the entire nation of Israel, such as the prayer, the supplication, the fasting on the eve of Rosh Chodesh, and more," his rationale for relocation also has to do with wanting more Jews to celebrate the holiday. "Having it take place at the *kotel* will allow other communities to participate," he asserts. "We call upon everyone to share with us the ideas and significance of the Sigd day, and thus this holy community [i.e., the Beta Israel] will be able to contribute its part to the entire nation of Israel."[27]

While Qes Semai (Shimon) Elias—the director of the Council of Kohanim of Ethiopian Jews in Israel, the organization representing the several dozen qessotch living in the country—echoes the opinions of Qes Emaha and Qes Mula about politicians interrupting and disrupting the religious proceedings, he feels the qessotch have recently been making some headway in limiting the intrusiveness of such speeches and in reclaiming the religious focus of the holiday at the Armon Hanatziv Promenade. An additional helpful move in that direction, Qes Semai proposes, would be to have a religiously observant member of the Ethiopian Jewish community fill the role of Master of Ceremonies. For his part, despite the current disturbances, Qes Mula feels the Armon Hanatziv Promenade remains the most suitable location for realizing "our [i.e., Ethiopian Jewry's] holiday tradition as we know and are familiar with it."

Among those offering educational programs at the Armon Hanatziv Promenade during the 2012 and 2013 Sigd celebrations was Shoshana Ben-Dor, the Israeli director of the North American Conference on Ethiopian Jewry. Ben-Dor, too, is confident that all Jews would benefit from celebrating the holiday. "The Sigd brings together elements that exist in several Jewish holidays in a way that no other Jewish holiday does," she maintains. "It has the aspects of repentance, asking for mercy, and hoping that God has forgiven us that are found in the High Holy Days. It has the mourning for Jerusalem found in Tisha B'Av. It has the returning to Zion found in Yom HaAtzma-ut. It has the covenant and giving of the Torah found in Shavuot. The Sigd is the only day in the entire calendar that brings these all together—and also includes an annual renewal of the covenant. There is an importance in the Sigd for all Jews."[28]

For a number of years, however, Ben-Dor has been warning that the Sigd might not sustain its religious focus in Israel and that the likelihood of this happening is exacerbated by insufficient instruction about the significance of its prayers and by the lack of a holiday prayer book for worshipers to use:[29]

> [T]he overwhelming majority of youths who come to the Sigd do not at present relate to the religious aspects of the holiday, but rather know little about the holiday and come to meet friends and relatives.
> Also, the day has become a focal point for a whole string of cultural activities that take place in various cultural centers (Beit Avi Chai, Inbal Theater, the Zionist Confederation House) and in towns and cities around the country that include various musical and artistic performances that are called Sigd, but are not.
> This trend has been encouraged by the President's House forum, the leadership of which has made it clear that to them—and the assumption is that [also] to most Ethiopian Jews and other Israelis—the Sigd as a religious holiday has little appeal, so that the day should be used as a focal point for any cultural activity that exposes the general Israeli public to "the best in Ethiopian culture," and so many theater groups and municipalities have jumped on this band wagon.[30]

In collaboration with the Council of Kohanim of the Ethiopian Jews in Israel, as well as Ziva Mekonen-Degu (the executive director of the Israel Association of Ethiopian Jews), Ben-Dor has been working on a Sigd prayer book for over six years. The first of its kind, it is near completion and slated to be published in time for the 2014 festival. The prayers will be written in four columns—in Ge'ez, in Ge'ez transliterated into Hebrew, in Amharic, and in Hebrew. She hopes the prayer book will make the holiday accessible to more Jews, as well as help preserve its religious core. "When the siddur comes out, more people will realize how beautiful and powerful the prayers are," Ben-Dor predicts.[31] The beauty of the prayers, she proposes—such as these verses from the Sigd hymn "Let us Prostrate"[32]—themselves warrant ensuring the holiday's survival:[33]

> All of the earth will prostrate and give thanks to You and Your name
> They will bring flocks of sheep and herds of cattle and prostrate in Jerusalem
> They will bring gold and silver and prostrate in Jerusalem
> And they will bring golden clothing and prostrate in Jerusalem
> And they will bring fine garments and prostrate in Jerusalem
> And priests and prophets will come and prostrate in Jerusalem
> And kings and princes will come and prostrate in Jerusalem
> And great ones and judges will come and prostrate in Jerusalem
> And they will come from east and from west and prostrate in Jerusalem
> And they will come from north and from south and prostrate in Jerusalem
> And they will come from four directions and prostrate in Jerusalem
> Prostrate before God in the courtyard of His Holy Temple

By the afternoon, the hours of worship and study at the Armon Hanatziv Promenade build to a religious crescendo. Women raise their hands, ululate, and prostrate, pressing their foreheads to the ground. When the qessotch descend from their platform at the conclusion of the services, they are quickly surrounded by hundreds of congregants, who accompany them with ululation, applause, trumpet blasts, and dancing to a nearby tent, there to break the fast communally following the repentance and renewal of the covenant. Speaking with me outside of the tent in 2012, the government-appointed chief rabbi of the Jewish community from Ethiopia, Yosef Hadane,[34] stressed the significance of continuing to celebrate the Sigd in the state of Israel, as well as in other countries where Jews reside. "Our forefathers in Ethiopia always prayed to return to Jerusalem and always prayed in the direction of Jerusalem. We are here, but something else is built on the spot of the Holy Temple and the vast majority of the Jewish nation is still in the diaspora," he said. "This day and these prayers are very important for ingathering the exiles and for the coming of the Messiah. This is not just an event. This is an entirely pure day, a day of prayer. Therefore, I would suggest that Jews in Israel and the rest of the world adopt this holiday. I would say this is not only for the Jews from Ethiopia. It is for the entire nation."[35]

Rabbi Hadane has been stating that case in various ways for upwards of thirty years now. In Jon Abbink's "Seged Celebration in Ethiopia and Israel: Continuity and Change of a Falasha Religious Holiday" (1983), for example, Rabbi Hadane (obliquely referred to as Rabbi A.) is quoted as saying about Ethiopian Jewry, the Sigd, and Israel: "It is not only that we want something of our own . . . we have brought a very ancient custom, which was forgotten by the rest of the Jews, back to Israel!"[36] Similar sentiments about the holiday's pan-Judaic relevance have more recently been echoed by Qes Semai, the director of the Council of Kohanim of Ethiopian Jews in Israel. In a 2009 address before Shimon Peres at the President's House, for example, Qes Semai stated that the Sigd contained the "essence of the tradition of Israel as it was expressed in the Ethiopian exile," and argued that the Sigd's inauguration as an Israeli national holiday in 2008 was a "tremendous and heartwarming achievement," but was not enough. "Our next ambition in connection with the holiday is to claim a worthy place for it among the Jewish holidays of the Hebrew calendar, and to thus impart to the month of Marcheshvan, which is otherwise devoid of holidays, our own festive contribution," the qes told President Peres and his guests. "If we persist and believe in our suggestion, perhaps this dream will also be realized."[37] Qes Semai also used the occasion to point out that the Israeli rabbinate does not recognize the status of the qessotch and that the government does not treat them equitably.

Likewise, Qes Avihu Azariah, chairman of the Council of Kohanim of Ethiopian Jews in Israel, called for greater recognition of the qessotch's authority, as well as for rabbinic endorsement of the holiday, in his address during the 2011 Sigd celebration in Jerusalem:

> At this festive time, it is appropriate to mention that for my fellow qessotch and for me the difficulty [of absorption in Israel] is as personal as anyone else's, and even more so. Most difficult was the understanding that here in the Holy Land that we longed for we lost the authority to lead: a difficult and painful blow.

Happily, lately, with the addition of young qessotch who perform holy work, and with the establishment of the Council of Kohanim of Ethiopian Jews in Israel, which works with great success to repair this injustice, there has come a breath of positive fresh air in everything connected with strengthening the status of the qessotch.

... I once again call and turn in our name [i.e., the Beta Israel community] from every possible platform to the chief rabbis with a request to add the Sigd to the Hebrew calendar on the twenty-ninth day of the month of Cheshvan.[38]

The following year (2012), again speaking at the President's House, Qes Semai reiterated the significance of the Sigd and promised to "continue to try and convince anyone who is willing to listen to us and has influence that this is a worthy and honourable holiday, a holiday we are all proud of. It can be a leading holiday in each and every town, extending beyond the boundaries of the community and touching each and every person in Israeli society."[39] Qes Avihu began his 2012 Sigd address at the Armon Hanatziv Promenade by stressing that the holiday belongs not only to Ethiopian Jews, but "is a holiday of the entire Jewish nation."

Rabbi Sharon Shalom is equally adamant that Jews from Ethiopia should carry on the Sigd's traditions in Israel and that other Israeli Jews would benefit from celebrating the holiday as well. "The Jews from Ethiopia will continue to mark the Sigd, which is an ancient holiday, and was once perhaps kept by all of Israel," he writes in *From Sinai to Ethiopia*. "Moreover, we, the nation of Israel dwelling in Zion, are in great need of the messages and foci that surrounded the Sigd holiday in Ethiopia. Love and unity, the establishment of the covenant with the God of Israel and Jerusalem, are always relevant."[40]

While Sigd celebrations in Israel have differed from celebrations in Ethiopia, and in some ways have even changed from year to year,[41] one constant has continued to be the qessotch's centrality to the holiday.[42] Rabbi Hadane was particularly pleased with how evident that centrality was throughout the 2012 Sigd celebration: "This day is a day of unity. So many people came and answered amen to the prayers of the qessotch ... The spiritual leaders—the qessotch—pray and embrace the community. This is what was traditionally done in Ethiopia."[43]

Among those attending the 2013 Sigd celebration was the newly-appointed Rishon Lezion, the Sephardi Chief Rabbi of Israel, Rabbi Yitzhak Yosef. His father, the late Rabbi Ovadia Yosef, who was himself a Sephardi chief rabbi, passed away in early October 2013 at the age of ninety-three. (The funeral, attended by hundreds of thousands of mourners in Jerusalem, was the largest in Israel's history.) Rabbi Ovadia Yosef was considered a great supporter and friend of Ethiopian Jewry, having issued rabbinic rulings that paved the way for their mass *aliyah* to the state of Israel and that reiterated that they are Jewish according to halachah. When it was announced that Rabbi Yitzhak Yosef had arrived at the Armon Hanatziv Promenade, a ripple of ululations spread through the crowd of worshipers, and people rose from their seats as a sign of respect upon seeing him. Wearing the traditional embroidered hat and robe of a Rishon Lezion, Rabbi Yitzhak Yosef joined the qessotch on the platform from which they conduct the Sigd services, and offered his greetings.

"I wish to bless you on the occasion of your holiday," he told the worshipers. He also used the occasion to remember his late father: "I wish to mention my father, Rabbi Ovadia Yosef, who issued the rabbinic ruling that the Jews of Ethiopia are Jews in every sense, basing himself on the words of the Radbaz [i.e., Rabbi David ben Shelomo ibn Zimra] and Rabbi [Yaakov] Castro, and others." He explained that his father had issued that historic ruling "in order to safeguard the Judaism of the nation of Israel and the uniqueness of the nation of Israel." The chief rabbi then urged the qessotch to continue laboring for Judaism and the Torah, and to "strengthen your entire holy congregation." While his brief attendance at the celebration—as both a chief rabbi and a son of the late Rabbi Ovadia Yosef—was clearly appreciated by the worshipers, it should be noted that in his speech Rabbi Yitzhak Yosef referred to the Sigd as "your holiday," meaning one unique to Ethiopian Jewry, rather than "our holiday," the pan-Judaic festival envisioned by the qessotch and rabbis from the Ethiopian Jewish community.

The qessotch have not yet been able to make the Sigd a pan-Judaic holiday, nor succeeded in gaining the same state recognition and funding that is granted to rabbis and rabbinic students in Israel. The early encounters between non-Ethiopian Jews and Ethiopian Jewry were often characterized by a lack of concern "with the loss of ancient and accepted Falasha customs" that ensued as these made way for Rabbinic Judaism,[44] and this religious trend continued with the community's mass immigration to the state of Israel.[45] By 1993, some one hundred years after those first encounters, Steven Kaplan and Chaim Rosen proclaimed: "Whatever our intention or desires, Beta Israel culture as it developed and flourished in Ethiopia has come to an end. Its demise, which began in Ethiopia, has continued in Israel as one of the inevitable side-effects of the community's wholesale immigration. Its passing should be respectfully mourned; and its history should be recorded and studied, while some informants still retain accurate memories."[46] In many ways, it is difficult to disagree with their assessment,[47] and the process they describe has visibly—perhaps even permanently—impacted the status and role of the qessotch.[48] Recently, however, the first-ever Israeli-born qes—Efraim Zion-Lawi of Karmiel—was ordained, a promising indication that despite their current marginalization, the qessotch will persist as a religious institution in Israel,[49] will remain an influential and guiding force for members of the Jewish community from Ethiopia, and will ensure the continuance of the Sigd holiday.

Notes

1. Steven Kaplan and Chaim Rosen, "Ethiopian Immigrants in Israel: Between Preservation of Culture and Invention of Tradition," *Jewish Journal of Sociology* 35 (1993): 38; Jon Abbink, "Ethnic Trajectories in Israel: Comparing the 'Bené Israel' and 'Beta Israel' Communities, 1950–2000," *Anthropos* 97 (2002): 6. For a discussion of some of the early encounters between Ethiopian and non-Ethiopian Jews, see Kaplan, "'Race' as a Category in the Historical Encounter between Ethiopian Jews and World Jewry," *Pe'amim* 80 (1999): 83–92 [Hebrew].
2. David Ribner and Ruben Schindler, "The Crisis of Religious Identity Among Ethiopian Immigrants in Israel," *Journal of Black Studies* 27 (1996): 108–110.
3. According to a November 12, 2012 press release by the State of Israel's Central Bureau of Statistics, "The Ethiopian Community in Israel—A Collection of Data on the Occasion of the Sigd Holiday" (Jerusalem, 307/2012), "At the end of 2011 the Ethiopian community in Israel numbered 125,500 residents."
4. I attended the Sigd celebration at the Armon Hanatziv Promenade on November 14, 2012; at the conclusion of the ceremonies there, I proceeded to the Western Wall plaza. The following year,

I attended the Sigd celebration at the Armon Hanatziv Promenade on October 31, 2013.

5. In particular, this article is informed by interviews with four qessotch: Qes Emaha (Amaha) Negat (Netanya, November 13, 2012 and November 3, 2013), Qes Mula Zerihoon (Ramat Gan, November 13, 2012), and Qes Semai Elias (Rishon Lezion, November 15, 2012 and November 1, 2013, as well as subsequent phone conversations and email correspondence); and Qes Efraim Zion-Lawi (Karmiel, November 2, 2013, as well as subsequent phone conversations and email correspondence). Portions of those and other interviews appeared in my articles "Past in the Present: An inside look at Sigd — the holiday of Ethiopian Jewry — and the struggle to secure its survival, *Ami Magazine* 97 (2012): 78–85; "The Gift of Sigd," *CJ: Voices of Conservative/Masorti Judaism* 7 (2013): 30–33; and "Israel's Ethiopian Jewish community celebrates annual Sigd holiday in Jerusalem," The Jewish Voice 19 (2013): 22–23, 42.

6. Tishrei was already regarded as the first month of the year in Nehemiah's time. See Allan M. Langner, "The History of the Tishrei Conundrum," *Jewish Bible Quarterly* 40 (2012): 133

7. Sharon Shalom, *From Sinai to Ethiopia* (Israel: Yedioth Ahronoth and Chemed Books, 2012), 212 [Hebrew]. As mentioned, the position that the Sigd was once celebrated by all Jews, at least in the Land of Israel, is certainly not unique to Rabbi Shalom. Compare his opinion on the Sigd's origins and the question of why it has not been observed by other Jewish communities with, for example, that of Qes Emaha below. However, Rabbi Shalom also believes there is Talmudic evidence supporting his opinion. See *From Sinai to Ethiopia,* 212.

8. Shalom, *From Sinai to Ethiopia*, 209.

9. Shalom, *From Sinai to Ethiopia*, 210; interview with Qes Mula Zerihoon.

10. Abbink, "Seged Celebrations in Ethiopia and Israel: Continuity and Change of a Falasha Religious Holiday," *Anthropos* 78 (1983): 796; Shoshana Ben-Dor, "The Sigd of Beta Israel: Testimony to a Community in Transition," in *Ethiopian Jews and Israel*, eds. Michael Ashkenazi and Alex Weingrod (New Brunswick: Transaction Books, 1987), 141.

11. Ben-Dor, "The Sigd of Beta Israel" 141.

12. Ben-Dor, "The Sigd of Beta Israel," 142.

13. Ben-Dor, "Sigd," in *Ethiopia*, ed. Hagar Salamon (Jerusalem: Machon Ben-Tsvi, 2008), 138 [Hebrew].

14. Mabrato Solomon, "From the *tayelet* to the *kotel*," *Makor Rishon* ("Musaf 'Shabbat'") 797, November 16, 2012 [Hebrew]. Rabbi Solomon's Hebrew article was also printed in a special Sigd

pamphlet put out by T'nuat Haimanot, which he heads [*Alon Kehilat Yehude Etiopia* 14 (Sigd 5773): 1–2]. Among other places, the pamphlet was distributed at the Armon Hanatziv Promenade during the 2012 Sigd celebration.

15. See Kaplan, "The Beta Israel (Falasha) Encounter with Protestant Missionaries: 1860.1905," *Jewish Social Studies* 49 (1987): 27–42; Kaplan, "Falasha Christians: A Brief History," *Midstream* 39 (1993): 20–21.

16. Converts to Christianity sometimes continued to attend Jewish celebrations. See Kaplan, "The Beta Israel (Falasha) Encounter with Protestant Missionaries," 37; Kaplan, "Falasha Christians," 20. See also See Yossi Friedman and Galia (Sabar) Friedman, "Changes Among the Jews of Ethiopia 1974–1983," *Pe'amim* 33 (1987):137 [Hebrew]; or Galia Sabar Friedman, "Religion and the Marxist State in Ethiopia: the Case of the Ethiopian Jews," *Religion in Communist Lands* 17 (1989): 251. And see Emanuela Trevisan Semi, "The Conversion of the Beta Israel in Ethiopia: A Reversible 'Rite of Passage,'" *Journal of Modern Jewish Studies* 1 (2002): 93.

17. Religious and social dimensions of the Sigd's celebration (see below, note **29**), as well as other areas of Jewish practice, were impeded during the Marxist Derg's rule of Ethiopia. See Friedman and Friedman, "Changes Among the Jews of Ethiopia," 131, 136–137 [Hebrew]; or Friedman, "Religion and the Marxist State in Ethiopia," 247, 250–252. Qes Mula alludes to this in his statement, contrasting that state of affairs in Ethiopia with the absence of religious persecution in Israel.

18. For some discussion of the continued evolution of Ethiopian Judaism, see Simon Messing, "Journey to the Falashas," *Commentary* 22 (1956): 34; John T. Pawlikowski, "The Judaic Spirit of the Ethiopian Orthodox Church: A Case Study in Religious Acculturation," *Journal of Religion in Africa* 4 (1971–72): 195; Kay Kaufman Shelemay, "A Quarter-Century in the Life of a Falasha Prayer," *Yearbook of the International Folk Music Council* 10 (1978): 84–85, 95–97; Kaplan and Rosen "Ethiopian Immigrants in Israel: Between Preservation of Culture and Invention of Tradition," 35–48; Abbink, "An Ethiopian Jewish 'Missionary' as Culture Broker," in *Ethiopian Jews and Israel*, **21**–32; Kaplan, "The Origins of the Beta Israel: Five Methodological Cautions," *Pe'amim* 33 (1987): 41–43 [Hebrew]; Kaplan, "'Falasha' Religion: Ancient Judaism or Evolving Ethiopian Tradition" (Review article), *Jewish Quarterly Review* 89 (1988): 49–65; Monika D. Edelstein, "Lost Tribes and Coffee Ceremonies: Zar Spirit Possession and the Ethno-Religious Identity of Ethiopian Jews in Israel," *Journal of Refugee Studies* 15 (2002): 156, 158; Semi, *Jacques Faitlovitch and the Jews of Ethiopia* (London: Vallentine Mitchell, 2007), xvi–xvii, 67–68.

19. Jeff Halper, "The Absorption of Ethiopian Immigrants: A Return to the Fifties," in *Ethiopian Jews and Israel*, 126–127.
20. Kaplan and Rosen, "Ethiopian Immigrants in Israel: Between Preservation of Culture and Invention of Tradition," 41; Ribner and Schindler, "The Crisis of Religious Identity Among Ethiopian Immigrants in Israel," 109; Kaplan and Hagar Salamon, "Ethiopian Immigrants in Israel: Experience and Prospects," *Jewish Policy Research* Report No. 1 (1998): 15, 17.
21. Kaplan and Salamon, "Ethiopian Immigrants in Israel: Experience and Prospects," 15, 17.
22. Edelstein, "Lost Tribes and Coffee Ceremonies," 163.
23. Speaking to me in Jerusalem at the conclusion of the 2013 Sigd celebration, one rabbi from the Beta Israel community expressed his hope that future Sigd celebrations would "also have Hebrew and a role for rabbis, as well as qessotch."
24. Interview with Adgo Salehu, Jerusalem, November 14, 2012. Salehu was also one of the first worshipers I encountered in Jerusalem on the morning of the 2013 Sigd celebration. He was already at the Armon Hanatziv Promenade, dressed in white and draped in a red, yellow, and green sash, by the time I arrived there early that day.
25. Kaplan and Salamon, "Ethiopian Immigrants in Israel: Experience and Prospects," 15. But see Shelemay, "Seged: A Falasha Pilgrimage Festival," *Musica Judaica* 3 (1980–81): 55–56.
26. Ben-Dor, "Sigd," 147.
27. Solomon, "From the *tayelet* to the *kotel*." See also Rosen, "Similarities and Differences between the Beta Israel of Gondar and Tigre," *Pe'amim* 33 (1987): 106–107. Rosen mentions the last two reasons when discussing the preference of some for celebrating the Sigd at the *kotel*. He appears to find the third reason especially compelling. See also Ben-Dor, "The Sigd of Beta Israel," 150–153; Kaplan, "The Beta Israel and the Rabbinate: law, ritual and politics," *Social Science Information* 27 (1988): 366. Compare Rabbi Solomon's comments on being able to contribute to the wider Jewish world with those of Qes Semai (below, note 37). On the importance to Ethiopian Jews of being "able to give" and not "just to receive" in a different context—that of donating blood in Israel—see Don Seeman, "'One People, One Blood': Public Health, Political Violence, and HIV in an Ethiopian-Israeli Setting," *Culture, Medicine and Psychiatry* 23 (1999): 173.
28. Interview with Ben-Dor, Jerusalem, November 15, 2012.
29. See for example, Ben-Dor, "Sigd," 147–148. Even in Ethiopia, "a degree of secularization of the Sigd" had become apparent by 1980 (see Ben-Dor, "The Sigd of Beta Israel," 146), if not earlier. Furthermore, the Sigd holiday always "had dimensions that

were not religious," but primarily social (see Ben-Dor, "Sigd," 146). In his interview, Qes Mula enumerated five primary facets of the holiday, four of which of which were religious, but one of which also had a clearly social-**communal** function: "This was a day of gathering of all the remote villages which had not met for a year. Relatives would meet and strengthen their bond, and the connection between the villages was maintained." See also Shelemay, "Seged," 56.

30. Email from Ben-Dor, August 8, 2013.
31. Interview with Ben-Dor, Jerusalem, November 15, 2012.
32. The selection was recorded in Ge'ez by Shoshana Ben-Dor and incorporates recordings from a joint project of the Center for Jewish Music of the Hebrew University and the Laboratoire de anciennes cultures et traditiones orales, as well as additional field work with Qes Semai Elias. It is reprinted here with permission, in my translation into English. See also Shelemay, "Seged," 49, 57.
33. Email from Ben-Dor, December 2, 2012.
34. The rabbi's last name is sometimes spelled *Adane*. See below, note 36.
35. Interview with Rabbi Yosef Hadane, Jerusalem, November 14, 2012.
36. Quoted in Abbink, "Seged Celebrations in Ethiopia and Israel," 808. See also the reference to Rabbi A. (i.e., Rabbi [H]adane) on p. 807.
37. Semai Elias, "B'racha l'regel Chag HaSigd," speech delivered at the President's House, Jerusalem, November 2, 2009 [Hebrew]. Text provided by Qes Semai.
38. Avihu Azariah, "B'racha l'regel Chag HaSigd," speech delivered at Armon Hanatziv Promenade, Jerusalem, November 24, 2011[Hebrew]. Text provided by Qes Semai Elias.
39. Elias, "B'racha l'regel Chag HaSigd," speech delivered at the President's House, Jerusalem, October 31, 2012 [Hebrew]. Text provided by Qes Semai.
40. Shalom, *From Sinai to Ethiopia*, 212.
41. Shelemay, "Seged," 55–56; Ben-Dor, "The Sigd of Beta Israel," 147, 155; Kaplan and Rosen, "Ethiopian Immigrants in Israel: Between Preservation of Culture and Invention of Tradition," 39.
42. This was the case in Ethiopia and has also been the case in Israel since the 1983 Sigd celebration. See Ben-Dor, "The Sigd of Beta Israel," 150.
43. Interview with Rabbi Hadane, Jerusalem, November 14, 2012.
44. Semi, *Jacques Faitlovitch and the Jews of Ethiopia*, xvii.
45. Rosen and Kaplan, "Ethiopian Immigrants in Israel: Between Preservation of Culture and Invention of Tradition," 40–41.

46. Rosen and Kaplan, "Ethiopian Immigrants in Israel: Between Preservation of Culture and Invention of Tradition," 39.
47. See also Kaplan and Salamon, "Ethiopian Immigrants in Israel: Experience and Prospects," 18–19.
48. Rosen and Kaplan, "Ethiopian Immigrants in Israel: Between Preservation of Culture and Invention of Tradition," 41.
49. Germaw Mengistu " The Israeli-born ques"/"'To integrate into Israeli society, but to preserve the way of our forefathers,'" *Yedioth Negat* 69 (May 2012): 1, 7 [Hebrew and Amharic]. The significance of continuing to have qessotch extends well beyond the preservation of the Sigd holiday, for as Marc Shapiro notes, "without priests there is no way [for Ethiopian Jews] to carry on their religious traditions." See Shapiro, "The Falasha of Ethiopia," *The World & I* 12 (1987): 524; and Shapiro, "Return of a Lost Tribe," *The World & I* 3 (1988): 484, 488. See also Kaplan, "The Beta Israel (Falasha) Encounter with Protestant Missionaries," 31–33.

Poetry

To a Grandson Yet to Be Born

Reeve Robert Brenner

Well shuttered until your space
gives way to the earth's own
contours created to clothe you,
a few centimeters long, already proudly Jewish
in my daughter's womb
vestigially tailed
pre-intellectual proto-graduate student
advanced degree candidate
about ninety-days. Sounds can see you
music can see you.
Nurete your host, Mitch your sire
I your saba introduce you to them—
she a thinker, he a doctor
she a lover, he so wise
already saving for your
schooling, ready to carry you on his shoulders
to museums and galleries walled with portraits.
Nurete, your mother, holds you close and inward.
She will teach you, *tayerl*
the joys and sorrows of speaking, reading, writing
lashon kodesh.
May you spend many happy hours
with the aleph bet
washing ink from your fingers.
You will make the walls
of Jerusalem
your own ramparts,
You will see that they stand
long after I am gone.

RABBI REEVE ROBERT BRENNER (NY64) serves Bet Chesed Congregation, Bethesda, Maryland, and is the retired Sr. Staff Chaplain of the National Institutes of Health. His *Faith and Doubt of Holocaust Survivors* has been republished with a new introduction by Rutgers University Transaction Press.

Who am I your saba?
Something like a tree
seen through your window,
providing shade in summer, in winter
my branches heavy with snow will
skip to the wind along the hardened earth
may shelter pussy cats and turtles,
wild deer and a teddy bear,
and you.

POETRY

Rising Higher

Israel Zoberman

In the Synagogue
Of my childhood,
My father would remind
Me to stand still at the *Amidah*.
But, how can one,
While standing still,
Rise higher and higher?

ISRAEL ZOBERMAN, D. Min. (C74) is the founding rabbi of Beth Chaverim, Virginia Beach, Virginia.

Book Reviews

Women's Bible Commentary, 3rd edition
Carol A. Newsom, Sharon H. Ringe, Jacqueline E. Lapsley, eds.
(Louisville, KY: Westminster John Knox, 2012), 679 pp.

The New Reform Judaism: Challenges and Reflections
by Dana Evan Kaplan
(Philadelphia: Jewish Publication Society; Lincoln: University of Nebraska Press, 2013), 382 pp.

The last three to four decades have seen a flourishing of women's scholarship in the area of biblical studies. There are more women biblical scholars, Jewish and non-Jewish alike. Further, their books and articles are readily accessible to an interested readership. What is now available is an updated, revised, and expanded edition of the one-volume *Women's Bible Commentary* that was originally published in 1992. This superb work, at over six hundred fifty pages, contains some of the finest contemporary thinking by many of the leading lights of women biblical scholars in North America. In a quiet nod to the authors of the Septuagint, here some seventy women scholars have come together to offer their insights into the books of the Jewish Bible, the Apocrypha, and the New Testament. Yet there is more! In addition to those books themselves, which, by the way, follow the order found in Protestant bibles with Apocrypha, there are additional special articles dedicated to many connected subjects. For the Jewish Bible there are: "Eve and Her Interpreters," "Sarah, Hagar, and Their Interpreters," "Miriam and Her Interpreters," and Jephtha's Daughter and Her Interpreters." In terms of the New Testament, there are articles on "Mary and Her Interpreters," and "Mary Magdalene and Her Interpreters." Other articles of special note include "When Women Interpret the Bible," "Women as Biblical Interpreters Before the Twentieth Century," "Women's Religious Life in Ancient Israel," "Beyond the Canon," and "The Religious Lives of Women in the Early Church." There also are special articles in the Apocrypha section: "Introduction to the Apocrypha," "Judith and Her Interpreters," and "Susannah and Her Interpreters." Since the Christian Orthodox tradition also recognizes the canonicity of 3 Maccabees, and Psalm 151, there also are articles on those books, as well as an article on 4 Maccabees.

Two of the current editors, Carol Newsom and Sharon H. Ringe had edited the original 1992 version of this work. In the Introduction to that book, which they also include in this volume, they wrote: Women scholars have raised new questions. They "have posed . . . new ways of reading that . . . have challenged the very way biblical studies are done. [Feminist biblical studies take] many different directions . . . Some commentators have attempted to reach 'behind the text' to recover knowledge about the actual conditions of women's lives in the biblical period . . . Still others have tried to discover the extent to which even the biblical writings that pertain to women are shaped by the concerns and perspectives of men and yet how it can still be possible at times to discover the presence of women and their own points of view between the lines." Yet, in the mere two decades between the publication of the first edition and this third version, there have been profound changes in feminist biblical criticism. A new introduction explains, "Issues that were just beginning to be explored . . . the hermeneutical significance of sexual identity, analysis of masculinity, and postcolonial positioning" are now part of feminist criticism. Further, there has been an explosion of feminist biblical critics—women as well as men. The editors agonized over several issues: whether to limit this volume to women writers (and that answer was "yes"), which articles to include from previous volumes, and which younger women working in the field to ask to write new articles. Happily the authors of previous chapters not included here "not only accepted but cheered [the editors] initiative to include the work of younger scholars." Those authors who reappear from earlier volumes revised their previous work, in some cases significantly.

One of the salient features of this volume is that while many chapters are but a half-dozen pages in length, others that are of particular interest in terms of feminist studies, are longer, some ten to twenty pages. Chapters addressing each of the biblical books, as well as those devoted to the literature of the Apocrypha/Deuterocanonical writings, feature three sections: Introduction, Content, and Bibliography. The newest additional articles, which address the reception history of such women as those mentioned above (Eve, Sarah, Hagar . . . but also Rahab, Deborah, Jael, Delilah, Jezebel, Job's wife) have merely some comments and a bibliography. The relevant reception history might include observations on Jewish, Christian, and Muslim responses to these women, as well as how they are depicted in the arts, along with illustrations.

One of the editors, Sharon H. Ringe, in the chapter, "When Women Interpret the Bible," explains what makes this such a special work. The contributors made a "commitment to read the biblical texts through the varied lenses of women's experiences in ancient and modern religious and cultural contexts." Ringe further points out that women face a particular challenge. For all readers, irrespective of gender, the Bible "bears a variety of kinds of religious authority: guide for conduct, rule of faith, inerrant source of truth (factual and/or moral), and revelation of God." Yet at the same time, for many, but not all within "these communities, the authority of the Bible is explicit, as well as implicit, but often ambiguous and finally ambivalent, especially for women." Women read and experience the Bible differently from men. Ringe explains, "women reading the Bible have found themselves on alien and even hostile turf." Indeed, both "the silence of women and their silencing—the contempt in which they are held and the violence with which they are treated—in the Bible mirror the realities of many women's lives. For them, the Bible is experienced as giving a divine stamp of approval to their suffering." She also points out "the problem of language and gender . . . [the] so-called generic use of words like 'man,' 'brother,' and 'mankind,'. . . [which] obscures or even negates the participation of women," as well as the problematic use of the male pronouns referring to God (he, him) and how to convey the idea that "God is beyond human categories of gender." This exciting and vibrant volume, which has a place in our own as well as synagogue or community libraries, will appeal to rabbis and laity alike. By providing brief bibliographies, the authors offer direction for further study.

* * *

Without doubt, the Judaism of 2035 or 2065 will look a lot different than it does in 2015. The Judaism of today is radically different than it was in 1935 or 1965. As that is true of Judaism as whole, the same can be said about American Judaism, and more specifically American Reform Judaism. In this thoughtful volume, which features an Index, a Timeline of Significant Events, and a Glossary, our colleague Dana Evan Kaplan provides for the reader a portrayal of Reform Judaism in North America half way through the second decade of the 21st century. While focusing on the present, in this, his fourth book on American Judaism, he offers historical context why Reform Judaism is where it is and what it is. Many of Kaplan's examples focus on the past thirty or forty years as he explains important decisions made by the leadership of the Union of Reform Judaism (formerly the Union of American Hebrew Congregations), as they steered through the turbulent post-World War Two years, a time that saw serious upheavals in American demographics and social thought. Yet this is more than just a socio-religious history of Reform Judaism, for he consciously weaves in the stories of many present-day examples of laity and rabbis who are the living faces of Reform Judaism. Reform Judaism, as Kaplan notes, prides itself on flexibility, but this too has its downsides: not all religious identities fit. He writes, "the Reform movement will need to take a clear look at where those boundaries should be drawn" (p. 9). Yet Reform Judaism has no accepted methodology for predetermining how to evaluate any particular issue. One of its great challenges is "how to present Jewish religious belief in the absence of a consensus over what we believe" (p. 3).

There are eight chapters in this work, each about thirty-to-forty pages in length. Kaplan immediately engages the reader as he begins his opening chapter titled In Search of a Reform Jewish Theology. He relates the story of a woman who moved from a lifetime in Conservative Judaism to become an active member in her congregation because "Reform theology allowed for ritual flexibility that greatly enriched her personal religious experience" (p. 19). This then leads into a discussion about a history of Judaism and more specifically Reform Judaism. A Brief History of the American Reform Movement follows, with a major focus on the post-WWII years. He recalls the names and writes about the achievements of Maurice Eisendrath at the UAHC, Nelson Glueck at HUC-JIR, and Joe Glaser at the CCAR. A major section of this chapter discusses the years at the UAHC and the leadership offered by Alexander Schindler. He also covers the tenures of Alfred Gottschalk and David Ellenson at HUC-JIR, and Eric Yoffie at UAHC/URJ and then includes Rick Jacobs' recent election to that post. To Observe or Not to Observe, the chapter that follows looks at how Reform Judaism, and in particular American

Reform Judaism has struggled with such issues as kashrut, Shabbat observance, and marriage and divorce.

Unquestionably the past two decades have seen, as Kaplan titles his next chapter, a New Reform Revolution in Worship and Practice. He recalls the CCAR's 1999 adoption of the "Statement of Principles for Reform Judaism," showing how the seeds of this document were sown more than twenty-five years earlier in the landmark publications of the early 1970s, Leonard Fein's *Reform is a Verb*, and Theodore Lenn's *Rabbi and Synagogue in Reform Judaism*. Kaplan notes his regret that in the process, that while "the freedom to explore alternative religious beliefs was liberating" it also undermined "the theological consistency necessary for coherency" and that this "legacy of the sixties" continues to "haunt us" and ultimately holds back Reform Judaism from what it could become (p. 138). He takes note of the new Reform prayerbook, *Mishkan T'filah*, and while he sees it as a creative effort, he also criticizes it for its lack of a "sound Jewish theology" (p. 157).

In the chapter A New Reform Revolution in Values and Ethics, Kaplan covers a lot of ground including women's ordination, comments on the issues of ethical behavior, and Social Justice as understood and practiced by Reform Judaism, Zionism and Israel (where he briefly details the increasing involvement of Reform Judaism with and in Israel), inclusivity for women, and sexual equality, as well as a commitment to environmental responsibility. The chapter Who Is a (Reform) Jew, discusses the struggles Reform Jews and Reform congregations have with the realities of increased mixed marriages and synagogue participation. He addresses the conflicting goals of encouraging non-Jewish spouses to raise their children as active Jews in synagogue life, and yet how to avoid the introduction of non-Jewish ideas and practices which threaten the religious integrity of this institution. Next he writes about On the Boundaries of Reform, addressing Messianic Judaism, Jubus (Jewish Buddhists), and Judaism with a Humanistic Perspective. He concludes with the statement that while "American Jews embrace a variety of spiritual approaches that they find religiously meaningful" that this inevitability brings with it a "blurring of boundaries and a violation of traditional norms" so that "Reform Judaism will need to cultivate a sophisticated 'discourse of disagreement' in order to meet this challenge" (p. 269). Seeking the Spiritual, chapter eight, highlights additional challenges for contemporary Judaism.

The world of cyberspace is colliding with traditional institutions. Descriptions about PunkTorah, the Virtual Congregational Experience (i.e. the CyberSanctuary), Second Life, what Kaplan defines as Creative Expressions of Spirituality through Art, Music, and Dance, Storahtelling, as well as Gonzo Judaism, Adventure Religion, and Wilderness Judaism are addressed here.

One of the strengths of this volume is that it concentrates more on description than prescription. Nonetheless, Kaplan is clear that the Reform movement faces enormous challenges in the coming years, and that it "will need to develop new and convincing justifications for maintaining the Jewish people as a separate ethno-religious group in an era where boundaries and borders of all kinds are fading, if not disappearing (p. 313). In his view, this will necessitate creating a Judaism that will focus not on "loyalty to community" but how to "engage the individual in a search for existential meaning" (p. 315). Kaplan argues for a direction away from the "current focus on pluralism" and instead to build to a "committed core" by refocusing on ethical monotheism, "the idea that there is one and only one God, and that God demands ethical behavior" (p. 316). In short, Kaplan argues that Reform Judaism cannot be the limitless Big Tent that makes room for all ideas. As he states slightly earlier, "every religious movement has to have some set of boundaries, delineating what is acceptable and what is not" (p. 267).

David J. Zucker, PhD (C-'70) is recently retired as Rabbi/Chaplain at Shalom Cares, a senior continuum of care center, Aurora, Colorado. His newest books are *The Bible's PROPHETS: An Introduction for Christians and Jews,* and *The Bible's WRITINGS: An Introduction for Christians and Jews,* (Wipf & Stock 2013). He publishes in a variety of areas. See his website, www.DavidJZucker.org

Call for Papers: *Maayanot*

The CCAR Journal: The Reform Jewish Quarterly is committed to serving its readers' professional, intellectual, and spiritual needs. In pursuit of that objective, the *Journal* created a new section known as *Maayanot* (Primary Sources), which made its debut in the Spring 2012 issue.

We continue to welcome proposals for *Maayanot* —translations of significant Jewish texts, accompanied by an introduction as well as annotations and/or commentary. *Maayanot* aims to present fresh approaches to materials from any period of Jewish life, including but not confined to the biblical or Rabbinic periods. When appropriate, it is possible to include the original document in the published presentation.

Please submit proposals, inquiries, and questions to *Maayanot* editor, Daniel Polish, dpolish@optonline.net.

Along with submissions for *Maayanot*, the *Journal* encourages the submission of scholarly articles in fields of Jewish Studies, as well as other articles that fit within our Statement of Purpose.

The *CCAR Journal: The Reform Jewish Quarterly*
Published quarterly by the Central Conference of American Rabbis.

Volume LXI, No. 4. Issue Number: Two hundred forty-two.
Fall 2014

STATEMENT OF PURPOSE

The *CCAR Journal: The Reform Jewish Quarterly* seeks to explore ideas and issues of Judaism and Jewish life, primarily—but not exclusively—from a Reform Jewish perspective. To fulfill this objective, the Journal is designed to:

1. provide a forum to reflect the thinking of informed and concerned individuals—especially Reform rabbis—on issues of consequence to the Jewish people and the Reform Movement;

2. increase awareness of developments taking place in fields of Jewish scholarship and the practical rabbinate, and to make additional contributions to these areas of study;

3. encourage creative and innovative approaches to Jewish thought and practice, based upon a thorough understanding of the traditional sources.

The views expressed in the Journal do not necessarily reflect the position of the Editorial Board or the Central Conference of American Rabbis.

The *CCAR Journal: The Reform Jewish Quarterly* (ISSN 1058-8760) is published quarterly by the Central Conference of American Rabbis, 355 Lexington Avenue, 18th Floor, New York, NY, 10017. Application to mail at periodical postage rates is pending at New York, NY and at additional mailing offices.

Subscriptions should be sent to CCAR Executive Offices, 355 Lexington Avenue, 18th Floor, New York, NY, 10017. Subscription rate as set by the Conference is $100 for a one-year subscription, $150 for a two-year subscription. Overseas subscribers should add $36 per year for postage. POSTMASTER: Please send address changes to CCAR Journal: The Reform Jewish Quarterly, c/o Central Conference of American Rabbis, 355 Lexington Avenue, 18th Floor, New York, NY, 10017.

Typesetting and publishing services provided by Publishing Synthesis, Ltd., 39 Crosby Street, New York, NY, 10013.

The *CCAR Journal: The Reform Jewish Quarterly* is indexed in the *Index to Jewish Periodicals*. Articles appearing in it are listed in the *Index of Articles on Jewish Studies* (of *Kirjath Sepher*).

© Copyright 2014 by the Central Conference of American Rabbis.
All rights reserved.
ISSN 1058-8760

ISBN: 978-0-88123-215-8

GUIDELINES FOR SUBMITTING MATERIAL

1. The *CCAR Journal* welcomes submissions that fulfill its Statement of Purpose whatever the author's background or identification. Inquiries regarding publishing in the CCAR Journal and submissions for possible publication (including poetry) should be sent to the editor, Rabbi Paul Golomb, journaleditor@ccarnet.org.

2. Other than commissioned articles, submissions to the *CCAR Journal* are sent out to a member of the editorial board for anonymous peer review. Thus submitted articles and poems should be sent to the editor with the author's name omitted. Please use MS Word format for the attachment. The message itself should contain the author's name, phone number, and e-mail address, as well as the submission's title and a 1–2 sentence bio.

3. Books for review and inquiries regarding submitting a review should be sent directly to the book review editor, Rabbi Evan Moffic, at *emoffic@gmail.com*.

4. Inquiries concerning, or submissions for, *Maayanot* (Primary Sources) should be directed to the *Maayanot* editor, Rabbi Daniel Polish, at *dpolish@optonline.net*.

5. Based on Reform Judaism's commitment to egalitarianism, we request that articles be written in gender-inclusive language.

6. The *Journal* publishes reference notes at the end of articles, but submissions are easier to review when notes come at the bottom of each page. If possible, keep this in mind when submitting an article. Notes should conform to the following style:

   a. Norman Lamm, *The Shema: Spirituality and Law in Judaism* (Philadelphia: Jewish Publication Society, 1998), 101–6. **[book]**

   b. Lawrence A. Hoffman, "The Liturgical Message," in *Gates of Understanding*, ed. Lawrence A.Hoffman (New York: CCAR Press, 1977), 147–48, 162–63. **[chapter in a book]**

   c. Richard Levy, "The God Puzzle," *Reform Judaism* 28 (Spring 2000): 18–22. **[article in a periodical]**

   d. Lamm, *Shema*, 102. **[short form for subsequent reference]**

   e. Levy, "God Puzzle," 20. **[short form for subsequent reference]**

   f. Ibid., 21. **[short form for subsequent reference]**

7. If Hebrew script is used, please include an English translation. If transliteration is used, follow the guidelines abbreviated below and included more fully in the **Master Style Sheet**, available on the CCAR website at *www.ccarnet.org*:

   "ch" for *chet* and *chaf* "ei" for *tzeirei*

   "f" for *fei* "a" for *patach* and *kamatz*

   "k" for *kaf* and *kuf* "o" for *cholam* and *kamatz katan*

   "tz" for *tzadi* "u" for *shuruk* and *kibbutz*

   "i" for *chirik* "ai" for *patach* with *yod*

   "e" for *segol*

   Final "h" for final *hei*; none for final *ayin* (with exceptions based on common usage): *atah*, *Sh'ma*, <u>but</u> *Moshe*.

   Apostrophe for *sh'va nah*: *b'nei*, *b'rit*, *Sh'ma*; no apostrophe for *sh'va nach*.

   Hyphen for two vowels together where necessary for correct pronunciation: *ne-eman*, *samei-ach*, <u>but</u> *maariv*, Shavuot.

   No hyphen for prefixes unless necessary for correct pronunciation: *babayit*, HaShem, Yom HaAtzma-ut.

   Do not double consonants (with exceptions based on dictionary spelling or common usage): *t'filah*, *chayim*, <u>but</u> *tikkun*, Sukkot.

www.ingramcontent.com/pod-product-compliance
Lightning Source LLC
Chambersburg PA
CBHW071425160426
43195CB00013B/1811